Better Homes and Gardens®

BUDGET
MEAL$

Save big $$$ with smart ways to shop and efficient ways to cook.

WILEY

Better Homes and Gardens® Budget Meals
Art Director: Matt Strelecki
Contributing Project Editors: Spectrum Communication Services, Inc.,
Lois White, Mary Williams
Contributing Writers: Nancy Byal, Jan Hazard
Contributing Graphic Designers: Ken Carlson/Waterbury Publications, Inc;
Chad Jewell; Diana Van Winkle
Editorial Assistant: Sheri Cord
Book Production Manager: Mark Weaver
Contributing Copy Editor: Carol DeMasters
Contributing Proofreaders: Jean Baker, Stephanie Boeding, Sara Henderson
Contributing Indexer: Elizabeth T. Parson
Test Kitchen Director: Lynn Blanchard
Test Kitchen Product Supervisor: Jill Moberly
Test Kitchen Culinary Specialists: Marilyn Cornelius, Juliana Hale,
Maryellyn Krantz, Colleen Weeden, Lori Wilson
Test Kitchen Nutrition Specialists: Elizabeth Burt, R.D., L.D.;
Laura Marzen, R.D., L.D.

Meredith® Books
Editorial Director: John Riha
Deputy Editor: Jennifer Darling
Managing Editor: Kathleen Armentrout
Brand Manager: Gina Rickert
Group Editor: Jan Miller
Copy Chief: Doug Kouma
Senior Copy Editors: Kevin Cox, Jennifer Speer Ramundt,
Elizabeth Keest Sedrel
Assistant Copy Editor: Metta Cederdahl
Proofreader: Joleen Ross

Executive Director, Sales: Ken Zagor
Director, Operations: George A. Susral
Director, Production: Douglas M. Johnston
Business Director: Janice Croat

Vice President and General Manager, SIP: Jeff Myers

Better Homes and Gardens® Magazine
Editor in Chief: Gayle Goodson Butler
Deputy Editor, Food and Entertaining: Nancy Hopkins

Meredith Publishing Group
President: Jack Griffin
Executive Vice President: Doug Olson

Meredith Corporation
Chairman of the Board: William T. Kerr
President and Chief Executive Officer: Stephen M. Lacy

In Memoriam: E. T. Meredith III (1933–2003)

All of us at Meredith® Books are
dedicated to providing you with the
information and ideas you need to
create delicious foods. We welcome
your comments and suggestions.
Write to us at: Meredith Special
Interest Media, 1716 Locust St.,
Des Moines, IA 50309-3023.

Our seal assures you that every
recipe in *Budget Meals* has been
tested in the Better Homes and
Gardens Test Kitchen®. This means
that each recipe is practical and
reliable and meets our high standards
of taste appeal. We guarantee your
satisfaction with this book for as
long as you own it.

TABLE OF CONTENTS

NEW!

LOOK!
MONEY-SAVING TIPS and HINTS

WELCOME TO BUDGET MEALS

Time, money, energy—we all feel the crunch. As budgets tighten and prices escalate for all household goods including food, you may feel challenged to feed your family healthful, well-balanced, and delicious meals that also are easy on the pocketbook.

BUDGET MEALS comes to your rescue with 350 recipes. The chapters are filled with everyday and party-special ideas for main dishes, soups, stews, skillet dinners, slow cooker meals, pasta side dishes, salads, and yes, even desserts. Our meal-planning advice encourages you to cook inventively, inexpensively, and without sacrificing taste. Nutritional information is included with each recipe.

Look for practical, easy-to-use information you can put to work right now. "Take Stock in the Pantry" shows how to have a well-stocked, well-organized pantry that saves on time, money, and trips to the supermarket. You will enjoy putting "Money-Saving Tips and Hints" to work and will not feel like a tightwad. Have you ever been caught short of an ingredient? "In-a-Pinch" identifies clever ingredient substitutions. For the busiest of the busy (isn't that all of us?), every recipe in "Cook Once, Eat Twice" produces an extra meal for later in the week or for the freezer. If you feel as if there is nothing in the house to eat, 50 "No-Recipe Recipes" will feed your creative juices. Search your pantry and voilà, you have a satisfying dinner on the table quickly and easily.

Whether you are just learning how to save money or have been at it for years, you will find a wealth of helpful ideas in **BUDGET MEALS**. Happy cooking, happy dining, happy saving!

Take Stock IN THE PANTRY

$AVE!

If the heart and soul of the home is the kitchen, then the pantry is the engine that powers it. Think of the pantry as a reservoir of consumable goods. Locate the pantry anywhere in your home that is cool and dark. It may be a walk-in pantry, a designated cupboard, or shelves in the garage or basement. For honest-to-goodness savings, organize and manage your pantry. Good planning, sensible shopping, and careful storage ensure fresh, flavorful, and safe foods on-call when you need them.

HOW TO START

Admittedly, planning takes time. If you want your pantry to work for you and control costs, it is worth the effort to plan it. Build a pantry that meets your needs. After all, you know your likes and dislikes. First, write a three- or four-week menu plan for breakfast, lunch, dinner, and even snacks. Plan all of the meals even if you know many of them may not be served at home, such as breakfast on the run or lunches at school or the office.

Next, think about the cooking categories that are part of your weekly meals. Make a list of all the ingredients and food products you need for your three-week plan. Organize the foods into shopping categories to save you time at the supermarket. Also, plan the pantry storage zones in advance so unloading food ingredients goes smoothly and quickly.

THE PANTRY PLAN

Organize the pantry to save time and energy. Start by either drafting a schematic plan, drawing it on paper, or making a mental plan. A walk-in pantry off the kitchen works best. If you do not have one, then convert a cupboard closet or a freestanding cabinet as the pantry. Arrange shelves and bins to hold the food in zones according to how you cook. For instance, designate zones for easy weeknight meals, lunch on the run, quick breakfasts, snacks, traditional staple food, and baking supplies. Place the most-used zones in the easiest-to-reach areas.

THE CLEAN-OUT

If you already have a kitchen full of food, pull everything out of the cupboards, clean the shelves, and audit what you have. Remember, the pantry consists of many areas: shelf-stable foods and supplies, and refrigerated and freezer products. With your menus and zones in mind, review the foods you have not used in more than a year and will not use. Donate them to a food pantry or toss them if they are outdated. For the foods you keep, date them with a permanent marker so you use them first. Cross these items off your pantry-stocking list.

PANTRY Organizing Tips

1. **RESTOCK THE FOODS** by use or in pantry cooking zones. Breakfast items such as cooked and ready-to-eat cereals, breakfast bars, coffee, and tea go in one zone. Lunch foods such as peanut butter, jellies, canned tuna, and lunch bags go in the lunch zone. Put nonperishable ingredients that you use in one week (marinara sauce and pasta, taco night dinner) in another pantry zone.

2. **STORE THE STAPLES** such as flour, sugar, baking powder, baking soda, olive oils, and vinegars in one convenient area. The foods you usc daily for meal preparation need to be in easy reach.

3. **BASKETS, BINS, AND TRAYS** are handy for containing zoned foods. Canisters, wall and door mounts, and turntables for corners and hard-to-reach places organize the zones. Container/organization stores, home improvement centers, and office supply stores are sources for buying these items.

4. **TO SIMPLIFY CLEANUP** after food shopping and meal preparation, designate one handy spot for utility items such as plastic wrap, foil, and storage containers.

5. **IF YOU BUY FOODS SUCH AS FLOUR AND SUGAR IN BULK,** plan to transfer them into useable portions in smaller containers. Select clean, transparent containers that are airtight, stackable, and space-efficient. Store bulk portions in airtight containers out of the way.

6. **ARRANGE HERBS AND SPICES IN ALPHABETICAL ORDER** so they are easy to find, simple to return to the shelf, and easy to replace when needed. Involve your children in this activity to reinforce or improve their alphabet skills.

7. **IF SPACE ALLOWS, STORE SPECIALTY APPLIANCES IN THE PANTRY.** Hang bulky or seldom-used utensils from hooks mounted on the wall or on the back of a door.

8. **CLEARLY LABEL SHELVES AND BINS.** Bold, readable labeling, such as large print from a computer, is a key tactic to make this plan work. It helps you and your family to remove and return items to their rightful place. Use magnetic labels on metal shelving and self-stick labels from office supply stores for wood or plastic shelves.

READY, SET, *Shop*

1. **KEEP A NOTEPAD OR CLIPBOARD AND PEN/PENCIL IN A CONVENIENT PLACE THAT THE ENTIRE FAMILY CAN USE TO RECORD SHOPPING NEEDS.** When the last jar of peanut butter is opened, it should be noted on the shopping list. Also, have your children record when foods are completely used, especially if it is their favorite treat. It is good training and helps them to be part of food pantry budgeting.

2. **ORGANIZE ITEMS ON THE LIST INTO GROUPS THAT FOLLOW THE LAYOUT OF THE SUPERMARKET.** It results in a fast way to shop and reduces the chance of missing an item on the grocery list.

3. **HAVE AN ENVELOPE OR PAPER CLIP TO HOLD COUPONS FOR FOODS YOU PLAN TO BUY.** Position it near the shopping list to grab as you head out the door to the supermarket.

4. **STORE CANVAS SHOPPING BAGS NEAR THE SHOPPING LIST.** Many markets reduce your grocery bill by a few cents per bag if you supply your own shopping bags.

5. **SET ASIDE PART OF YOUR WEEKLY FOOD BUDGET FOR PANTRY STAPLES.** That way you have money for sales or to buy in bulk.

6. **KNOW FOOD COSTS OR THE BASE PRICE OF MOST STAPLES.** Then you can determine if a food is really "on sale." Take advantage of the supermarket unit price code. Generally listed on the shelf below the food item, this code tells you the cost per serving or the price per ounce. With this information, you can compare prices of different brands. Another good reason to know base prices is that some warehouse stores do not offer unit price coding. Use a calculator to determine if bulk food really is a value. Then ask yourself, "Will I use this while it is still fresh?" If not, don't buy it.

7. **SHOP FOR SPECIALS OR ON-SALE FOODS AND PRODUCTS YOU USE.** Read the grocery store ads, specials, and/or flyers. Clip cents-off coupons for items you use.

8. **SOMETHING MIGHT BE A BARGAIN, BUT NOT FOR YOU.** Purchasing foods you do not like is never a bargain.

PANTRY *Storage Guidelines*

Pantry staples fare best in a cool, dry place.
Here are recommended storage times for common pantry items.

- **BAKING POWDER:** Once open, it lasts 6 months at room temperature.

- **BANANAS:** Store at room temperature.

- **BREAD CRUMBS:** Store dried up to 6 months; refrigerate for up to 2 years.

- **CANNED GOODS** (no dented or damaged cans): Store up to 2 years.

- **EGGS:** Store in the egg carton in the refrigerator up to 4 weeks. Look for the "sell by" date stamped on the carton.

- **FLOUR:** Store in an airtight container in a cool, dark place up to 6 months. Keep it in the freezer for longer storage. Bring to room temperature before using.

- **HONEY:** It lasts indefinitely. If it crystallizes, heat it in the opened jar set in a pan of hot water on low heat until crystals dissolve.

- **MAYONNAISE:** Refrigerate it after opening for up to 2 months.

- **ONIONS:** Store in a cool, dark place, away from potatoes, up to 2 months. Sweet onions last up to 2 weeks.

- **PASTA, DRY:** Store in cool, dark place up to 1 year.

- **PEANUT BUTTER:** Store unopened up to 1 year at room temperature. Once open, refrigerate it to avoid rancidity.

- **POTATOES:** Store in cool, dark place up to 6 weeks.

- **RICE:** Store long-grain white rice in airtight container up to 2 years. Store brown rice in an airtight container in the freezer up to 1 year.

- **SALAD/VEGETABLE AND OLIVE OIL:** Store in a cool dark place up to 6 months.

- **SOY SAUCE:** Unopened, it keeps at room temperature for 1 year. Refrigerate it after opening for an additional year.

- **SPICES AND HERBS:** Store in a cool, dark place away from the stove or oven for up to 1 year. Smell before using. If the aroma is weak, discard it. Write the date of purchase on the label.

- **TOMATOES:** Store at room temperature and refrigerate only when really ripe.

- **VINEGAR:** Store unopened indefinitely. After opening, it is good up to 6 months at room temperature.

PANTRY *Staples List*

Start with this list of basics.
Add to it based on your needs and preferences.

SHELF STABLE

- ☐ Baking powder and baking soda
- ☐ Beans, canned
- ☐ Bread/crackers
- ☐ Bread crumbs, dry
- ☐ Broth or bouillon granules, chicken and beef broth
- ☐ Couscous
- ☐ Flour, all purpose
- ☐ Fruit, canned
- ☐ Garlic: powders and salts
- ☐ Herbs and spices
- ☐ Ketchup
- ☐ Maple syrup
- ☐ Nonstick cooking spray
- ☐ Oatmeal
- ☐ Oils: olive, vegetable/salad
- ☐ Onions
- ☐ Pasta
     long (spaghetti, linguine)
     flat (lasagna, pappardelle)
     shaped, short, tube (penne, elbow, fusilli, bow ties)
- ☐ Peanut butter
- ☐ Potatoes
- ☐ Rice: long-grain, brown, rice mixes
- ☐ Salt
- ☐ Soups: cream of mushroom, tomato, dried soup mixes
- ☐ Sugar: granulated, brown, and powdered
- ☐ Tuna and salmon, canned
- ☐ Tomatoes: canned, tomato sauce, tomato paste
- ☐ Vanilla
- ☐ Vegetables, canned
- ☐ Vinegar: cider, wine, balsamic, red wine, white wine

REFRIGERATOR

- ☐ Bacon
- ☐ Beef, ground
- ☐ Butter or margarine
- ☐ Cheese: cream, cheddar, Monterey Jack
- ☐ Chicken
- ☐ Dairy: milk, yogurt, butter, sour cream
- ☐ Eggs
- ☐ Fruits: apples, oranges, lemons
- ☐ Juices
- ☐ Vegetables: carrots and celery

FREEZER

- ☐ Desserts: ice cream or frozen yogurt
- ☐ Fruits
- ☐ Juices
- ☐ Vegetables

Vegetable CHART

VEGETABLE	AVAILABILITY	HOW TO STORE
Artichokes	Available twice a year: March through May and September through November	Refrigerate untrimmed in a closed plastic bag up to I week.
Asparagus	Available March through June with peak season in April and May; available year-round in some areas	Wrap the bases of fresh asparagus spears in wet paper towels and keep tightly sealed in a storage container in the refrigerator for up to 4 days.
Avocado: Hass (dark and bumpy), Fuerte (large, green, smooth skin)	Available year-round	When ripe, refrigerate uncovered for 2 to 3 days.
Beans: green, snap or string, yellow wax	Available April through September; available year-round in some areas	Refrigerate in a covered container for up to 5 days.
Broccoli	Available year-round	Keep unwashed broccoli in a covered container in the refrigerator for up to 4 days.
Brussels sprouts	Available year-round with peak season from August through April	Refrigerate in a covered container for up to 2 days.
Beets	Available year-round with peak season from June through October	Trim beet greens, leaving I to 2 inches of stem. Do not cut the long root. Store unwashed beets in an open container in the refrigerator for up to I week.
Cabbage: green, napa, red, savoy	Available year-round	Refrigerate in a covered container for up to 5 days.
Carrots	Available year-round	Refrigerate in a plastic bag for up to 2 weeks.
Cauliflower	Available year-round	Refrigerate in a covered container for up to 4 days.
Celery	Available year-round	Refrigerate, tightly wrapped, for up to 2 weeks.
Celery root (celeriac)	Available September through March	Refrigerate in closed plastic bag for 7 to 10 days.
Corn	Available July through September; available year-round in some areas	Best used the day of picking or purchase. Cover and refrigerate in husks up to 2 days.
Cucumbers	Available year-round with peak season from late May through early September	Refrigerate salad cucumbers in refrigerator up to I week. Pickling cucumbers should be picked and used the same day.
Eggplant	Available year-round with peak season from July through September	Refrigerate whole eggplants uncovered for up to 4 days.
Fennel	Available October through April; available year-round in some areas	Refrigerate, tightly wrapped, for up to 5 days.

VEGETABLE	PEAK SEASON	HOW TO STORE
Garlic	Available year-round	Keep in cool, dark place. Whole up to 6 weeks.
Ginger (fresh)	Available year-round	Store at room temperature 5 days; wrap in paper towel and refrigerate 3 to 4 weeks. For longer storage, slice ginger into a jar, cover with dry sherry, and refrigerate covered.
Greens: chard, Swiss chard, beet, turnip, collard, mustard	Available year-round	Refrigerate unwashed in closed plastic bag for 2 to 3 days.
Leeks	Available year-round	Refrigerate, tightly wrapped, for up to 5 days.
Mushrooms (all varieties)	Available year-round; morel mushrooms available April through June	Store unwashed mushrooms in the refrigerator for up to 2 days. A paper bag or damp cloth lets them breathe so they stay firm longer.
Onions (all varieties)	Variety determines availability. Some varieties, such as white, red, pearl, and boiling onions, are available year-round. Sweet onion varieties, such as Vidalia, Maui, Osso Sweet, and Walla Walla, are available on and off throughout the year.	Keep in a cool, dry, well-ventilated place; sweet varieties for 2 weeks, others up to 2 months.
Peas, pea pods, and sugar snaps	Peas: Available January through June with peak season from March through May. Pea pods: Available February through August.	Store, tightly wrapped, in the refrigerator for up to 3 days.
Peppers: hot or sweet	Available year-round	Refrigerate in a covered container for up to 5 days.
Potatoes: Russet, Yukon gold, creamer, red, purple, heirloom	Available year-round	Store for several weeks in a dark, well ventilated, cool place that is slightly humid but not wet. Bright light causes potatoes to get green patches that have a bitter flavor. Do not refrigerate; cold temperatures cause potatoes to turn overly sweet and to darken when cooked.
Root vegetables: parsnips, rutabagas, turnips	Available year-round. Parsnips: Peak season from November through March. Rutabagas: Peak season from September through March. Turnips: Peak season from October through March.	Refrigerate for up to 2 weeks.
Spinach	Available year-round	Rinse leaves in cold water and thoroughly dry. Place the leaves in a storage container with a paper towel and refrigerate for up to 3 days.
Squash, winter: hubbard, acorn, kabocha, butternut	Some varieties available year-round with peak season September through March.	Store whole squash in a cool, dry place for up to 2 months. Refrigerate cut squash, wrapped in plastic, for up to 4 days.
Sweet potatoes, yams	Available year-round with peak season from October through January.	Store in a cool, dry, dark place for up to I week.
Tomatoes	Available year-round with peak season from June through early September	Store at room temperature for up to 3 days. Do not store tomatoes in the refrigerator unless very ripe or they will lose their flavor.
Zucchini, summer squash	Some varieties available year-round with peak season from June through September	Refrigerate squash, tightly wrapped, for up to 5 days; fresh-from-the-garden squash may be stored for up to 2 weeks.

No-Recipe RECIPES

EASY!

NO-FUSS SALADS

1. **THE CLASSIC: C**ombine torn romaine lettuce, chopped tomatoes, and chopped seeded cucumber. Toss with balsamic vinaigrette.

2. **RANCH HAND: P**air ranch dressing with torn mixed salad greens, shredded carrots, and chopped seeded cucumber.

3. **QUICK SPINACH: H**oney-mustard salad dressing adds appeal to torn spinach, tomato wedges, and sliced mushrooms.

4. **GREENS AND BERRIES: M**ix torn spinach, sliced mushrooms, and raspberries or halved strawberries with poppy seed dressing.

5. **VERY VEGGIE: M**ix a can of rinsed and drained black-eyed peas, a drained can of corn with sweet peppers, and chopped celery. Embellish with Italian dressing.

6. **FRUIT KABOBS: S**kewer strawberry halves, watermelon chunks, pineapple chunks, and kiwifruit pieces. If desired, serve with bottled poppy seed salad dressing or lemon yogurt.

7. **ROWS AND ROWS: O**n a serving platter arrange rows of shredded iceberg lettuce, sliced cucumber, sliced red sweet pepper, sliced red onion, shredded carrot, sliced mushroom, and shredded cheddar cheese. If desired, sprinkle with crumbled cooked bacon. Serve with your favorite bottled salad dressing.

8. **PENNE, HAM, AND CHEESE: C**ombine cooked penne pasta, cubed ham, cubed cheddar cheese, and halved green and/or red seedless grapes. Mix a little shredded orange peel into bottled poppy seed dressing. Add to pasta mixture; toss.

EASY SIDES

9. **PASTA PRIMAVERA: T**oss hot cooked vermicelli and broccoli florets with olive oil, finely chopped garlic, crushed red pepper, and finely chopped tomatoes.

10. **BERRY-NUT COUSCOUS: T**oss hot cooked couscous with dried cranberries, orange juice, a few drops of olive oil, and toasted almonds.

11. **PESTO ROLL-UPS: S**eparate a package of refrigerated crescent rolls into triangles and spread with purchased basil pesto. Cut each triangle in half to make 16 long triangles. Roll triangles; bake as directed on the package.

12. **APPETIZER KABOBS: T**hread cubes of salami or cheese, cooked tortellini, and vegetables alternately onto 6-inch skewers. Marinate in bottled Italian salad dressing in the refrigerator for several hours. Drain and serve.

13. **CHIPOTLE-CHEDDAR MASHED POTATOES:** Stir a small amount of finely chopped chipotle peppers in adobo sauce, a dab of adobo sauce, and finely shredded cheddar cheese into mashed potatoes. Stir in milk to achieve desired consistency.

14. **HERBED BREADSTICKS:** Cut a loaf of French bread into 1-inch-wide sticks about 4 to 6 inches long. Place on a baking sheet. Brush breadsticks with a mixture of melted butter, snipped fresh or dried basil, and garlic salt. Bake until breadsticks are golden brown.

15. **WASABI POTATOES:** Prepare mashed potatoes as usual. Stir 1 to 2 teaspoons wasabi powder into melted butter, then into the potatoes.

SIMPLE SANDWICHES

16. **PB AND APPLE WRAP:** Spread peanut butter on a flour tortilla. Sprinkle evenly with chopped apple and low-fat granola. Tightly roll tortilla; cut in half.

17. **MEDITERRANEAN WRAPS:** Spread a flour tortilla with purchased hummus then plain low-fat yogurt. Top with cooked chicken strips, chopped tomato, and thinly sliced cucumber. Roll and enjoy.

18. **BARBECUE BEEF WRAP:** Top a flour tortilla with shredded barbecue beef, shredded Monterey Jack cheese, and broccoli slaw mix. Top with salsa; roll.

19. **DELI ROAST BEEF:** Lay thinly sliced cooked roast beef on pumpernickel, rye, or whole wheat bread. Top with coleslaw, herb-pepper seasoning, and another slice of bread.

20. **MOCK MONTE CRISTO:** Spread honey mustard on one side of two slices of frozen French toast. Top one slice with thinly sliced cooked turkey breast, ham, and Swiss cheese. Cover with the other slice of French toast, mustard side down. Bake at 400°F for 15 to 20 minutes.

21. **TURKEY RUSSIANS:** Spread cut sides of kaiser rolls or other shaped rolls with Russian salad dressing. On bottom bun halves layer thinly sliced deli turkey and sliced Swiss cheese. Add bun tops, dressing side down. Bake at 350°F until cheese melts and sandwich is heated through.

22. **BARBECUE CHICKEN SANDWICHES:** Heat together chopped or shredded cooked chicken and barbecue sauce. Spoon onto split toasted kaiser rolls. Top with sliced cheddar cheese, sliced red onion, and roll tops.

23. **PB AND STRAWBERRY POCKETS:** Spread the inside of halved white or whole grain pita halves with peanut butter. Fill pita halves with raisins, sliced strawberries, and dry-roasted sunflower kernels.

FIX-QUICK MAIN DISHES

24. **ITALIAN GRILLED CHICKEN:** Marinate skinless, boneless chicken breast halves in bottled Italian salad dressing. Drain and grill chicken over medium heat for 12 to 15 minutes or until no longer pink.

25. **TEX-MEX FILLETS:** Place codfish fillets in a baking dish, top with bottled salsa and shredded Monterey Jack cheese and/or shredded cheddar cheese. Bake at 425°F about 10 minutes. Serve with flour tortillas.

26. HAM AND BROCCOLI SPUDS: Heat a package of frozen cut broccoli in cheese sauce according to package directions. Stir in chopped cooked ham; season to taste with caraway seeds. Heat through; spoon mixture into split hot baked potatoes.

27. PIZZA BURGERS: Broil 4 hamburgers. Spoon warmed bottled mushroom tomato-based pasta sauce over burgers. Top with a slice of provolone cheese. Broil for 1 to 2 minutes. Sprinkle with snipped fresh basil. If you like, serve on toasted slices of sourdough bread or in split hamburger buns.

28. FRESH TOMATO PIZZA: Place a 12-inch Italian bread shell on a large baking sheet. Bake according to package directions. Sprinkle with shredded pizza cheese and snipped fresh basil. Top with sliced tomatoes. Drizzle with olive oil. Bake until cheese melts.

29. CHICKEN-VEGGIE COUSCOUS: Cook desired vegetables in hot olive oil until tender; add chopped cooked chicken. Sprinkle with Italian seasoning and stir into hot cooked couscous.

30. ONE-POT SPAGHETTI: In a large Dutch oven, brown ground beef and chopped onion. Drain off fat. Stir in one jar of pasta sauce and a jar full of water. Add one-half box dried penne pasta or other shaped pasta. Simmer, uncovered, until pasta is tender, stirring often.

31. HERBED PASTA: Toss hot cooked pasta with olive oil, salt, and coarsely ground black pepper. Toss in snipped fresh herbs such as sage, rosemary, and/or basil. Top with shaved Parmesan cheese.

32. BAKED PARMESAN CHICKEN: Combine crushed cornflakes, grated Parmesan cheese, and dried Italian seasoning, crushed. Dip skinless, boneless chicken breast halves in melted butter; roll in cornflake mixture. Place on a baking sheet. Bake at 375°F for 30 minutes.

33. BARBECUE CHICKEN PIZZA: Bake a 12-inch Italian bread shell according to package directions. Spread purchased barbecue sauce over crust. Top with chopped cooked chicken, chopped red onion, chopped green sweet pepper, and shredded mozzarella cheese. Bake until cheese melts.

34. WEEKNIGHT OMELET: Fill an omelet with leftover cooked vegetables, chopped cooked meat, and cheese. If necessary, warm the veggies and meat in a little hot butter before adding to the omelet.

35. BALSAMIC CHICKEN: Marinate skinless, boneless chicken breasts in bottled balsamic vinegar dressing, finely chopped garlic, and crushed red pepper. Bake or grill as desired until chicken is no longer pink.

36. PORK SALSA: Combine trimmed pork shoulder, sliced onion, and bottled salsa in a slow cooker. Cover and cook 8 to 10 hours on low setting. Shred pork with two forks. Serve in split hamburger buns.

37. PASTA CARBONARA: Cook sliced bacon and chopped onion. Remove from heat; add cooked spaghetti, $\frac{1}{4}$ to $\frac{1}{2}$ cup refrigerated or thawed frozen egg substitute, milk or cream, and shredded Parmesan cheese. Toss; serve with grated Parmesan cheese.

38. LEMON CHICKEN: Stuff a quartered fresh lemon, half an onion, and a clove of garlic into the cavity of a whole chicken. Roast at 400°F for an hour or until the chicken is no longer pink.

39. CHILLED TUNA PASTA DINNER: Toss cooked elbow macaroni with drained tuna, shredded carrot, chopped green onion, and creamy Caesar salad dressing. Chill.

40. TURKEY WORCESTER: Marinate turkey cutlets in white wine Worcestershire sauce for 30 minutes; drain, reserving marinade. Cook cutlets in equal parts cooking oil and butter until no longer pink. Remove from pan. Add marinade; cook until thick. Pour over cutlets. Sprinkle with snipped chives.

41. SESAME BEEF: Season beef minute steaks with garlic salt and pepper. Coat both sides of meat with sesame seeds. Cook on both sides in hot oil to desired doneness. Remove meat from pan; add red wine or beef broth to pan. Cook, stirring browned bits of meat off bottom of skillet. Serve meat and pan juices over hot steamed spinach.

DELISH DESSERTS

42. TROPICAL FRUIT DESSERT: Top fresh or canned pineapple chunks, coarsely chopped mango, and/or coarsely chopped papaya with toasted coconut.

43. PEACHES AND CREAM: Top scoops of vanilla ice cream or frozen yogurt with fresh or canned sliced peaches. Drizzle with honey. Sprinkle with chopped toasted pecans.

44. BROWNIE TRIFLES: In dessert glasses layer brownies with whipped cream, prepared chocolate pudding, and chocolate-covered toffee pieces.

45. ICE CREAM SANDWICHES: Place spoonfuls of your favorite flavor of ice cream between oatmeal or chocolate chip cookies; roll edges in chopped nuts, miniature chocolate pieces, or sprinkles.

46. CRANBERRY FLOAT: In tall glasses combine equal parts cranberry-apple juice and chilled ginger ale. Add a scoop of vanilla ice cream or orange sherbet to each glass.

47. CHOCO-CHERRY FLOAT: Drizzle chocolate syrup into tall glasses. Stir in chilled cherry-flavor cola. Add cherry-nut ice cream to each glass.

48. DECADENT CARAMEL BROWNIES: Spread baked and cooled brownies with caramel ice cream topping. Sprinkle with toasted macadamia nuts and semisweet chocolate pieces.

49. PEANUT BUTTER CUP BROWNIES: Spread baked and cooled brownies with a thin layer of creamy peanut butter. Top with coarsely chopped chocolate-covered peanut butter cup candy and chopped peanuts or honey-roasted peanuts.

50. PEPPERMINT STICK PIE: Spoon softened peppermint ice cream onto a chocolate-flavor crumb pie shell. Freeze until firm. Serve with warm fudge ice cream topping.

LOOK!
MONEY-SAVING TIPS and HINTS

Quality

Trendy yet less-expensive ethnic recipes such as pasta main dishes, chilis, risottos, and curries are perfect for entertaining on a budget.

Check the pantry for party foods such as crackers, olives, and nuts before shopping. Check the crisper for veggies to cut for a crudite platter.

BUY day-old baguette bread. Slice and toast it to use for appetizers and crostini.

 Store-bought precut veggies and fruit cost at least twice as much as whole fruits and veggies.

If you give more than one party in a short period of time, make double or triple appetizers, such as meatballs and chicken wings. Freeze the extras for the next party.

 Purchase store-brand chips and/or crackers at a <u>fraction</u> of the cost of major brands.

For a party menu, prepare recipes that have similar ingredients so you can purchase larger quantities or use a whole package. For instance, if one recipe calls for 4 ounces of cream cheese, plan to make another recipe that will use the remaining 4 ounces of an 8-ounce package.

Stock up on cocktail breads and rolls in bulk from superstores and bakery outlets. They freeze well up to one month.

TIP! **Control wine and liquor costs by serving "mixed" beverages such as fruit punch or wine coolers. Make them rather than buying bottled versions.** **TIP!**

CHAPTER 1

DISCOUNT DAYS
PARTY FOOD

Most everyone loves a party, especially now that entertaining is more relaxed and casual. That is great news when finding time to prepare and serve party food can be a challenge. To keep hosting expenses under control, remember that starter foods, such as dips and snack mixes, feed many on fewer dollars. Here is a collection of favorite budget-friendly starters that taste more expensive than they are. Party on!

Greek
LAYER DIP

Serve this yogurt and hummus dip with pita wedges. Toast the pita for a crisp bite and fresh flavor.

Makes 10 servings

Start to Finish: **30 minutes**

1 6-ounce carton plain yogurt
½ cup finely chopped unpeeled
   cucumber
1 tablespoon finely chopped
   red onion
1 teaspoon snipped fresh mint
1 10-ounce container plain
   hummus
½ cup chopped seeded tomato
   (1 medium)
½ cup crumbled feta cheese
   (2 ounces)
3 large plain and/or whole
   wheat pita bread rounds

1. In a small bowl combine yogurt, ¼ cup of the cucumber, the red onion, and mint. Set aside.

2. Spread hummus in the bottom of a 10-inch quiche dish or 9-inch pie plate. Spread yogurt mixture over hummus. Sprinkle with the remaining ¼ cup cucumber, the tomato, and cheese.

3. Split each pita round in half horizontally; cut each half into 8 wedges. Serve dip with pita wedges.

Per serving: 128 cal., 4 g total fat (1 g sat. fat), 6 mg chol., 241 mg sodium, 18 g carbo., 2 g fiber, 5 g pro.

Red
PEPPER DIP

Vegetable dippers make this a healthful appetizer. *Makes 1¾ cups*

Start to Finish: 15 minutes

1 8-ounce package cream
    cheese, cut up
½ of a 15.5-ounce jar (1 cup)
    roasted red sweet peppers,
    drained
2 tablespoons olive oil
1 tablespoon honey
1 fresh red chile pepper,
    seeded and coarsely
    chopped (see note, page
    22), or 1 to 2 teaspoons
    drained and chopped
    bottled sliced jalapeño chile
    pepper
½ teaspoon bottled minced
    garlic (1 clove)
1 tablespoon snipped fresh
    rosemary, basil, or oregano
    or 1 teaspoon dried
    rosemary, basil, or oregano,
    crushed
    Assorted vegetable dippers
    and/or tortilla chips

1. In a food processor or blender
combine cream cheese, roasted
sweet peppers, oil, honey, chile
pepper, and garlic. Cover and
process or blend until smooth,
stopping to scrape down sides as
necessary. Add herb; cover and
pulse until combined.
2. Transfer dip to a serving bowl.
Serve dip with vegetables and/or
tortilla chips.

Test Kitchen Tip: Use a
combination of fresh herbs for
an even more interesting flavor,
or use dried Italian seasoning for
the dried herb.

Make-Ahead Directions: Prepare
as directed. Cover and chill for
up to 2 days.

Per 2 tablespoons dip: 83 cal., 8 g total fat (4 g sat.
fat), 18 mg chol., 49 mg sodium, 3 g carbo., 0 g fiber, 1 g pro.

Creamy
SPINACH DIP

About half of a 10-ounce bag of prewashed spinach leaves makes the 3 cups of chopped spinach you need to make this dip. *Makes 2 cups*

Prep: **25 minutes** Chill: **4 to 36 hours**

5 slices bacon
2 cups sliced fresh mushrooms
⅓ cup finely chopped onion
   (1 small)
1 teaspoon bottled minced
   garlic (2 cloves)
1 tablespoon olive oil
1 tablespoon red wine vinegar
1 tablespoon Dijon-style
   mustard
¼ teaspoon ground black
   pepper
3 cups chopped fresh spinach
1 3-ounce package cream
   cheese, softened
½ cup dairy sour cream
2 tablespoons milk
   Milk
   Bagel chips or pita chips

1. In a large skillet cook bacon over medium heat until crisp. Remove bacon and drain on paper towels, discarding drippings. Crumble 4 of the bacon slices; set aside. Crumble the remaining bacon slice; wrap and chill for garnish.

2. In the same skillet cook mushrooms, onion, and garlic in hot oil over medium heat until mushrooms are tender. Stir in vinegar, mustard, and pepper. Stir in spinach; cook and stir about 30 seconds or just until spinach is wilted. Add cream cheese, stirring until melted. Remove from heat. Stir in the 4 slices crumbled bacon, the sour cream, and the 2 tablespoons milk. Transfer mixture to a serving bowl. Cover and chill for 4 to 36 hours.

3. Before serving, stir dip. If necessary, stir in additional milk to reach dipping consistency. Garnish with the chilled crumbled bacon. Serve dip with bagel chips.

Per 2 tablespoons dip: 60 cal., 5 g total fat (2 g sat. fat), 11 mg chol., 105 mg sodium, 2 g carbo., 0 g fiber, 2 g pro.

Too-Easy
GUACAMOLE

Why is this too easy? You use a plastic bag with a zipper closure as the mixing bowl and also for airtight storage. See photo on page 97. *Makes about 1 cup*

Start to Finish: 15 minutes

2 ripe medium avocados, halved, seeded, and peeled
2 tablespoons dairy sour cream
2 tablespoons snipped fresh cilantro or parsley
1 tablespoon lime juice
⅛ teaspoon salt
　Tortilla chips
　Chopped tomato (optional)
　Sliced green onion (optional)

1. In a sturdy, resealable plastic bag combine avocado, sour cream, cilantro, lime juice, and salt; seal bag. Knead bag with your hands to combine ingredients.
2. To serve, snip a hole in one corner of the bag. Squeeze avocado mixture onto tortilla chips. If desired, sprinkle with tomato and green onion.

Test Kitchen Tip: Ripe avocados feel soft to gentle palm pressure. (Don't press them with your finger; they'll bruise.) To speed ripening, place avocados in a closed paper bag at room temperature. Ripe ones can be refrigerated for several days.

Make-Ahead Directions: Prepare as directed in Step 1. Chill guacamole in the plastic bag for up to 8 hours before serving.

Per 1 tablespoon guacamole: 39 cal., 4 g total fat (1 g sat. fat), 1 mg chol., 21 mg sodium, 2 g carbo., 1 g fiber, 0 g pro.

Homemade
SALSA

You can't beat homemade salsa's flavor or value when in-season tomatoes are used. *Makes 1 cup*

Start to Finish: **20 minutes**

1⅓ cups coarsely chopped, seeded tomato (4 small)
⅓ cup chopped onion (1 small)
2 tablespoons lime juice
1 to 2 fresh jalapeño chile peppers, seeded and finely chopped*
1 to 2 tablespoons snipped fresh cilantro or parsley
¼ teaspoon salt
Tortilla chips

1. In a food processor combine tomato, onion, lime juice, chile pepper, cilantro, and salt. Cover and process with several on/off pulses until mixture is evenly chopped.
2. Serve salsa with tortilla chips. Store in an airtight container in the refrigerator for up to 3 days.

Per ¼ cup salsa: 20 cal., 0 g total fat (0 g sat. fat), 0 mg chol., 150 mg sodium, 5 g carbo., 1 g fiber, 1 g pro.

*Test Kitchen Tip: Because hot chile peppers contain oils that can burn your skin and eyes, avoid direct contact with them as much as possible. When working with chile peppers, wear plastic or rubber gloves. If your bare hands do touch the chile peppers, wash your hands well with soap and water.

Creamy Dip
FOR FRUIT

The cream cheese, sour cream, and brown sugar combo complements any kind of fruit. For the best value, purchase the fruit currently in season. *Makes 2 cups*

Prep: 15 minutes Chill: 1 hour

1 8-ounce package cream
cheese, softened
1 8-ounce carton dairy sour
cream
¼ cup packed brown sugar
1 teaspoon vanilla
2 to 3 tablespoons milk
Dark sweet cherries,
strawberries, and/or apple,
pear, or banana slices

1. In a small bowl beat cream cheese with an electric mixer on low speed until smooth. Gradually add sour cream, beating until combined. Add brown sugar and vanilla; beat just until combined. Stir in enough of the milk to reach dipping consistency.
2. Cover and chill for at least 1 hour before serving. Serve with cherries, strawberries, and/or apple, pear, or banana slices.

Spice Dip for Fruit: **Prepare as** directed, except add ½ teaspoon ground cinnamon or pumpkin pie spice to the mixture.

Per 2 tablespoons Creamy or Spice Dip: 95 cal., 8 g total fat (5 g sat. fat), 22 mg chol., 52 mg sodium, 5 g carbo., 0 g fiber, 2 g pro.

Creamy Marshmallow Dip for Fruit: **Prepare as directed, except** omit brown sugar and stir in one 7-ounce jar marshmallow creme.

Per 2 tablespoons dip: 70 cal., 5 g total fat (3 g sat. fat), 13 mg chol., 35 mg sodium, 6 g carbo., 0 g dietary fiber, 1 g protein.

Lower-Calorie Creamy Dip for Fruit: **Prepare as directed, except** substitute reduced-fat cream cheese and light sour cream for the regular cream cheese and sour cream.

Per 2 tablespoons dip: 70 cal., 5 g total fat (3 g sat. fat), 13 mg chol., 35 mg sodium, 6 g carbo., 0 g dietary fiber, 1 g protein.

Chili
CON QUESO

Pasteurized prepared cheese product melts to a satiny smooth consistency for this classic tortilla dip.

Makes 2½ cups dip

Start to Finish: **30 minutes**

½ cup finely chopped onion
(1 medium)

1 tablespoon butter or
margarine

1⅓ cups chopped, seeded
tomato (2 medium)

1 4-ounce can diced green
chile peppers, undrained

8 ounces pasteurized prepared
cheese product, cut into
cubes

½ cup shredded Monterey
Jack cheese with jalapeño
peppers (2 ounces)

1 teaspoon cornstarch

Tortilla chips or corn chips

1. In a medium saucepan cook onion in hot butter until tender. Stir in tomato and undrained chile peppers. Bring to boiling; reduce heat. Simmer, uncovered, for 10 minutes.

2. In a medium bowl toss the cheeses with cornstarch. Gradually add cheese mixture to saucepan, stirring until cheeses are melted. Heat through. Serve with chips.

Per ¼ cup dip: 125 cal., 9 g total fat (6 g sat. fat), 28 mg chol., 394 mg sodium, 4 g carbo., 0 g fiber, 7 g pro.

White Chili Con Queso: **Prepare as directed, except substitute 8 ounces softened, cubed cream cheese for the cheese product.**

Per ¼ cup dip: 122 cal., 11 g total fat (7 g sat. fat), 34 mg chol., 146 mg sodium, 3 g carbo., 0 g fiber, 4 g pro.

Slow-Cooker Directions: **Omit butter and Step 1. In a 2½- to 3½-quart slow cooker toss cheeses with cornstarch. Add the onion, tomato, and undrained chile peppers. Cover and cook on low-heat setting for 3 to 3½ hours or on high-heat setting for 1½ hours. Whisk well before serving. Keep warm, covered, on low-heat setting for up to 2 hours.**

Hot
REUBEN DIP

For significant savings, opt for blocks of cheese and shred it yourself. The savings is about half the price of the packaged, pre-shredded cheese. *Makes 4½ cups*

Prep: 20 minutes Bake: 25 minutes Oven: 350°F

1 14- or 16-ounce can
  sauerkraut, rinsed and well
  drained
1½ cups shredded cheddar
  cheese (6 ounces)
1½ cups shredded Swiss cheese
  (6 ounces)
6 ounces corned beef, chopped
1 cup mayonnaise or salad
  dressing
  Party rye bread, toasted
  baguette-style French bread
  slices, and/or assorted
  crackers

1. Preheat oven to 350°F. Pat sauerkraut dry with paper towels. In a large bowl combine sauerkraut, cheddar cheese, Swiss cheese, corned beef, and mayonnaise. Spread in an ungreased 9-inch quiche dish or 1½-quart casserole.

2. Bake, uncovered, about 25 minutes or until bubbly. Cool slightly before serving. Serve dip with rye bread, baguette slices, and/or crackers.

Make-Ahead Directions: Prepare as directed through Step 1. Cover and chill for up to 24 hours. Preheat oven to 350°F. Bake, uncovered, about 30 minutes or until bubbly.

Per ¼ cup dip: 190 cal., 17 g total fat (6 g sat. fat), 32 mg chol., 396 mg sodium, 2 g carbo., 1 g fiber, 7 g pro.

Asiago CHEESE DIP

This hot dip works well when the gang is over to watch televised sporting events. The slow cooker keeps the dip warm and creamy for up to 2 hours after cooking, assuming it lasts that long! *Makes 6½ cups*

Prep: 15 minutes   Cook: Low 3 hours, High 1½ hours

1 cup chicken broth or water
4 ounces dried tomatoes (not oil-packed)
2 16-ounce cartons dairy sour cream
1½ cups shredded Asiago cheese (6 ounces)
1¼ cups mayonnaise or salad dressing
½ of an 8-ounce package cream cheese, cut up
1 cup sliced fresh mushrooms
1 cup thinly sliced green onion (8)
Thinly sliced green onion
Baguette-style French bread slices, toasted

1. In a small saucepan bring broth to boiling. Remove from heat. Add dried tomatoes; let stand, covered, for 5 minutes. Drain, discarding liquid. Chop tomatoes (you should have about 1¼ cups).
2. Meanwhile, in a 3½- or 4-quart slow cooker combine sour cream, Asiago cheese, mayonnaise, and cream cheese. Stir in mushrooms and the 1 cup green onion. Stir in chopped tomato.

3. Cover and cook on low-heat setting for 3 to 4 hours or on high-heat setting for 1½ to 2 hours. Stir before serving.
4. Serve immediately or keep warm, covered, on low-heat setting for up to 2 hours. Sprinkle dip with additional green onion and serve with toasted baguette slices.

Per ¼ cup dip: 195 cal., 18 g total fat (8 g sat. fat), 29 mg chol., 237 mg sodium, 5 g carbo., 1 g fiber, 4 g pro.

Bacon-Horseradish
CHEDDAR DIP

Serve crispy scoopers with this sharply flavored dip. *Makes 5 cups*

Prep: 20 minutes Cook: Low 4 hours, High 2 hours

3 8-ounce packages cream
  cheese, softened and cut up

3 cups shredded cheddar
  cheese (12 ounces)

1 cup half-and-half or light
  cream

⅓ cup chopped green onion (3)

3 tablespoons prepared
  horseradish

1 tablespoon Worcestershire
  sauce

1½ teaspoons bottled minced
  garlic (3 cloves)

½ teaspoon coarsely ground
  black pepper

12 slices bacon, crisp-cooked,
  drained, and finely crumbled
  Corn chips, toasted pita
  wedges, and/or assorted
  crackers

1. In a 3½- or 4-quart slow cooker combine cream cheese, cheddar cheese, half-and-half, green onion, horseradish, Worcestershire sauce, garlic, and pepper.

2. Cover and cook on low-heat setting for 4 to 5 hours or on high-heat setting for 2 to 2½ hours, stirring once halfway through cooking. Stir in bacon.

3. Serve immediately or keep warm, covered, on low-heat setting for up to 2 hours. Serve dip with corn chips, toasted pita wedges, and/or crackers.

Per ¼ cup dip: 227 cal., 21 g total fat (13 g sat. fat), 63 mg chol., 282 mg sodium, 2 g carbo., 0 g fiber, 8 g pro.

IN-A-PINCH TIPS!

INSTEAD OF HALF-AND-HALF OR LIGHT CREAM, USE 1 TABLESPOON MELTED BUTTER AND ENOUGH WHOLE MILK TO EQUAL 1 CUP.

Hot
ARTICHOKE SPREAD

Remember to shorten the baking time when heating small portions in au gratin dishes. *Makes 5 cups*

Prep: 25 minutes   Bake: 30 minutes   Oven: 350°F

1 tablespoon butter or margarine

¾ cup finely chopped onion

1 teaspoon bottled minced garlic (2 cloves)

2 8-ounce packages reduced-fat cream cheese (Neufchâtel), softened

1½ cups grated Parmesan cheese

¼ cup milk

¼ cup light mayonnaise or salad dressing

¼ cup light dairy sour cream

¼ teaspoon ground black pepper

3 cups chopped fresh spinach

1 14-ounce can artichoke hearts, drained and chopped

Bagel chips, crostini, or sliced French bread

1. Preheat oven to 350°F. In a medium skillet melt butter over medium heat. Add onion and garlic; cook for 3 to 4 minutes or until tender. Cool slightly.

2. In a large bowl stir together cream cheese, Parmesan cheese, milk, mayonnaise, sour cream, and pepper. Stir in the onion mixture, spinach, and artichokes. Spread mixture in an ungreased 10-inch quiche dish or deep-dish pie plate or use 2 smaller au gratin dishes.

3. Bake, uncovered, for 30 to 35 minutes (20 to 25 minutes if using au gratin dishes) or until spread is heated through and starting to brown.

4. Serve spread with bagel chips.

Make-Ahead Directions: Prepare as directed through Step 2. Cover and chill for up to 24 hours. Preheat oven to 350°F. Bake, uncovered, about 40 minutes (about 25 minutes if using au gratin dishes) or until spread is heated through and starting to brown.

Per 2 tablespoons spread: 58 cal., 4 g total fat (2 g sat. fat), 14 mg chol., 138 mg sodium, 2 g carbo., 0 g fiber, 2 g pro.

Simple
SALMON SPREAD

Anchovy paste gives this salmon spread a distinctive nutty flavor. *Makes 1¾ cups*

Prep: 15 minutes Chill: 2 hours

1 14.75-ounce can red sockeye salmon, drained and skin and bones removed
¼ cup oil-packed dried tomatoes, drained and chopped
2 tablespoons lemon juice
2 tablespoons mayonnaise or salad dressing
1 teaspoon bottled minced garlic (2 cloves)
1 teaspoon anchovy paste
1 teaspoon capers, drained (optional)
¼ teaspoon ground white or black pepper
   Mayonnaise or salad dressing (optional)
   Assorted crackers

1. In a food processor* combine salmon, dried tomato, lemon juice, the 2 tablespoons mayonnaise, the garlic, anchovy paste, capers (if desired), and pepper. Cover and process until smooth. If necessary, stir in enough additional mayonnaise to reach desired consistency.

2. Transfer mixture to a serving bowl. Cover and chill for 2 hours to allow flavors to blend. Serve spread with crackers.

*Test Kitchen Tip: If you don't have a food processor, in a medium bowl combine salmon, dried tomato, lemon juice, the 2 tablespoons mayonnaise, the garlic, anchovy paste, capers (if desired), and pepper. Mash with a potato masher until combined. If necessary, stir in enough additional mayonnaise to reach desired consistency.

Make-Ahead Directions: Prepare as directed, except cover and chill for up to 24 hours.

Per 2 tablespoons spread: 67 cal., 4 g total fat (1 g sat. fat), 12 mg chol., 189 mg sodium, 2 g carbo., 0 g fiber, 6 g pro.

Blue Cheese
WALNUT SPREAD

Soft, piquant cheese and crunchy walnuts characterize this quickly prepared, elegant cheese dip. Serve it with crackers, of course, or sliced apples and pears tossed with lemon juice. *Makes 1 cup*

Start to Finish: 15 minutes

1 3-ounce package cream cheese, softened
½ cup crumbled blue cheese (2 ounces)
¼ cup dairy sour cream
½ teaspoon Worcestershire sauce
¼ cup chopped walnuts, toasted
1 tablespoon snipped fresh chives or thinly sliced green onion
   Assorted crackers, apple slices, and/or pear slices

1. In a bowl stir together cream cheese, blue cheese, sour cream, and Worcestershire sauce. Stir in walnuts and chives.

2. Serve spread with crackers, apple, and/or pear.

Per 2 tablespoons spread: 100 cal., 9 g total fat (5 g sat. fat), 20 mg chol., 138 mg sodium, 1 g carbo., 0 g fiber, 3 g pro.

Apple-Spice
HUMMUS

This chickpea dip is based on the Mediterranean favorite—hummus, which is usually quite garlicky and rich. We kept the same protein-rich blend of chickpeas and nuts while lightening the flavor by omitting garlic, and adding intriguing flavor with apple and spices. *Makes 3 cups*

Start to Finish: **20 minutes**

2 15-ounce cans garbanzo beans (chickpeas), rinsed and drained
²⁄₃ cup chopped, peeled sweet apple (such as Golden Delicious) (1 medium)
¹⁄₃ cup lemon juice
¼ cup creamy peanut butter or tahini (sesame seed paste)
2 to 3 tablespoons water
½ teaspoon salt
½ teaspoon apple pie spice
¼ teaspoon cayenne pepper (optional)
   Apple slices, carrot slices, and/or whole wheat crackers

1. In a food processor or blender combine half of the following ingredients: drained beans, apple, lemon juice, peanut butter, the water, salt, apple pie spice, and, if desired, cayenne pepper. Cover and process or blend until smooth. Transfer mixture to a serving bowl. Repeat with the remaining half of the above ingredients.

2. Serve dip with apple, carrot, and/or crackers.

Per 2 tablespoons dip: 62 cal., 2 g total fat (0 g sat. fat), 0 mg chol., 167 mg sodium, 10 g carbo., 2 g fiber, 2 g pro.

MASH AWAY: IF YOU DON'T HAVE A FOOD PROCESSOR OR BLENDER, USE A FORK OR POTATO MASHER TO MASH THE BEANS, AND FINELY CHOP THE APPLE WITH A KNIFE. COMBINE MASHED BEANS, FINELY CHOPPED APPLE, AND REMAINING DIP INGREDIENTS IN A BOWL AND STIR UNTIL NEARLY SMOOTH.

Fruited

CHEESE BALL

If you prefer, shape the sweet and savory cream cheese mixture into two 5-inch logs instead of a ball.

Makes 2½ cups

Prep: **20 minutes**   Stand: **30 minutes**   Chill: **4 to 24 hours**

2 cups shredded Monterey Jack cheese (8 ounces)
½ of an 8-ounce package cream cheese
½ cup snipped dried apricots
⅓ cup golden raisins, snipped
¼ cup pitted dates, snipped
2 tablespoons orange juice
¼ teaspoon salt
Coarsely chopped almonds, toasted
Assorted crackers and/or apple slices

1. In a medium bowl combine Monterey Jack cheese and cream cheese. Let stand at room temperature for 30 minutes. Meanwhile, in a small bowl combine apricots, raisins, and dates; add enough warm water to cover. Let stand about 30 minutes or until softened; drain well.

2. Add orange juice to cheese mixture. Beat with an electric mixer on medium speed until combined. Stir in apricots, raisins, dates, and salt. Cover and chill for 4 to 24 hours.

3. Shape mixture into a ball. Roll in almonds to coat. Serve with crackers and/or apple slices.

Per 2 tablespoons spread: 95 cal., 6 g total fat (3 g sat. fat), 16 mg chol., 107 mg sodium, 6 g carbo., 1 g fiber, 4 g pro.

I'm-So-Stuffed
MUSHROOMS

For uniform baking, select mushrooms of the same size. *Makes 24 stuffed mushrooms*

Prep: **25 minutes** Bake: **13 minutes** Oven: **425°F**

24 large fresh mushrooms,
    1½ to 2 inches in diameter
    Nonstick cooking spray
¼ cup butter or margarine
¼ cup sliced green onion (2)
½ teaspoon bottled minced
    garlic (1 clove)
½ cup fine dry bread crumbs
½ cup shredded cheddar
    cheese (2 ounces)
2 slices bacon, crisp-cooked,
    drained, and crumbled

1. Preheat oven to 425°F. Clean mushrooms, remove stems, and set stems aside. Place mushroom caps, stem sides down, in a 15×10×1-inch baking pan. Lightly coat mushroom caps with cooking spray. Bake for 5 minutes. Drain mushroom caps, stem sides down, on a double thickness of paper towels.

2. Chop enough of the reserved mushroom stems to make 1 cup. In a medium saucepan melt butter over medium heat. Add chopped mushroom stems, green onion, and garlic; cook until tender, stirring occasionally. Stir in bread crumbs, cheese, and bacon. Turn mushrooms stem sides up. Spoon crumb mixture into mushroom caps.

3. Return stuffed mushrooms to baking pan. Bake, uncovered, for 8 to 10 minutes or until heated through.

Per stuffed mushroom: 45 cal., 4 g total fat (2 g sat. fat), 8 mg chol., 101 mg sodium, 2 g carbo., 0 g fiber, 2 g pro.

Chilly
VEGGIE PIZZA

This recipe is perfect for all occasions. Part of this pizza's appeal comes from the variety of vegetables topping the cream-cheese-covered crust. See photo on page 98. *Makes 12 servings*

Prep: **25 minutes** Bake: **8 minutes** Chill: **2 to 4 hours** Oven: **375°F**

1 8-ounce package (8) refrigerated crescent rolls
1 8-ounce package cream cheese, softened
⅓ cup mayonnaise or salad dressing
2 tablespoons thinly sliced green onion (1)
½ teaspoon dried dill
½ cup shredded lettuce
⅓ cup sliced, pimiento-stuffed green olives or pitted ripe olives
¼ cup chopped green and/or yellow sweet pepper
¼ cup chopped seeded cucumber
⅔ cup crumbled garlic-and-herb feta cheese
½ cup chopped seeded tomato (1 medium)

1. Preheat oven to 375°F. Grease a 12-inch pizza pan or 13×9×2-inch baking pan. Unroll crescent rolls. Press dough onto the bottom and sides of the prepared pizza pan (or onto the bottom and about ½ inch up the sides of the prepared baking pan). Press dough perforations to seal. Bake, uncovered, for 8 to 10 minutes or until light brown. Cool.

2. Meanwhile, in a medium bowl combine cream cheese, mayonnaise, green onion, and dill. Spread cream cheese mixture over cooled crust. Top with lettuce, olives, sweet pepper, and cucumber. Sprinkle with feta cheese and tomato. Cover and chill for 2 to 4 hours.

Per serving: 206 cal., 17 g total fat (7 g sat. fat), 28 mg chol., 334 mg sodium, 9 g carbo., 0 g fiber, 4 g pro.

# Deviled
EGGS

This classic is always a hit appetizer at gatherings. For these party favorites, check the price of all sizes of eggs, then purchase the least expensive dozen. *Makes 12 servings*

Start to Finish: **25 minutes**

6 hard-cooked eggs
¼ cup mayonnaise or salad
   dressing
1 teaspoon yellow mustard
1 teaspoon vinegar
   Salt and ground black pepper
   Paprika or fresh parsley
     sprigs (optional)

1. Halve hard-cooked eggs lengthwise; remove yolks. Set whites aside. Place yolks in a small bowl; mash with a fork. Stir in mayonnaise, mustard, and vinegar. Season to taste with salt and pepper.

2. Stuff egg white halves with yolk mixture. Cover and chill for up to 24 hours. If desired, garnish with paprika.

Per serving: 73 cal., 6 g total fat (1 g sat. fat), 108 mg chol., 109 mg sodium, 0 g carbo., 0 g fiber, 3 g pro.

Greek-Style Deviled Eggs: Prepare as directed, except fold 2 tablespoons crumbled feta cheese, 1 tablespoon finely chopped pitted kalamata olives or ripe olives, and 2 teaspoons snipped fresh oregano into yolk mixture.

Per serving: 78 cal, 7 g fat (2 g sat fat), 109 mg chol, 134 mg sodium, 1 g carbo, 0 g fib, 3 g pro.

Curry-and-Crab Deviled Eggs: Prepare as directed, except omit mustard and vinegar. Stir the mayonnaise, 2 teaspoons Dijon-style mustard, 1 teaspoon snipped fresh chives, and ½ teaspoon curry powder into mashed yolks. Fold in ¼ cup drained and flaked canned crabmeat.

Per serving: 77 cal, 6 g fat (1 g sat fat), 111 mg chol, 136 mg sodium, 0 g carbo, 0 g fib, 4 g pro.

Chipotle Deviled Eggs: **Prepare** as directed, except omit mayonnaise, mustard, and vinegar. Stir ¼ cup dairy sour cream, 1 tablespoon finely chopped green onion, and 1 teaspoon finely chopped canned chipotle pepper in adobo sauce (see note, page 22) into mashed yolks.

Per serving: 48 cal, 4 g fat (1 g sat fat), 108 mg chol, 84 mg sodium, 1 g carbo, 0 g fib, 3 g pro.

Polynesian Glazed
CHICKEN WINGS

Keep a package of frozen drummettes in the freezer along with the ingredients for the spicy-sweet glaze in your cupboard. You will be able to savor these wings whenever you like. *Makes 15 servings*

Prep: 15 minutes Bake: 1 hour Oven: 400°F

3 pounds frozen plain chicken wing drummettes (about 30)
½ cup packed brown sugar
1 tablespoon cornstarch
2 teaspoons grated fresh ginger
¼ to ½ teaspoon crushed red pepper
½ cup unsweetened pineapple juice
½ cup chicken broth
¼ cup finely chopped green sweet pepper
2 tablespoons soy sauce
Thinly sliced green onion (optional)

1. Preheat oven to 400°F. Place frozen chicken drummettes in an ungreased 15×10×1-inch baking pan. Bake, uncovered, for 50 to 60 minutes or until chicken is no longer pink and skin is crispy.

2. Meanwhile, for glaze, in a small saucepan combine brown sugar, cornstarch, ginger, and crushed red pepper. Stir in pineapple juice, broth, sweet pepper, and soy sauce. Cook and stir over medium heat until thickened and bubbly. Cook and stir for 2 minutes more.

3. Carefully drain off any fat from baking pan. Brush drummettes with some of the glaze. Bake, uncovered, for 10 minutes more. Brush with additional glaze. Transfer to a serving platter. If desired, sprinkle with green onion. Pass the remaining glaze.

Make-Ahead Directions: Prepare glaze as directed in Step 2. Cool slightly. Transfer to an airtight container; seal. Chill for up to 24 hours before using. Transfer glaze to a small saucepan; cook over low heat until heated through, stirring occasionally.

Per serving: 231 cal., 15 g total fat (3 g sat. fat), 93 mg chol., 251 mg sodium, 9 g carbo., 0 g fiber, 16 g pro.

*Creole*

TURKEY MEATBALLS

Be warned, these tasty meatballs will be gobbled up quickly. *Makes 10 servings*

Prep: **25 minutes**   Bake: **25 minutes**   Oven: **375°F**

1 egg, lightly beaten
¾ cup chopped green sweet
    pepper (1 medium)
½ cup quick-cooking rolled oats
½ cup chopped onion
    (1 medium)
2 tablespoons milk
1 teaspoon dried Italian
    seasoning, crushed
1 teaspoon salt-free seasoning
    blend
1 teaspoon Creole seasoning
1 teaspoon bottled minced
    garlic (2 cloves)
1 pound uncooked ground
    turkey or ground chicken

1. Preheat oven to 375°F. Lightly grease a 15×10×1-inch baking pan; set aside. In a large bowl combine egg, sweet pepper, oats, onion, milk, Italian seasoning, salt-free seasoning, Creole seasoning, and garlic. Add ground turkey; mix well.
2. Using a slightly rounded tablespoon, shape turkey mixture into 1¼-inch meatballs. Arrange meatballs in the prepared baking pan.
3. Bake, uncovered, about 25 minutes or until no longer pink in center (165°F).*

Make-Ahead Directions: **Prepare** as directed through Step 2. Cover and chill for up to 24 hours. Uncover and bake as directed.

*Test Kitchen Tip: The internal color of a meatball is not a reliable doneness indicator. A poultry meatball cooked to 165°F is safe, regardless of color. To measure the doneness of a meatball, insert an instant-read thermometer into the center of the meatball.

Per serving: 98 cal., 5 g total fat (1 g sat. fat), 57 mg chol., 52 mg sodium, 5 g carbo., 1 g fiber, 9 g pro.

*Italian*

COCKTAIL MEATBALLS

These party appetizers make your life easy. Four ingredients, a few minutes preparation, and four hours in a slow cooker—that's all you need. *Makes 16 servings*

Prep: 10 minutes Cook: 4 hours

1 16-ounce package (32) frozen cooked meatballs, thawed
½ cup bottled roasted red and yellow sweet peppers, drained and cut into 1-inch pieces
⅛ teaspoon crushed red pepper
1½ cups purchased pasta sauce with onion and garlic

1. In a 1½-quart slow cooker combine meatballs, roasted pepper, and crushed red pepper. Pour pasta sauce over mixture in cooker.
2. Cover and cook for 4 to 5 hours (use low-heat setting if available).

3. Skim fat from sauce. Stir gently before serving. Serve immediately or keep warm, covered, for up to 2 hours (use low-heat setting if available).

Per serving: 99 cal., 8 g total fat (3 g sat. fat), 10 mg chol., 322 mg sodium, 4 g carbo., 1 g fiber, 4 g pro.

Cranberry-Barbecue
MEATBALLS

With a choice of three sauces and slow-cooker or saucepan directions, these tidbits are sure-to-please fare for any party. *Makes 64 servings*

Prep: 10 minutes Cook: Low 4 hours, High 2 hours

2 16-ounce packages
   (64 total) frozen cooked
   plain meatballs, thawed
1 16-ounce can jellied
   cranberry sauce
1 cup bottled barbecue sauce

1. Place meatballs in a 3½- or 4-quart slow cooker. In a medium bowl combine cranberry sauce and barbecue sauce. Pour over meatballs, stirring to coat.
2. Cover and cook on low-heat setting for 4 to 5 hours or on high-heat setting for 2 to 2½ hours.
3. Serve immediately or keep warm, covered, on low-heat setting for up to 2 hours. Use toothpicks to serve meatballs.

Saucepan Directions: In a large saucepan combine cranberry sauce and barbecue sauce; stir in meatballs. Bring to boiling; reduce heat. Simmer, uncovered, for 10 to 15 minutes or until heated through, stirring occasionally.

Per serving: 60 cal., 4 g total fat (2 g sat. fat), 5 mg chol., 156 mg sodium, 5 g carbo., 0 g fiber, 2 g pro.

Cranberry-Chipotle Meatballs: Prepare as directed, except add 1 to 2 tablespoons finely chopped canned chipotle chile pepper in adobo sauce (see note, page 22) to the cranberry-barbecue sauce mixture.

Per serving: 60 cal, 4 g total fat (2 g sat fat), 5 mg chol, 158 mg sodium, 5 g carbo, 0 g fiber, 2 g pro.

Mexi Meatballs: Prepare as directed, except substitute one 16-ounce jar salsa and one 10-ounce can enchilada sauce for the cranberry and barbecue sauces.

Per serving: 47 cal, 4 g total fat (2 g sat fat), 5 mg chol, 183 mg sodium, 2 g carbo, 0 g fiber, 2 g pro.

Bourbon-Glazed
COCKTAIL SAUSAGES

Here is another take on the ever-popular cocktail wiener. The three ingredients meld beautifully for a "wow, what is it?" sort of sauce. *Makes 12 servings*

Prep: **5 minutes** Cook: **4 hours**

1 16-ounce package cocktail wieners or small cooked smoked sausage links
½ cup apricot preserves
¼ cup maple syrup
1 tablespoon bourbon or orange juice

1. In a 1½-quart slow cooker combine cocktail wieners, preserves, syrup, and bourbon. Cover and cook for 4 hours (use low-heat setting if available).

2. Serve immediately or keep warm, covered, for up to 1 hour (use low-heat setting if available). Use toothpicks to serve wieners.

Test Kitchen Tip: To increase the recipe, double the ingredient amounts, using 1 package cocktail wieners and 1 package small cooked smoked sausage links, and use a 3½- or 4-quart slow cooker.

Per serving: 170 cal., 10 g total fat (4 g sat. fat), 23 mg chol., 383 mg sodium, 14 g carbo., 0 g fiber, 5 g pro.

Crunchy Cracker
SNACK MIX

Customize this snack mix by substituting some of your favorite bite-size crackers. Also, if you prefer a particular type of nut, substitute it for the mixed nuts. See photo on page 99. *Makes 13 cups*

Prep: 10 minutes   Bake: 25 minutes   Oven: 300°F

5 cups wheat stick crackers
4 cups bite-size cheese
   crackers
3 cups pretzel twists
2 cups mixed nuts
½ cup butter or margarine,
   melted
1 0.6- to 0.7-ounce envelope
   cheese-garlic or Italian dry
   salad dressing mix

1. Preheat oven to 300°F. In a large roasting pan combine wheat stick crackers and cheese crackers. Bake, uncovered, about 5 minutes or until warm. Stir in pretzels and nuts.
2. Pour melted butter over mixture. Sprinkle with salad dressing mix; stir gently to coat. Bake, uncovered, for 20 minutes more, stirring once.

3. Spread mixture on a large piece of foil to cool. Store in an airtight container for up to 1 week.

Per ¼ cup serving: 80 cal., 6 g total fat (2 g sat. fat), 5 mg chol., 165 mg sodium, 5 g carbo., 1 g fiber, 2 g pro.

LOOK!

MONEY-SAVING TIPS and HINTS

Buy ground beef in bulk. Package in 1-pound portions or whatever size works for you. Label and freeze in freezer wrap or bags.

Opt for larger cuts of meat and trim to the size you need. Wrap and freeze in freezer wrap or bags.

$AVE! Purchase large packages of beef cuts, such as family size. Repackage and freeze according to your needs.

Yes! For stew meat, purchase pot roast on sale and cut into pieces for stew meat rather than buying precut meat.

Take advantage of sales on heat-and-eat beef, such as pot roast, meatloaf, and barbecued beef. Freeze for last-minute meals.

Cook a chuck roast in broth in your slow cooker. Shred the meat and freeze in 2-cup containers. You'll have enough for *4* generous sandwiches. Thaw as needed for a quick lunch or dinner.

Save on work time, energy cost, and clean up when browning ground beef. Cook twice as much as you need. Freeze the remainder for another recipe. Having cooked ground beef on hand will simplify meals when time is short. Add the meat to pasta sauce, use in quick soups, or in tacos.

Make your own seasoned, ready-to-cook beef patties. Purchase ground beef on sale or in large quantity, jazz it up with spices, and freeze patties on baking sheets. When frozen, transfer to freezer bags.

$** Buy specialty beef items, such as bacon-wrapped tenderloins, on sale. Wrap and freeze in useful portions. **$

CHAPTER 2

BANK ON BEEF

Our love for beef never wavers. So step up to this "bank" of 58 recipes that help you enjoy your taste for beef without breaking the food budget. Many cook in the slow-cooker, the appliance "chef" for busy lives. Others take less than 30 minutes from start to finish with results that do not sacrifice flavor. With this cache of money-saving recipes, you'll never run out of great ways to serve beloved beef.

Sunday
OVEN POT ROAST

Cover the roasting pan with a tight-fitting lid or with a double thickness of foil. *Makes 6 to 8 servings*

Prep: **30 minutes** Roast: **2 hours, 5 minutes** Oven: **325°F**

2½- to 3-pound boneless beef chuck pot roast
    Salt and ground black pepper
2 tablespoons olive oil or cooking oil
1 14-ounce can beef broth
2 stalks celery, cut into 2-inch pieces
1 cup chopped onion (1 large)
5 cups assorted fresh vegetables such as peeled Yukon gold or sweet potatoes, cut into 2-inch pieces; parsnips, peeled and cut into 2-inch pieces; shallots or garlic bulbs, peeled and halved horizontally; and/or medium carrots, cut into 1½-inch pieces
¼ cup cold water
3 tablespoons all-purpose flour

1. Preheat oven to 325°F. Trim fat from meat. Sprinkle meat with salt and pepper. In a roasting pan or large ovenproof Dutch oven, cook meat in hot oil over medium-high heat until brown on all sides. Drain off fat. Add broth, celery, and onion.

2. Roast, covered, for 1¼ hours. Using a slotted spoon, remove and discard celery. Arrange assorted vegetables around meat. Roast, uncovered, for 50 to 60 minutes more or until meat and vegetables are tender, basting twice with pan juices. Using the slotted spoon, transfer meat and vegetables to a serving platter; cover and keep warm.

3. For gravy, measure pan juices; skim off fat. Discard enough juices or add enough water to juices to equal 1½ cups. In a small saucepan whisk together the cold water and flour; add the 1½ cups pan juices. Cook and stir over medium heat until thickened and bubbly. Cook and stir for 1 minute more. Season to taste with salt and pepper. Serve meat and vegetables with gravy.

Nutrition Facts per serving: 419 cal., 14 g total fat (4 g sat. fat), 112 mg chol., 584 mg sodium, 29 g carbo., 4 g dietary fiber, 43 g protein.

Slow-Cooker Directions: Trim fat from meat. Sprinkle meat with salt and pepper. If necessary, cut meat to fit into a 5- to 6-quart slow cooker. Omit cooking oil. Place all of the vegetables in cooker; add meat and broth. Cover and cook on low-heat setting for 9 to 11 hours or on high-heat setting for 4½ to 5½ hours. Remove meat and vegetables from cooker; cover and keep warm. Continue as directed in Step 3.

Cranberry-Chipotle
BEEF

Looking for a slow-cooked roast that serves just four? This fiery chipotle-seasoned chuck roast is a delicious choice. *Makes 4 servings*

Prep: 10 minutes   Cook: Low 6 hours, High 3 hours

1½ pounds boneless beef chuck pot roast
1 medium onion, cut into thin wedges
1 teaspoon bottled minced garlic (2 cloves)
¼ teaspoon salt
¼ teaspoon ground black pepper
1 16-ounce can whole cranberry sauce
1 to 2 teaspoons finely chopped canned chipotle chile pepper in adobo sauce (see note, page 22)
2 cups uncooked instant brown rice
Fresh jalapeño chile peppers, halved (optional)

1. Trim fat from meat. If necessary, cut meat to fit into a 4-quart slow cooker. Place onion in cooker; add meat. Sprinkle with garlic, salt, and black pepper. In a small bowl combine cranberry sauce and chipotle pepper; pour over mixture in cooker.

2. Cover and cook on low-heat setting for 6 to 8 hours or on high-heat setting for 3 to 4 hours.

3. To serve, cook brown rice according to package directions, except omit butter and salt. Serve meat mixture with brown rice. If desired, garnish with jalapeño pepper.

Per serving: 506 cal., 7 g total fat (2 g sat. fat), 101 mg chol., 296 mg sodium, 71 g carbo., 4 g fiber, 40 g pro.

Cola
POT ROAST

Different and delicious, this slow cooker pot roast with veggies and brown gravy obtains a sweet note from a can of cola. The meat is tender, and the gravy is thick. *Makes 6 servings*

Prep: 15 minutes Cook: Low 7 hours, High 3½ hours

1 2½- to 3-pound boneless beef chuck pot roast
   Nonstick cooking spray
2 16-ounce packages frozen stew vegetables
1 12-ounce can cola
1 envelope (½ of a 2.2-ounce package) onion soup mix
2 tablespoons quick-cooking tapioca

1. Trim fat from meat. Coat a large skillet with cooking spray; heat skillet over medium-high heat. Cook meat in hot skillet until brown on all sides.

2. Transfer meat to a 4½- or 5-quart slow cooker. Top with frozen vegetables. In a small bowl stir together cola, dry soup mix, and tapioca. Pour over meat and vegetables.

3. Cover and cook on low-heat setting for 7 to 8 hours or on high-heat setting for 3½ to 4 hours.

Per serving: 278 cal., 5 g total fat (2 g sat. fat), 75 mg chol., 582 mg sodium, 28 g carbo., 2 g fiber, 29 g pro.

Cowboy
BEEF

Pot roast heads for the untamed West when slow-cooked with chili beans, corn, tomatoes, and spicy chile peppers in adobo sauce. *Makes 6 servings*

Prep: 10 minutes   Cook: Low 10 hours, High 5 hours

1 2- to 2½-pound boneless beef chuck pot roast
1 15-ounce can chili beans in chili gravy, undrained
1 11-ounce can whole kernel corn with sweet peppers, drained
1 10-ounce can diced tomatoes and green chiles, undrained
1 to 2 teaspoons finely chopped canned chipotle chile pepper in adobo sauce (see note, page 22)

1. Trim fat from meat. If necessary, cut meat to fit into a 3½- or 4-quart slow cooker. Place meat in cooker. In a medium bowl combine undrained chili beans in gravy, drained corn, undrained tomatoes, and chipotle pepper. Pour bean mixture over meat in cooker.

2. Cover and cook on low-heat setting for 10 to 12 hours or on high-heat setting for 5 to 6 hours.

3. Remove meat from cooker and place on a cutting board. Slice meat; arrange in a shallow serving bowl. Using a slotted spoon, spoon bean mixture over meat. Drizzle with enough of the cooking liquid to moisten.

Per serving: 307 cal., 7 g total fat (2 g sat. fat), 89 mg chol., 655 mg sodium, 23 g carbo., 5 g fiber, 37 g pro.

Beef
BURGUNDY

A fruity wine infuses rich flavor into thrifty beef stew meat and frozen vegetables. *Makes 6 servings*

Prep: **20 minutes**   Cook: **Low 7 hours, High 3½ hours**

Nonstick cooking spray
2 pounds beef stew meat, cut into 1-inch pieces
1 16-ounce package frozen stew vegetables
1 10.75-ounce can condensed golden mushroom soup
⅔ cup Burgundy wine
⅓ cup water
1 tablespoon quick-cooking tapioca
3 cups hot cooked wide noodles or garlic mashed potatoes (optional)
Snipped fresh parsley (optional)

1. Lightly coat a large skillet with cooking spray; heat skillet over medium-high heat. Cook meat, half at a time, in hot skillet until brown.
2. Place frozen vegetables in a 3½- or 4-quart slow cooker. Add meat. In a medium bowl combine soup, Burgundy wine, the water, and tapioca. Pour over meat and vegetables.

3. Cover and cook on low-heat setting for 7 to 9 hours or on high-heat setting for 3½ to 4½ hours.
4. If desired, serve meat mixture over hot cooked noodles and sprinkle with parsley.

Per serving: 291 cal., 8 g total fat (3 g sat. fat), 91 mg chol., 535 mg sodium, 14 g carbo., 1 g fiber, 34 g pro.

Old-Time
BEEF STEW

There's nothing like a bowl of old-fashioned beef stew. Served with corn bread or biscuits, this is a hearty, comforting meal—ready when you walk in the door. *Makes 6 servings*

Prep: **30 minutes** Cook: **Low 9 hours, High 4½ hours**

1½ pounds beef stew meat, cut into 1-inch pieces

1 tablespoon cooking oil

3 medium potatoes (1 pound), cut into 1-inch pieces

4 medium carrots, cut into ¾-inch slices

½ of a 16-ounce package (about 2 cups) frozen small whole onions

2 bay leaves

3 tablespoons quick-cooking tapioca

2 tablespoons Worcestershire sauce

1 tablespoon snipped fresh thyme or 1 teaspoon dried thyme, crushed

¼ teaspoon salt

¼ teaspoon ground black pepper

2 14-ounce cans beef broth
Corn bread, warmed (optional)

1. In a large skillet cook meat, half at a time, in hot oil over medium-high heat until brown. Drain off fat.

2. In a 3½- to 5-quart slow cooker combine potato, carrot, and frozen onions. Add meat and bay leaves. Sprinkle with tapioca, Worcestershire sauce, dried thyme (if using), salt, and pepper. Pour broth over mixture in cooker.

3. Cover and cook on low-heat setting for 9 to 11 hours or on high-heat setting for 4½ to 5½ hours.

4. Discard bay leaves. Stir in fresh thyme (if using). If desired, serve with corn bread.

Per serving: 310 cal., 8 g total fat (2 g sat. fat), 53 mg chol., 593 mg sodium, 27 g carbo., 4 g fiber, 31 g pro.

Beef Stew
WITH CORNMEAL DUMPLINGS

This is a hearty, comforting stew topped with Southern-style dumplings. *Makes 8 servings*

Prep: **30 minutes** Cook: **1 hour 40 minutes**

2 pounds beef stew meat, cut into 1-inch pieces
1 tablespoon cooking oil
1 28-ounce can diced tomatoes, undrained
1 cup beef broth
¼ cup coarse-grain Dijon-style mustard
1 teaspoon dried thyme, crushed
1 teaspoon bottled minced garlic (2 cloves)
½ teaspoon salt
½ teaspoon dried oregano, crushed
½ teaspoon ground black pepper
1 20-ounce package refrigerated diced potatoes with onions
1 cup packaged peeled baby carrots
1 9-ounce package frozen cut green beans
1 recipe Cornmeal Dumplings

1. In a 4-quart Dutch oven cook meat, half at a time, in hot oil over medium-high heat until brown. Drain off fat. Return all of the meat to Dutch oven. Stir in undrained tomatoes, broth, mustard, thyme, garlic, salt, oregano, and pepper. Bring to boiling; reduce heat. Simmer, covered, for 1 hour.

2. Add potatoes and carrots. Return to boiling; reduce heat. Simmer, covered, for 20 minutes. Stir in frozen green beans. Return to boiling; reduce heat.

3. Drop Cornmeal Dumplings batter from a tablespoon into 8 mounds on top of stew. Cook, covered, about 20 minutes or until a toothpick inserted into a dumpling comes out clean.

Cornmeal Dumplings: In a medium bowl stir together one 8.5-ounce package corn muffin mix, ½ cup shredded cheddar cheese (2 ounces), and ¼ cup sliced green onion (2). Stir in 1 lightly beaten egg and ¼ cup dairy sour cream just until moistened (batter will be thick).

Per serving: 446 cal., 13 g total fat (4 g sat. fat), 104 mg chol., 1092 mg sodium, 47 g carbo., 4 g fiber, 33 g pro.

Fajita-Style
FLANK STEAK

When broiling flank steak, take care not to overcook the beef. It's most tender and flavorful cooked just to medium doneness. *Makes 6 servings*

Prep: 15 minutes   Marinate: 8 to 24 hours   Broil: 15 minutes

1   1½-pound beef flank steak
¼ cup bottled Italian salad
     dressing
¼ cup bottled salsa
½ teaspoon finely shredded
     lime peel
1   tablespoon lime juice
1   tablespoon snipped fresh
     cilantro or parsley
⅛ teaspoon bottled hot pepper
     sauce

1. Trim fat from meat. Place meat in a resealable plastic bag set in a shallow dish.

2. For marinade, in a small bowl combine salad dressing, salsa, lime peel, lime juice, cilantro, and hot pepper sauce. Pour marinade over meat. Seal bag; turn to coat meat. Marinate in the refrigerator for 8 to 24 hours, turning bag occasionally. Drain meat, reserving marinade.

3. Preheat broiler. Place meat on the unheated rack of a broiler pan. Broil 3 to 4 inches from the heat for 15 to 18 minutes for medium (160°F), turning and brushing once with marinade halfway through broiling.

4. Pour the remaining marinade into a small saucepan; bring to a full boil. Thinly slice meat diagonally across the grain. Serve meat with marinade.

Per serving: 208 cal., 11 g total fat (4 g sat. fat), 40 mg chol., 288 mg sodium, 2 g carbo., 0 g fiber, 24 g pro.

Asian Beef
AND NOODLE BOWL

This colorful beef and noodle soup is flavored with ginger and soy sauce. *Makes 4 servings*

Start to Finish: **30 minutes**

12 ounces beef flank steak or boneless top round steak

4 cups water

2 3-ounce packages ramen noodles (any flavor)

2 teaspoons chili oil, or 2 teaspoons cooking oil plus ⅛ teaspoon cayenne pepper

1 teaspoon bottled minced garlic (2 cloves)

1 teaspoon grated fresh ginger

1 cup beef broth

2 tablespoons soy sauce

2 cups fresh baby spinach or torn fresh spinach leaves

1 cup shredded carrot (2 medium)

¼ cup snipped fresh cilantro or parsley

1. Trim fat from meat. Thinly slice meat diagonally across the grain into bite-size strips; set aside. In a large saucepan bring the water to boiling. If desired, break up noodles; drop noodles into boiling water. (Reserve the flavor packets for another use.) Return to boiling; boil for 2 to 3 minutes or until noodles are tender but still firm, stirring occasionally. Drain noodles.

2. Meanwhile, in a very large skillet, heat oil over medium-high heat. Add meat, garlic, and ginger; cook and stir for 2 to 3 minutes or until meat is slightly pink in center. Stir in broth and soy sauce.

3. Bring to boiling; reduce heat. Stir in cooked noodles, spinach, and carrot; heat through. Before serving, stir in cilantro.

Per serving: 381 cal., 17 g total fat (3 g sat. fat), 34 mg chol., 1,503 mg sodium, 30 g carbo., 2 g fiber, 26 g pro.

IN-A-PINCH TIPS!

CILANTRO TIP: FOR EACH ¼ CUP FRESH CILANTRO, USE 1 TEASPOON DRIED CILANTRO AND ¼ CUP CHOPPED FRESH PARSLEY.

Easy
BEEF STROGANOFF

A combination of noodles and broccoli stretches the yummy meat and sauce base of the stroganoff.

Makes 4 servings

Start to Finish: **35 minutes**

3 cups dried wide noodles

12 ounces broccoli spears

½ cup light dairy sour cream

1½ teaspoons prepared
   horseradish

½ teaspoon snipped fresh dill

1 pound boneless beef ribeye
   or sirloin steak

1 tablespoon cooking oil

1 small onion, cut into ½-inch
   slices

½ teaspoon bottled minced
   garlic (1 clove)

4 teaspoons all-purpose flour

½ teaspoon ground black
   pepper

1 14-ounce can beef broth

3 tablespoons tomato paste

1 teaspoon Worcestershire
   sauce

1. Cook noodles according to package directions, adding broccoli during the last 5 minutes of cooking; drain. Return noodle mixture to hot pan; cover and keep warm.

2. Meanwhile, in a small bowl stir together sour cream, horseradish, and dill. Cover and chill until ready to serve.

3. Trim fat from meat. Thinly slice meat across the grain into bite-size strips. In a large skillet heat oil over medium-high heat. Add half of the meat, the onion, and garlic. Cook and stir until meat is slightly pink in center and onion is tender. Remove meat and onion from skillet. Add the remaining meat; cook and stir until meat is slightly pink in center. Return all of the meat to skillet. Sprinkle with flour and pepper; stir to coat. Stir in broth, tomato paste, and Worcestershire sauce. Cook and stir until thickened and bubbly. Cook and stir for 1 minute more.

4. Divide noodle mixture among 4 bowls. Spoon meat mixture over noodle mixture. Top with sour cream mixture.

Per serving: 368 cal., 15 g total fat (5 g sat. fat), 81 mg chol., 454 mg sodium, 32 g carbo., 4 g fiber, 29 g pro.

Beef
FAJITAS

Shredded carrot and lettuce provide a fresh crunch to slow-simmered meat and vegetables.
Makes 8 servings

Prep: **25 minutes**   Cook: **Low 7 hours, High 3½ hours**

1 large onion, cut into thin
  wedges
2 pounds boneless beef sirloin
  steak
1 teaspoon ground cumin
1 teaspoon ground coriander
½ teaspoon salt
½ teaspoon ground black
  pepper
2 cups thin bite-size strips red
  and/or green sweet pepper
  (2 medium)
¼ cup beef broth
8 7- to 8-inch whole wheat or
  plain flour tortillas
1 cup shredded carrot
  (2 medium)
1 cup coarsely shredded
  lettuce
  Bottled salsa, purchased
  guacamole, and/or dairy
  sour cream

1. Place onion in a 3½- or 4-quart slow cooker. Trim fat from meat. Sprinkle one side of meat with cumin, coriander, salt, and black pepper; rub in with your fingers. Thinly slice meat across the grain into bite-size strips. Add meat and sweet pepper to cooker. Pour broth over mixture in cooker.

2. Cover and cook on low-heat setting for 7 to 8 hours or on high-heat setting for 3½ to 4 hours.

3. Using a slotted spoon, spoon meat mixture onto tortillas. Top with carrot and lettuce. Fold tortillas over filling. Serve with salsa, guacamole, and/or sour cream.

Per serving: 327 cal., 10 g total fat (3 g sat. fat), 70 mg chol., 642 mg sodium, 22 g carbo., 12 g fiber, 33 g pro.

Chicken
FRIED STEAK

Pounding does the trick for tenderizing round steak, a less tender, more economical cut of meat. After cooking the meat, reserve the pan drippings to make milk gravy to serve over the meat and, if you like, mashed potatoes. *Makes 4 servings*

Prep: **30 minutes** Cook: **45 minutes**

1 pound boneless beef top round steak, cut ½ inch thick
1 egg, lightly beaten
1 tablespoon milk
¾ cup fine dry bread crumbs
1½ teaspoons snipped fresh basil or oregano or ½ teaspoon dried basil or oregano, crushed
½ teaspoon salt
¼ teaspoon ground black pepper
2 tablespoons cooking oil
1 small onion, sliced and separated into rings
2 tablespoons all-purpose flour
1⅓ cups milk
Salt and ground black pepper

1. Trim fat from meat. Cut meat into 4 serving-size pieces. Place each piece between 2 pieces of plastic wrap. Working from center to edges, pound lightly with the flat side of a meat mallet to ¼-inch thickness. Remove plastic wrap.

2. In a shallow dish combine egg and the 1 tablespoon milk. In another shallow dish or on waxed paper, combine bread crumbs, basil, the ½ teaspoon salt, and the ¼ teaspoon pepper. Dip meat into egg mixture, then into bread crumb mixture, turning to coat.

3. In a 12-inch skillet cook meat, half at time, in hot oil over medium-high heat until brown on both sides. (Add more oil, if necessary.) Return all of the meat to skillet. Reduce heat to medium-low. Cook, covered, for 45 to 60 minutes or until meat is tender. Transfer meat to a serving platter, reserving drippings in skillet. Cover meat and keep warm.

4. For the gravy, cook onion in the reserved drippings over medium heat until tender. (Add more oil, if necessary.) Stir in the flour. Gradually stir in the 1⅓ cups milk. Cook and stir until thickened and bubbly. Cook and stir for 1 minute more. Season to taste with additional salt and pepper. Serve meat with gravy.

Per serving: 351 cal., 13 g total fat (3 g sat. fat), 108 mg chol., 578 mg sodium, 23 g carbo., 1 g fiber, 34 g pro.

Salsa
SWISS STEAK

We turned up the flavor a bit by adding salsa to this family-pleasing saucy steak. *Makes 6 servings*

Prep: 15 minutes   Cook: Low 9 hours, High 4½ hours

2 pounds boneless beef round steak, cut 1 inch thick

1 to 2 large red and/or green sweet peppers, seeded and cut into bite-size strips

1 medium onion, sliced

1 10.75-ounce can condensed cream of mushroom soup

1 cup bottled salsa

2 tablespoons all-purpose flour

1 teaspoon dry mustard
  Hot cooked rice, corn bread, or mashed potatoes (optional)

1. Trim fat from meat. Cut meat into 6 serving-size pieces. In a 3½- or 4-quart slow cooker place meat, sweet pepper, and onion. In a medium bowl stir together soup, salsa, flour, and mustard. Pour over meat and vegetables.

2. Cover and cook on low-heat setting for 9 to 10 hours or on high-heat setting for 4½ to 5 hours. If desired, serve meat mixture with hot cooked rice.

Per serving: 251 cal., 6 g total fat (2 g sat. fat), 65 mg chol., 574 mg sodium, 10 g carbo., 1 g fiber, 37 g pro.

Italian Round
STEAK DINNER

In Italy, the traditional food movement called "Slow Food" is highly revered. A slow cooker makes this no-watch, long, slow cooking reverential. *Makes 8 servings*

Prep: **20 minutes** Cook: **Low 9 hours, High 4½ hours**

2¼ pounds boneless beef round steak

Salt and ground black pepper

1 tablespoon cooking oil

1 large fennel bulb, cut into thin wedges

1 large onion, halved and thinly sliced

1 cup packaged fresh julienned carrot

1 28-ounce can crushed tomatoes

1 15-ounce can tomato sauce

½ cup beef broth

2 teaspoons dried Italian seasoning, crushed

⅛ teaspoon crushed red pepper

6 cups hot cooked pasta

¼ cup finely shredded Parmesan cheese (1 ounce)

1. Trim fat from meat. Cut the meat into 8 serving-size pieces. Sprinkle lightly with salt and black pepper. In a large skillet cook the meat, half at a time, in hot oil over medium-high heat until brown on both sides. Drain off fat.

2. In a 4- or 4½-quart slow cooker, combine fennel, onion, and carrot. Add meat. In a large bowl combine tomatoes, tomato sauce, broth, Italian seasoning, and crushed red pepper. Pour over meat and vegetables.

3. Cover and cook on low-heat setting for 9 to 10 hours or on high-heat setting for 4½ to 5 hours.

4. To serve, divide hot cooked pasta among 8 dinner plates. Spoon meat mixture over pasta. Sprinkle with cheese.

Per serving: 434 cal., 9 g total fat (3 g sat. fat), 72 mg chol., 764 mg sodium, 47 g carbo., 6 g fiber, 38 g pro.

IN-A-PINCH TIPS!

TOMATO SAUCE SUB: FOR A 15-OUNCE CAN TOMATO SAUCE, USE ¾ CUP TOMATO PASTE PLUS 1 CUP WATER.

Chili for
A CROWD

Pair this crowd-pleasing entrée with one or more suggested toppings. If you like, replace the meat listed with ground beef or pork that's cooked and drained before it's added to the slow cooker.
Makes 10 to 12 servings

Prep: 15 minutes Cook: Low 10 hours, High 5 hours

2 pounds boneless beef round steak or boneless pork shoulder roast

2½ cups chopped yellow, red, and/or green sweet pepper (2 large)

2 cups chopped onion (2 large)

2 15-ounce cans chili beans in chili gravy, undrained

2 14.5-ounce cans Mexican-style stewed tomatoes, undrained and cut up

1 15-ounce can red kidney beans or pinto beans, rinsed and drained

1 cup beer or beef broth

2 to 3 teaspoons chopped canned chipotle chile pepper in adobo sauce (see note, page 22)

2 teaspoons garlic salt

2 teaspoons ground cumin

1 teaspoon dried oregano, crushed

Toppings such as shredded cheese, dairy sour cream, sliced green onion, and/or lime wedges (optional)

1. Trim fat from meat. Cut meat into ½-inch pieces. In a 5½- or 6-quart slow cooker, combine meat, sweet pepper, and onion. Stir in undrained chili beans in gravy, undrained tomatoes, drained kidney beans, beer, chipotle pepper, garlic salt, cumin, and oregano.

2. Cover and cook on low-heat setting for 10 to 12 hours or on high-heat setting for 5 to 6 hours. Spoon off fat. If desired, serve with toppings.

Per serving: 296 cal., 5 g total fat (1 g sat. fat), 52 mg chol., 821 mg sodium, 34 g carbo., 8 g fiber, 29 g pro.

Goulash
SOUP

Chilly outside? Plan to ladle up this hearty soup of beef chunks and veggies simmered with Hungarian paprika, caraway, and finished with sour cream. Serve it with caraway or rye bread cut into chunks.
Makes 6 to 8 servings

Prep: 30 minutes Cook: Low 9 hours, High 4½ hours

I pound boneless beef top round steak
I tablespoon cooking oil
3 14-ounce cans chicken broth
3 cups cubed, peeled potato (3 medium)
I 14.5-ounce can diced tomatoes, undrained
1½ cups sliced carrot (3 medium)
½ cup chopped onion (I medium)
2 tablespoons quick-cooking tapioca, crushed
2 tablespoons tomato paste
3 to 4 teaspoons Hungarian paprika
I teaspoon bottled minced garlic (2 cloves)
½ teaspoon dried marjoram, crushed
½ teaspoon caraway seeds, crushed
¼ teaspoon ground black pepper
½ cup dairy sour cream

I. Trim fat from meat. Cut meat into ½-inch pieces. In a large skillet cook meat, half at a time, in hot oil over medium-high heat until brown. Drain off fat.
2. Transfer meat to a 5- to 6-quart slow cooker. Stir in broth, potato, undrained tomatoes, carrot, onion, tapioca, tomato paste, paprika, garlic, marjoram, caraway seeds, and pepper.

3. Cover and cook on low-heat setting for 9 to 10 hours or on high-heat setting for 4½ to 5 hours. Top each serving with sour cream.

Per serving: 265 cal., 9 g total fat (3 g sat. fat), 51 mg chol., 983 mg sodium, 25 g carbo., 3 g fiber, 21 g pro.

IN-A-PINCH TIPS !

MARJORAM ALTERNATE: USE OREGANO—BUT A BIT LESS BECAUSE OREGANO IS MORE PUNGENT.

Beef and
CHIPOTLE BURRITOS

Chipotle peppers are smoked jalapeños that lend a great smoky flavor to foods. Find them at the supermarket with the other canned chile peppers. *Makes 6 servings*

Prep: **20 minutes**   Cook: **Low 8 hours, High 4 hours**

1½ pounds boneless beef round
   steak, cut ¾ inch thick
1 14.5-ounce can diced
   tomatoes, undrained
⅓ cup chopped onion (1 small)
1 to 2 canned chipotle chile
   peppers in adobo sauce,
   chopped (see note,
   page 22)
1 teaspoon dried oregano,
   crushed
½ teaspoon bottled minced
   garlic (1 clove)
¼ teaspoon ground cumin
6 9- to 10-inch flour tortillas,
   warmed
¾ cup shredded cheddar
   cheese (3 ounces)
1 recipe Pico de Gallo Salsa
   Shredded jicama or radishes
   (optional)
   Dairy sour cream (optional)

1. Trim fat from meat. If necessary, cut meat to fit into a 3½- or 4-quart slow cooker. Place meat in cooker. In a medium bowl combine undrained tomatoes, onion, chipotle pepper, oregano, garlic, and cumin. Pour over meat.

2. Cover and cook on low-heat setting for 8 to 10 hours or on high-heat setting for 4 to 5 hours.

3. Using a slotted spoon, remove meat from cooker, reserving cooking liquid. Shred meat by pulling two forks through it in opposite directions. Transfer meat to a medium bowl. Drizzle with enough of the reserved liquid to moisten.

4. Spoon meat onto tortillas just below the centers. Top with cheese, Pico de Gallo Salsa, and, if desired, jicama and sour cream. Roll up tortillas.

Pico de Gallo Salsa: In a small bowl combine 1 cup finely chopped tomato (2 medium); 2 tablespoons finely chopped onion; 2 tablespoons snipped fresh cilantro or parsley; 1 fresh serrano chile pepper, seeded and finely chopped (see note, page 22); and dash sugar. Cover and chill until ready to serve.

Per serving: 382 cal., 13 g total fat (5 g sat. fat), 69 mg chol., 663 mg sodium, 32 g carbo., 3 g fiber, 34 g pro.

Five-Spice
STEAK WRAPS

These wraps unite Asian and Mexican cuisines into one fresh fused dish. For easier slicing, place the steak in the freezer for 30 to 60 minutes to partially freeze before cutting it into thin strips. *Makes 4 wraps*

Start to Finish: **25 minutes**

2 cups packaged shredded cabbage with carrot (coleslaw mix)

¼ cup thin bite-size strips red or green sweet pepper

¼ cup thin bite-size strips carrot

¼ cup snipped fresh chives

2 tablespoons rice vinegar

½ teaspoon toasted sesame oil

12 ounces boneless beef round steak

½ teaspoon five-spice powder

¼ teaspoon salt
   Nonstick cooking spray

¼ cup plain low-fat yogurt or light dairy sour cream

4 8-inch flour tortillas

1. In a medium bowl combine cabbage, sweet pepper, carrot, and chives. In a small bowl combine vinegar and sesame oil. Pour vinegar mixture over cabbage mixture; toss gently to coat. Set aside.

2. Trim fat from meat. Thinly slice meat across the grain into bite-size strips. Sprinkle meat with five-spice powder and salt. Coat a large nonstick skillet with cooking spray; heat skillet over medium-high heat. Add meat; cook and stir for 2 to 3 minutes or until meat is slightly pink in center.

3. To assemble, spread 1 tablespoon of the yogurt down the center of each tortilla. Top with meat. Stir cabbage mixture; spoon over meat. Fold in sides of tortillas and roll up. If desired, secure with toothpicks.

Per wrap: 237 cal., 7 g total fat (2 g sat. fat), 51 mg chol., 329 mg sodium, 20 g carbo., 2 g fiber, 22 g pro.

Thai
BEEF STIR-FRY

Because it relies on bottled stir-fry sauce, frozen peppers, and precut beef strips, this stir-fry goes together in a flash. *Makes 4 servings*

Start to Finish: 15 minutes

4 ounces rice sticks
2 tablespoons cooking oil
1 16-ounce package frozen sweet pepper stir-fry vegetables
12 ounces packaged beef stir-fry strips
½ cup peanut stir-fry sauce

1. Prepare rice sticks according to package directions; drain. Set aside.
2. In a large skillet heat 1 tablespoon of the oil over medium-high heat. Add frozen vegetables; cook and stir for 2 to 3 minutes or until vegetables are crisp-tender. Drain, removing vegetables.

3. Add the remaining oil to skillet. Add meat; cook and stir for 3 to 4 minutes or until meat is slightly pink in center. Return vegetables to skillet. Add peanut sauce; stir all ingredients together to coat with sauce. Cook and stir until heated through. Serve meat mixture over rice sticks.

Per serving: 404 cal., 16 g total fat (4 g sat. fat), 50 mg chol., 597 mg sodium, 39 g carbo., 3 g fiber, 23 g pro.

Beef and
BOK CHOY

Better and faster than waiting on Chinese takeout, this stir-fry is made in your own kitchen.

Makes 4 servings

Start to Finish: **20 minutes**

4 teaspoons toasted sesame oil
12 ounces packaged beef stir-fry strips
1 teaspoon red chile paste
6 cups sliced bok choy
1 teaspoon bottled minced garlic (2 cloves)
1 tablespoon reduced-sodium soy sauce
2 teaspoons sesame seeds, toasted

1. In a 12-inch nonstick skillet heat 2 teaspoons of the oil over medium-high heat. Add meat and chile paste; cook and stir about 3 minutes or until meat is slightly pink in center. Remove from heat. Using a slotted spoon, remove meat from skillet, reserving liquid. Cover meat and keep warm.

2. Add the remaining 2 teaspoons oil to reserved liquid. Add bok choy and garlic; cook and stir for 2 to 3 minutes or until bok choy is crisp-tender. Transfer to a serving dish. Top with meat. Drizzle with soy sauce and sprinkle with toasted sesame seeds.

Per serving: 179 cal., 9 g total fat (2 g sat. fat), 52 mg chol., 271 mg sodium, 4 g carbo., 1 g fiber, 20 g pro.

BOK CHOY OPTIONS: SUBSTITUTIONS FOR BOK CHOY INCLUDE CHINESE CABBAGE, NAPA CABBAGE, OR GREEN CABBAGE.

Homestyle
MEAT LOAF

This brown sugar and ketchup-glazed meat loaf is outstanding in both flavor and moistness.

Makes 8 servings

Prep: **20 minutes**   Bake: **1 hour 10 minutes**   Stand: **10 minutes**   Oven: **350°F**

2 eggs, lightly beaten
¾ cup milk
⅔ cup fine dry bread crumbs or 2 cups soft bread crumbs
¼ cup finely chopped onion
2 tablespoons snipped fresh parsley
1 teaspoon salt
½ teaspoon dried sage, basil, or oregano, crushed
⅛ teaspoon ground black pepper
1½ pounds lean ground beef, ground lamb, or ground pork
¼ cup ketchup
2 tablespoons packed brown sugar
1 teaspoon dry mustard

1. Preheat oven to 350°F. In a medium bowl combine eggs and milk. Stir in bread crumbs, onion, parsley, salt, sage, and pepper. Add ground meat; mix well. Lightly pat mixture into an 8×4×2-inch loaf pan.

2. Bake for 1 to 1¼ hours or until meat is done (160°F). Spoon off fat. In a small bowl combine ketchup, brown sugar, and mustard; spread over meat loaf. Bake for 10 minutes more. Let stand for 10 minutes before slicing.

Homestyle Ham Loaf: Prepare as directed, except use the soft bread crumbs. Omit the salt and substitute ½ teaspoon dry mustard for the sage, basil, or oregano. Substitute 12 ounces lean ground beef or ground pork and 12 ounces ground cooked ham for the 1½ pounds ground beef, lamb, or pork. Bake and let stand as directed.

Per serving meat or ham loaf: 225 cal., 10 g total fat (4 g sat. fat), 108 mg chol., 676 mg sodium, 13 g carbo., 1 g fiber, 19 g pro.

Enchilada
MEAT LOAF

This is not your mother's meat loaf. The corn bread-topped loaf will bring shouts of "Ole!" when served.

Makes 6 servings

Prep: **20 minutes** Bake: **50 minutes** Stand: **10 minutes** Oven: **350°F**

1 egg, lightly beaten
½ cup finely chopped onion
   (1 medium)
¼ cup bottled salsa
2 tablespoons chili powder
1½ teaspoons bottled minced
   garlic (3 cloves)
½ teaspoon salt
1 pound lean ground beef
1 8.5-ounce package corn
   muffin mix
2 ounces sharp cheddar
   cheese, sliced and halved
   Bottled salsa (optional)

1. Preheat oven to 350°F. In a large bowl combine egg, onion, the ¼ cup salsa, the chili powder, garlic, and salt. Add ground beef; mix well. Shape meat mixture into a ball; place in an ungreased 9-inch pie plate. Flatten meat mixture to a 6-inch circle; set aside.

2. Prepare muffin mix according to package directions. Spread muffin batter over meat mixture. Bake, uncovered, about 50 minutes or until meat is done (160°F).

3. Arrange cheese on top of muffin mixture. Let stand, loosely covered, for 10 minutes before serving. If desired, serve with additional salsa.

Per serving: 573 cal., 33 g total fat (13 g sat. fat), 161 mg chol., 1069 mg sodium, 46 g carbo., 3 g fiber, 23 g pro.

Bistro Beef
WITH MUSHROOM SAUCE

A bottle of beer transforms brown gravy mix into a tasty complement for mushrooms and beef.

Makes 4 servings

Start to Finish: **30 minutes**

 1 medium onion, halved
1¼ pounds lean ground beef
¾ teaspoon salt
 3 cups sliced assorted fresh
    mushrooms (8 ounces)
 1 12-ounce bottle beer or
    nonalcoholic beer
 1 0.75- to 0.9-ounce envelope
    brown gravy mix
 2 teaspoons snipped fresh
    thyme or ½ teaspoon dried
    thyme, crushed

1. Finely shred half of the onion. Thinly slice the remaining onion; set aside.

2. In a large bowl combine shredded onion, ground beef, and salt; mix well. Shape meat mixture into four ½-inch-thick oval patties.

3. Heat a large nonstick skillet over medium heat. Add patties; cook for 10 to 12 minutes or until done (160°F),* turning once. Remove from skillet; cover and keep warm.

4. For sauce, add sliced onion, mushrooms, and ¼ cup of the beer to the same skillet. Cook over medium-high heat about 5 minutes or until vegetables are tender, stirring occasionally. In a small bowl combine gravy mix and the remaining 1¼ cups beer; stir into mushroom mixture. Stir in half of the thyme. Simmer, uncovered, about 1 minute or until thickened, stirring frequently.

5. Serve burgers with sauce. Sprinkle with the remaining thyme.

*Test Kitchen Tip: The internal color of a burger is not a reliable doneness indicator. A beef patty cooked to 160°F is safe, regardless of color. To measure the doneness of a patty, insert an instant-read thermometer through the side of the patty to a depth of 2 to 3 inches.

Per serving: 351 cal., 18 g total fat (7 g sat. fat), 89 mg chol., 732 mg sodium, 12 g carbo., 1 g fiber, 29 g pro.

Bull's-Eye ONION BURGERS

Not only are these scrumptious burgers shaped with a bull's-eye on top, but they are also tastefully targeted to hit the spot. *Makes 4 servings*

Prep: 20 minutes   Grill: 10 minutes

1 large sweet onion (such as Vidalia or Walla Walla)
1 pound lean ground beef
1½ teaspoons garlic powder
½ teaspoon salt
¼ teaspoon ground black pepper
4 slices Swiss cheese (4 ounces)
4 ¾-inch slices crusty country bread or Texas toast, toasted
Lettuce leaves (optional)
Tomato slices (optional)

1. Cut four ¼-inch slices from onion. (Reserve the remaining onion for another use.) Shape ground beef into four ½-inch-thick patties; sprinkle with garlic powder, salt, and pepper. Press 1 onion slice into the center of each patty; press edges of meat against onion, keeping meat flush with top of onion.

2. Grill patties, onion sides up, on the rack of an uncovered grill directly over medium coals for 10 to 13 minutes or until meat is done (160°F), turning once halfway through grilling and adding cheese during the last 1 minute of grilling. (For a gas grill, preheat grill. Reduce heat to medium. Place patties, onion sides up, on grill rack over heat. Cover and grill as above, adding cheese during the last minute of grilling.)

3. If desired, line toasted bread with lettuce and tomato. Add burgers, onion sides up.

Per serving: 378 cal., 17 g total fat (8 g sat. fat), 87 mg chol., 602 mg sodium, 21 g carbo., 2 g fiber, 34 g pro.

Burgers
ITALIANO

Everyone loves burgers! Served on a sourdough bread slice, this open-face sandwich is best eaten with a knife and fork. If you like, microwave the sauce in a 2-cup microwave-safe measuring cup, covered, on high until bubbly instead of heating it on the stovetop. *Makes 4 servings*

Prep: 15 minutes Broil: 11 minutes

1 pound lean ground beef
4 ¾-inch slices sourdough bread
1 cup purchased mushroom pasta sauce
1 cup shredded provolone or mozzarella cheese (4 ounces)
2 tablespoons shredded fresh basil

1. Preheat broiler. Shape ground beef into four ½-inch-thick patties. Place patties on the unheated rack of a broiler pan. Broil 3 to 4 inches from the heat for 10 to 12 minutes or until done (160°F), turning once halfway through broiling. While patties are broiling, add bread slices to broiler pan. Broil the bread slices for 2 to 3 minutes or until toasted, turning once halfway through broiling.

2. Meanwhile, in a medium saucepan heat pasta sauce over medium heat until bubbly, stirring occasionally.

3. Place patties on toasted bread slices. Spoon pasta sauce over patties; sprinkle with cheese. Broil for 1 to 2 minutes more or until cheese is melted. Sprinkle with basil.

Per serving: 504 cal., 30 g total fat (13 g sat. fat), 96 mg chol., 815 mg sodium, 27 g carbo., 2 g fiber, 30 g pro.

Garden
BURGERS

Plan on these burgers for a cookout in the summer months when tomatoes and summer squash are plentiful and inexpensive. *Makes 4 servings*

Prep: **20 minutes** Grill: **14 minutes**

2 tablespoons olive oil
2 tablespoons red wine vinegar
1 teaspoon snipped fresh thyme
¼ teaspoon cracked black pepper
1 pound lean ground beef
¼ teaspoon salt
¼ teaspoon ground black pepper
2 medium yellow summer squash, cut lengthwise into ¼- to ½-inch slices
4 hamburger buns, split and toasted
  Lettuce leaves
2 to 4 ounces blue cheese, cut into wedges
  Tomato slices (optional)
  Red onion slices (optional)
  Pickle slices (optional)

1. For dressing, in a screw-top jar combine oil, vinegar, thyme, and the cracked pepper. Cover and shake well. Set aside.
2. In a large bowl combine ground beef, salt, and the ground pepper; mix well. Shape meat mixture into four ¾-inch-thick patties. Brush squash with some of the dressing. Set the remaining dressing aside.
3. Grill patties on the rack of an uncovered grill directly over medium coals for 14 to 18 minutes or until done (160°F), turning once halfway through grilling. While patties are grilling, add squash to grill. Grill for 7 to 10 minutes or until tender, turning once halfway through grilling. (For a gas grill, preheat grill. Reduce heat to medium. Place patties on grill rack over heat. Cover and grill as above, adding squash for the last 7 to 10 minutes of grilling.)
4. Line bottoms of buns with lettuce. Add burgers, squash, blue cheese, and, if desired, tomato, red onion, and pickles. Drizzle cut sides of tops of buns with the remaining dressing. Replace tops of buns.

Per serving: 426 cal., 24 g total fat (8 g sat. fat), 82 mg chol., 592 mg sodium, 24 g carbo., 2 g fiber, 28 g pro.

IN-A-PINCH TIPS!

VEGGIE EXTRA: WHEN GRILLING VEGETABLES, GRILL A FEW EXTRAS FOR "LEFTOVERS." THEY ARE GREAT SERVED COLD IN A SALAD, FOLDED INTO AN OMELET, OR CHOPPED AND PILED ONTO FRENCH BREAD AS AN APPETIZER (CROSTINI).

Pizza BURGERS

Serve these cheese-topped burgers with your favorite pasta-vegetable salad. *Makes 8 servings*

Prep: **25 minutes** Grill: **10 minutes**

1 egg, lightly beaten
1¼ cups bottled meatless tomato pasta sauce
½ cup fine dry bread crumbs
⅓ cup chopped onion (1 small)
1 teaspoon dried basil or oregano, crushed
1 teaspoon bottled minced garlic (2 cloves)
1 pound lean ground beef
1 pound bulk Italian sausage
2 medium green, yellow, and/or red sweet peppers, seeded, cut into rings, and halved
1 tablespoon olive oil or cooking oil
8 kaiser rolls, split and toasted
1 6-ounce package sliced mozzarella cheese (8 slices)

1. In a large bowl combine egg and ¼ cup of the pasta sauce. Stir in bread crumbs, onion, basil, and garlic. Add ground beef and sausage; mix well. Shape meat mixture into eight ½-inch-thick patties.

2. Tear off an 18×12-inch piece of heavy foil. Place sweet pepper in center of foil; drizzle with oil. Bring up two opposite edges of foil; seal with a double fold. Fold the remaining ends to completely enclose sweet pepper, leaving space for steam to build.

3. Grill patties and foil packet on the rack of an uncovered grill directly over medium coals for 10 to 13 minutes or until patties are done (160°F) and sweet pepper is tender, turning patties and foil packet once halfway through grilling. (For a gas grill, preheat grill. Reduce heat to medium. Place patties and foil packet on gas grill over heat. Cover and grill as above.)

4. Meanwhile, in a small saucepan heat the remaining 1 cup pasta sauce until bubbly. Serve burgers in rolls with sweet pepper and cheese. Spoon some of the spaghetti sauce over burgers. Pass any remaining sauce.

Per serving: 583 cal., 29 g total fat (11 g sat. fat), 117 mg chol., 1,146 mg sodium, 44 g carbo., 3 g fiber, 31 g pro.

Norwegian
MEATBALLS

One good way to extend these nutmeg-accented meatballs in creamy mushroom sauce is to serve them over buttered noodles. *Makes 5 or 6 servings*

Prep: **20 minutes** Bake: **30 minutes** Oven: **350°F**

2 eggs, lightly beaten
½ cup milk
⅔ cup crushed saltine crackers
    (about 18 crackers)
⅓ cup finely chopped onion
    (1 small)
½ teaspoon celery salt
½ teaspoon ground nutmeg
½ teaspoon ground black
    pepper
2 pounds lean ground beef
1 10.75-ounce can condensed
    cream of mushroom soup
¾ cup milk

1. Preheat oven to 350°F. Grease a 3-quart rectangular baking dish or 13×9×2-inch baking pan; set aside.

2. In a large bowl combine eggs and the ½ cup milk. Stir in crackers, onion, celery salt, ¼ teaspoon of the nutmeg, and the pepper. Add ground beef; mix well. Shape meat mixture into 20 meatballs. Arrange meatballs in the prepared baking dish. Bake about 30 minutes or until meatballs are done (160°F).

3. For sauce, in a medium saucepan combine soup, the ¾ cup milk, and the remaining ¼ teaspoon nutmeg. Cook and stir over medium heat until heated through.

4. To serve, transfer meatballs to a serving bowl. Spoon sauce over meatballs.

Per serving: 469 cal., 26 g total fat (10 g sat. fat), 204 mg chol., 842 mg sodium, 17 g carbo., 1 g fiber, 39 g pro.

Stuffed
PEPPERS MOLE

Stuffed peppers with south-of-the-border flavor stretch ground beef with pizzazz. *Makes 4 servings*

Start to Finish: **20 minutes**

4 small or 2 large sweet
   peppers

10 to 12 ounces packaged
   precooked ground beef
   crumbles or 2 cups cooked
   ground beef

1 8.8-ounce pouch cooked
   Spanish-style rice or long
   grain and wild rice

½ cup frozen whole kernel corn

3 tablespoons bottled mole
   sauce*

2 tablespoons water

½ cup shredded Mexican
   cheese blend or shredded
   cheddar cheese (2 ounces)
   Salt and ground black pepper

2 tablespoons snipped fresh
   cilantro or parsley

1. Cut tops off small peppers or halve large peppers lengthwise. Remove seeds and membranes. In a 4-quart Dutch oven, immerse peppers in a large amount of boiling water for 3 minutes. Drain peppers, cut sides down, on paper towels.

2. For filling, in a medium saucepan combine beef crumbles, cooked rice, corn, mole sauce, and the water. Cook over medium heat until heated through, stirring frequently. Remove from heat; stir in cheese until melted.

3. Place peppers, cut sides up, on a serving platter. Sprinkle with salt and black pepper. Spoon filling into peppers. Sprinkle with cilantro.

*Test Kitchen Tip: If you can't find bottled mole sauce, substitute ¼ cup enchilada sauce and omit the 2 tablespoons water.

Per serving: 360 cal., 15 g total fat (7 g sat. fat), 75 mg chol., 732 mg sodium, 29 g carbo., 3 g fiber, 28 g pro.

Easy Beef
POT PIE

Savor the comfort and taste of a homemade pot pie without spending hours in the kitchen. Rely on prepared pastry, refrigerated potatoes, and frozen vegetables. *Makes 8 servings*

Prep: 15 minutes Bake: 18 minutes Stand: 10 minutes Oven: 400°F

½ of a 15-ounce package (1 crust) rolled refrigerated unbaked piecrust
1½ pounds lean ground beef
2 cups refrigerated diced potatoes with onions or frozen diced hash brown potatoes with onions and peppers, thawed
2 cups frozen mixed vegetables
1 15-ounce can Italian-style or regular tomato sauce
1 14.5-ounce can Italian-style stewed tomatoes, undrained
2 teaspoons sesame seeds

1. Preheat oven to 400°F. Let piecrust stand at room temperature while preparing meat mixture.
2. In a large skillet cook ground beef over medium-high heat until brown. Drain off fat. Stir in potatoes, mixed vegetables, tomato sauce, and undrained tomatoes. Bring to boiling; remove from heat. Meanwhile, unroll piecrust and cut into 8 wedges.

3. Spread meat mixture in an ungreased 3-quart rectangular baking dish. Place half of the pastry wedges, points toward center, along one long side of the dish, overlapping wedges slightly at the bases. Repeat with the remaining pastry wedges on the opposite side of the dish. Sprinkle with sesame seeds.
4. Bake, uncovered, for 18 to 20 minutes or until pastry is golden brown. Let stand for 10 minutes before serving.

Per serving: 342 cal., 16 g total fat (6 g sat. fat), 59 mg chol., 669 mg sodium, 32 g carbo., 3 g fiber, 19 g pro.

IN-A-PINCH TIPS!

GO ITALIAN: CAN'T FIND ITALIAN STEWED TOMATOES OR ITALIAN-SEASONED TOMATO PASTE? STIR 1 TEASPOON DRIED ITALIAN SEASONING INTO A CAN OF THE STEWED TOMATOES OR THE PASTE.

Shortcut
LASAGNA

The noodles are added uncooked in this no-fuss luscious lasagna. *Makes 8 servings*

Prep: **30 minutes** Bake: **40 minutes** Stand: **5 minutes** Oven: **350°F**

8 ounces lean ground beef
8 ounces bulk Italian sausage
1 26-ounce jar tomato-basil pasta sauce
1 egg, lightly beaten
1 15-ounce carton light ricotta cheese or cream-style cottage cheese
1 2.25-ounce can sliced, pitted ripe olives, drained
9 no-boil lasagna noodles
1 8-ounce package sliced mozzarella cheese
¼ cup grated Parmesan cheese
Snipped fresh basil (optional)

1. Preheat oven to 350°F. For sauce, in a large saucepan cook ground beef and sausage over medium-high heat until brown. Drain off fat. Stir in pasta sauce. Bring to boiling.

2. Meanwhile, in a medium bowl combine egg, ricotta cheese, and drained olives.

3. To assemble, spread about 1 cup of the sauce in the bottom of an ungreased 3-quart rectangular baking dish or 13×9×2-inch baking pan. Top with 3 of the lasagna noodles, making sure noodles do not touch sides of dish. Top with one-third of the ricotta mixture, one-third of the remaining sauce, and one-third of the mozzarella cheese. Repeat layering noodles, ricotta mixture, sauce, and mozzarella cheese two more times. (Make sure noodles are covered with sauce.) Sprinkle with Parmesan cheese.

4. Bake, covered, for 30 minutes. Bake, uncovered, for 10 to 15 minutes more or until noodles are tender and Parmesan cheese is golden brown. Let stand for 5 minutes before serving. If desired, garnish with fresh basil.

Per serving: 492 cal., 26 g total fat (12 g sat. fat), 109 mg chol., 987 mg sodium, 34 g carbo., 2 g fiber, 31 g pro.

Cheeseburger and
FRIES CASSEROLE

Even the name of this recipe sounds fun. This is a classic casserole that keeps coming back—all ages love it. *Makes 8 to 10 servings*

Prep: 15 minutes   Bake: 45 minutes   Oven: 350°F

2 pounds lean ground beef
1 10.75-ounce can condensed golden mushroom soup
1 10.75-ounce can condensed cheddar cheese soup
1 20-ounce package frozen french-fried crinkle-cut potatoes
Toppings such as ketchup, pickles, mustard, and/or chopped tomato (optional)

1. Preheat oven to 350°F. In a large skillet cook ground beef, half at a time, over medium-high heat until brown. Drain off fat. Transfer cooked meat to an ungreased 3-quart rectangular baking dish or 13×9×2-inch baking pan.

2. In a medium bowl combine mushroom soup and cheese soup; spread over meat. Sprinkle with potatoes.

3. Bake, uncovered, for 45 to 55 minutes or until potatoes are golden brown. If desired, serve with toppings.

Per serving: 348 cal., 18 g total fat (6 g sat. fat), 78 mg chol., 654 mg sodium, 24 g carbo., 2 g fiber, 24 g pro.

Easy
SHEPHERD'S PIE

Frozen mashed potatoes make quick work of this scrumptious family-style supper. *Makes 8 servings*

Prep: **30 minutes**   Bake: **25 minutes**   Oven: **425°F**

2 pounds lean ground beef
¼ cup all-purpose flour
1 envelope (½ of a 2.2-ounce package) onion soup mix
1 10.75-ounce can condensed cream of mushroom soup
1 8-ounce carton dairy sour cream
¾ cup water
1 tablespoon ketchup
1½ cups water
¼ cup butter or margarine
½ teaspoon salt
2 cups packaged instant mashed potato flakes
½ cup milk
2 eggs, lightly beaten
1 cup all-purpose flour
2 teaspoons baking powder

1. Preheat oven to 425°F. In a very large skillet cook ground beef over medium-high heat until brown. Drain off fat. Stir in the ¼ cup flour and the dry soup mix. Stir in mushroom soup, sour cream, the ¾ cup water, and the ketchup. Cook until heated through, stirring occasionally.

2. Meanwhile, in a medium saucepan combine the 1½ cups water, the butter, and salt. Bring to boiling; remove from heat. Stir in potato flakes and milk. Stir in eggs, the 1 cup flour, and the baking powder.

3. Transfer meat mixture to an ungreased 3-quart rectangular baking dish or 13×9×2-inch baking pan. Spoon potato mixture in mounds on top of meat mixture. Bake, uncovered, about 25 minutes or until potatoes are golden brown.

Per serving: 465 cal., 24 g total fat (11 g sat. fat), 143 mg chol., 911 mg sodium, 32 g carbo., 1 g fiber, 30 g pro.

*Baked*

CAVATELLI

This crowd-pleaser makes a great dish to star in an affordable party menu. *Makes 8 servings*

Prep: **25 minutes** Bake: **35 minutes** Stand: **10 minutes** Oven: **375°F**

1 pound dried cavatelli pasta or wagon wheel macaroni
1 pound lean ground beef or bulk Italian sausage
1¼ cups chopped onion
1½ teaspoons bottled minced garlic (3 cloves)
2 26- or 28-ounce jars tomato pasta sauce
1½ cups shredded mozzarella cheese (6 ounces)
¼ teaspoon ground black pepper

1. Preheat oven to 375°F. Cook pasta according to package directions; drain.
2. Meanwhile, in a large skillet cook ground beef, onion, and garlic over medium-high heat until sausage is brown and onion is tender. Drain off fat.
3. In a very large bowl stir together pasta sauce, 1 cup of the cheese, and the pepper. Add cooked pasta and sausage mixture; stir gently to combine. Transfer mixture to an ungreased 3-quart rectangular baking dish.
4. Bake, covered, for 30 to 35 minutes or until heated through. Sprinkle with the remaining ½ cup cheese. Bake, uncovered, about 5 minutes more or until cheese is melted. Let stand for 10 minutes before serving.

Per serving: 547 cal., 24 g total fat (9 g sat. fat), 57 mg chol., 1130 mg sodium, 59 g carbo., 5 g fiber, 24 g pro.

Taco
SPAGHETTI

Feel like Mexican cuisine tonight? This combination of pasta, salsa, ground beef, and cheese captures those south-of-the-border flavors. *Makes 6 servings*

Prep: **25 minutes**   Bake: **15 minutes**   Oven: **350°F**

5   ounces dried spaghetti, linguine, or fettuccine, broken
1   pound lean ground beef or uncooked ground turkey
1   cup chopped onion (1 large)
¾   cup water
½   of a 1.25-ounce envelope (2 tablespoons) taco seasoning mix
1   11-ounce can whole kernel corn with sweet peppers, drained
1   cup sliced, pitted ripe olives
1   cup shredded Colby Jack cheese or cheddar cheese (4 ounces)
½   cup bottled salsa
1   4-ounce can diced green chile peppers, drained
6   cups shredded lettuce
1   medium tomato, cut into thin wedges
    Tortilla chips (optional)
    Dairy sour cream (optional)

1. Preheat oven to 350°F. Lightly grease a 2-quart casserole; set aside. Cook pasta according to package directions; drain.

2. Meanwhile, in a large skillet cook ground beef and onion over medium-high heat until meat is brown and onion is tender. Drain off fat. Stir in the water and taco seasoning mix. Bring to boiling; reduce heat. Simmer, uncovered, for 2 minutes, stirring occasionally. Stir in cooked pasta, drained corn, olives, ½ cup of the cheese, the salsa, and drained chile peppers. Transfer mixture to the prepared casserole.

3. Bake, covered, for 15 to 20 minutes or until heated through. Sprinkle with the remaining ½ cup cheese. Serve with lettuce, tomato, and, if desired, tortilla chips and sour cream.

Per serving: 424 cal., 22 g total fat (8 g sat. fat), 65 mg chol., 978 mg sodium, 38 g carbo., 3 g fiber, 26 g pro.

Greek-Style Beef
AND VEGETABLES

Cinnamon and nutmeg add an unexpected but subtle flavor to this saucy dish. Serve it with warm pita bread. *Makes 6 servings*

Prep: 15 minutes   Cook: Low 6 hours, High 3 hours; plus 30 minutes on High

  1 pound lean ground beef
  1 cup chopped onion (1 large)
1½ teaspoons bottled minced garlic (3 cloves)
  3 cups frozen mixed vegetables
  1 14.5-ounce can diced tomatoes, undrained
  1 14-ounce can beef broth
  3 tablespoons tomato paste
  1 teaspoon dried oregano, crushed
  ⅛ teaspoon ground cinnamon
  ⅛ teaspoon ground nutmeg
  2 cups dried medium shell macaroni
  1 cup shredded Monterey Jack cheese or crumbled feta cheese (4 ounces)

1. In a large skillet cook ground beef, onion, and garlic over medium-high heat until meat is brown and onion is tender. Drain off fat. Transfer meat mixture to a 3½- or 4-quart slow cooker. Stir in mixed vegetables, undrained tomatoes, broth, tomato paste, oregano, cinnamon, and nutmeg.

2. Cover and cook on low-heat setting for 6 to 8 hours or on high-heat setting for 3 to 4 hours.

3. If using low-heat setting, turn to high-heat setting. Stir in macaroni. Cover and cook about 30 minutes more or until macaroni is tender. Sprinkle each serving with cheese.

Per serving: 446 cal., 16 g total fat (7 g sat. fat), 64 mg chol., 539 mg sodium, 46 g carbo., 5 g fiber, 28 g pro.

Chili
MACARONI

Wagon wheel macaroni provides a fun presentation and green beans replace the kidney beans in this chili-style dish. See photo on page 100. *Makes 4 servings*

Prep: 15 minutes Cook: 15 minutes

12 ounces lean ground beef or uncooked ground turkey
½ cup chopped onion (1 medium)
1 14.5-ounce can diced tomatoes and green chiles, undrained
1¼ cups tomato juice
2 teaspoons chili powder
½ teaspoon garlic salt
1 cup dried wagon wheel or elbow macaroni
1 cup frozen cut green beans
1 cup shredded cheddar cheese (4 ounces) (optional)
Tortilla chips (optional)

1. In a very large skillet cook ground beef and onion over medium-high heat until meat is brown and onion is tender. Drain off fat. Stir in undrained tomatoes, tomato juice, chili powder, and garlic salt. Bring to boiling.

2. Stir in macaroni and green beans. Return to boiling; reduce heat. Simmer, covered, about 15 minutes or until macaroni and beans are tender.

3. If desired, top each serving with cheese and serve with tortilla chips.

Per serving: 443 cal., 20 g total fat (9 g sat. fat), 83 mg chol., 881 mg sodium, 37 g carbo., 5 g fiber, 29 g pro.

IN-A-PINCH TIPS!

CHILI POWDER POINTER: SUBSTITUTE A FEW DASHES OF BOTTLED HOT PEPPER SAUCE ALONG WITH SOME DRIED OREGANO AND CUMIN POWDER. START WITH SMALL AMOUNTS, TASTE, THEN ADJUST ACCORDINGLY.

Slow-Cooker
TAMALE PIE

Don't skimp on the standing time. It allows the cheese to melt and the pie to cool just enough to eat.

Makes 8 servings

Prep: **25 minutes** Cook: **Low 6 hours, High 3 hours; plus 50 minutes on High** Stand: **20 minutes**

2 pounds lean ground beef

1 cup chopped onion (1 large)

1 teaspoon bottled minced garlic (2 cloves)

2 10-ounce cans enchilada sauce

1 11-ounce can whole kernel corn with sweet peppers, drained

1 4-ounce can diced green chile peppers, undrained

1 8.5-ounce package corn muffin mix

1 cup shredded cheddar cheese (4 ounces)

⅓ cup milk

1 egg, lightly beaten

1 tablespoon seeded and finely chopped fresh jalapeño chile pepper (see note, page 22) (optional)

1. In a very large skillet, cook ground beef, onion, and garlic over medium-high heat until meat is brown and onion is tender. Drain off fat. Transfer meat mixture to a 3½- or 4-quart slow cooker. Stir in enchilada sauce, drained corn, and undrained green chile peppers.

2. Cover and cook on low-heat setting for 6 to 8 hours or on high-heat setting for 3 to 4 hours.

3. In a medium bowl stir together muffin mix, ½ cup of the cheese, the milk, egg, and, if desired, jalapeño chile pepper just until combined.

4. If using low-heat setting, turn to high-heat setting. Stir meat mixture. Drop muffin batter from a spoon into 8 dumplings on top of meat mixture. Cover and cook for 50 minutes more (do not lift cover).

5. Sprinkle dumplings with the remaining ½ cup cheese. Remove liner from cooker, if possible, or turn off cooker. Let stand, uncovered, for 20 minutes before serving.

Per serving: 474 cal., 24 g total fat (9 g sat. fat), 113 mg chol., 805 mg sodium, 35 g carbo., 1 g fiber, 30 g pro.

 # One-Pot
SPAGHETTI

This easy spaghetti recipe allows the pasta to cook in the tomato sauce, so there is one less pan to wash. See photo on page 101. *Makes 4 servings*

Start to Finish: **40 minutes**

8 ounces lean ground beef or bulk pork sausage

1 cup sliced fresh mushrooms or one 4-ounce can (drained weight) sliced mushrooms, drained

½ cup chopped onion (1 medium)

½ teaspoon bottled minced garlic (1 clove)

1 14-ounce can chicken broth or beef broth

1¾ cups water

1 6-ounce can tomato paste

1 teaspoon dried Italian seasoning, crushed

¼ teaspoon ground black pepper

6 ounces dried spaghetti, broken

¼ cup finely shredded Parmesan cheese (1 ounce)

Fresh basil sprigs (optional)

1. In a large saucepan cook ground beef, fresh mushrooms (if using), onion, and garlic over medium-high heat until meat is brown and onion is tender. Drain off fat.

2. Stir in drained canned mushrooms (if using), broth, the water, tomato paste, Italian seasoning, and pepper. Bring to boiling.

3. Add broken spaghetti, a little at a time, stirring constantly. Return to boiling; reduce heat. Boil gently, uncovered, for 17 to 20 minutes or until spaghetti is tender and sauce is desired consistency, stirring frequently. Sprinkle each serving with cheese. If desired, garnish with fresh basil.

Per serving: 394 cal., 15 g total fat (6 g sat. fat), 39 mg chol., 926 mg sodium, 44 g carbo., 4 g fiber, 22 g pro.

 IN-A-PINCH TIPS!

GARLIC TIP: FOR ½ TEASPOON BOTTLED MINCED GARLIC, PEEL AND MINCE ONE FRESH GARLIC CLOVE, OR USE ½ TEASPOON GARLIC POWDER OR ½ TEASPOON BOTTLED, DRIED MINCED GARLIC.

Traditional
CINCINNATI CHILI

Cincinnatians enjoy what they call a "five-way." It is a plate of spaghetti topped with beans, chili, onions, and grated cheese. Skip one or two of the toppings and you have a "four-way" or a "three-way."

Makes 8 servings

Prep: **20 minutes** Cook: **45 minutes**

5 bay leaves
1 teaspoon whole allspice
2 pounds lean ground beef
2 cups chopped onion (2 large)
½ teaspoon bottled minced
  garlic (1 clove)
2 tablespoons chili powder
1 teaspoon ground cinnamon
¼ to ½ teaspoon cayenne
  pepper
4 cups water
1 15-ounce can red kidney
  beans, rinsed and drained
1 8-ounce can tomato sauce
1 tablespoon cider vinegar
1 teaspoon Worcestershire
  sauce
½ teaspoon salt
¼ teaspoon ground black
  pepper
  Hot cooked spaghetti
  (optional)
  Shredded Parmesan or
  cheddar cheese (optional)
  Sliced green onion (optional)

1. For spice bag, place bay leaves and allspice in the center of a double-thick, 6-inch square of 100-percent-cotton cheesecloth. Bring up corners and tie closed with clean kitchen string; set aside.

2. In a 4-quart Dutch oven, cook ground beef, onion, and garlic over medium-high heat until meat is brown and onion is tender. Drain off fat. Stir in the chili powder, cinnamon, and cayenne pepper. Cook and stir for 1 minute. Stir in the water, drained beans, tomato sauce, vinegar, Worcestershire sauce, salt, and black pepper. Add the spice bag.

3. Bring to boiling; reduce heat. Simmer, covered, for 30 minutes. Simmer, uncovered, for 15 to 20 minutes more or until chili reaches desired consistency, stirring occasionally. Remove and discard spice bag.

4. If desired, serve chili over hot cooked spaghetti and sprinkle with cheese and green onion.

Per serving: 257 cal., 11 g total fat (4 g sat. fat), 71 mg chol., 435 mg sodium, 16 g carbo., 5 g fiber, 25 g pro.

Taco
SOUP

We nicknamed this "dump" soup. Simply dump cans of vegetables and taco seasoning into ground beef and simmer. *Makes 8 servings*

Prep: 15 minutes   Cook: 1 hour

1 pound lean ground beef
1 15-ounce can black-eyed
   peas, undrained
1 15-ounce can black beans,
   undrained
1 15-ounce can chili beans in
   chili gravy, undrained
1 15-ounce can garbanzo
   beans (chickpeas),
   undrained
1 14.5-ounce can Mexican-
   style stewed tomatoes,
   undrained
1 11-ounce can whole kernel
   corn with sweet peppers,
   undrained
1 1.25-ounce envelope taco
   seasoning mix
   Dairy sour cream (optional)
   Bottled salsa (optional)
   Broken tortilla chips
   (optional)

1. In a 4-quart Dutch oven, cook ground beef over medium-high heat until brown. Drain off fat. Stir in undrained black-eyed peas, undrained black beans, undrained chili beans in gravy, undrained garbanzo beans, undrained tomatoes, undrained corn, and taco seasoning mix.

2. Bring to boiling; reduce heat. Simmer, covered, for 1 to 2 hours or until soup reaches desired consistency, stirring occasionally. If desired, top each serving with sour cream, salsa, and tortilla chips.

Per serving: 409 cal., 13 g total fat (5 g sat. fat), 41 mg chol., 1423 mg sodium, 52 g carbo., 12 g fiber, 26 g pro.

Stuffed Green
PEPPER SOUP

Love stuffed peppers? Try this soup that combines the same ingredients in a brand-new way.

Makes 6 servings

Prep: 15 minutes   Cook: 20 minutes

8 ounces lean ground beef
2 14.5-ounce cans diced
  tomatoes with green pepper
  and onion, undrained
3 cups water
1 14-ounce can beef broth
1 5.7-ounce package tomato-
  basil risotto mix
¾ cup chopped green sweet
  pepper (1 medium)

1. In a large saucepan cook ground beef over medium-high heat until meat is brown. Drain off fat. Stir in undrained tomatoes, the water, broth, risotto mix, and sweet pepper.

2. Bring to boiling; reduce heat. Simmer, covered, about 20 minutes or until rice is tender.

Per serving: 214 cal., 5 g total fat (2 g sat. fat), 24 mg chol., 1,103 mg sodium, 32 g carbo., 3 g fiber, 11 g pro.

Taco
PIZZA

Served either as a main dish or hearty appetizer, this Southwest-style pizza appeals to all ages. See photo on page 102. *Makes 6 servings*

Prep: 15 minutes Bake: 20 minutes Oven: 400°F

8 ounces lean ground beef and/or bulk pork sausage
¾ cup chopped sweet pepper (1 medium)
1 11.5-ounce package (8) refrigerated corn bread twists
½ cup bottled salsa
3 cups shredded taco cheese (12 ounces)
Crushed tortilla chips (optional)
Dairy sour cream (optional)
Chopped tomato (optional)
Sliced green onion (optional)

1. Preheat oven to 400°F. Grease a 12-inch pizza pan; set aside. In a medium skillet cook ground beef and sweet pepper over medium-high heat until meat is brown. Drain off fat.

2. Unroll corn bread dough (do not separate into strips). Press dough onto the bottom and up the sides of the prepared pizza pan. Spread salsa over dough. Sprinkle with meat mixture and cheese.

3. Bake about 20 minutes or until bottom of crust is golden brown when lifted slightly with a spatula. If desired, top with tortilla chips, sour cream, tomato, and green onion. Cut into wedges.

Per serving: 465 cal., 30 g total fat (15 g sat. fat), 73 mg chol., 870 mg sodium, 27 g carbo., 1 g fiber, 22 g pro.

IN-A-PINCH TIPS!

TACO CHEESE ALTERNATE: COMBINE EQUAL PARTS SHREDDED COLBY JACK AND CHEDDAR OR USE SHREDDED MEXICAN CHEESE BLEND.

Cheeseburger
PIZZA

You can make and bake this pizza in less time than it takes to have one delivered from a pizza parlor.

Makes 4 servings

Prep: **20 minutes** Bake: **8 minutes** Oven: **425°F**

8 ounces lean ground beef

½ cup chopped onion (1 medium)

1½ cups shredded cheddar cheese (6 ounces)

2 tablespoons ketchup

1 tablespoon sweet pickle relish

1 tablespoon yellow mustard

1 12-inch thin-crust Italian bread shell (such as Boboli brand)

1. Preheat oven to 425°F. In a large skillet cook ground beef and onion until meat is brown and onion is tender. Drain off fat. Stir in ½ cup of the cheese, the ketchup, pickle relish, and mustard. Cook and stir until cheese is melted.

2. Place bread shell on an ungreased baking sheet. Spread meat mixture over bread shell. Sprinkle with the remaining 1 cup cheese.

3. Bake for 8 to 10 minutes or until heated through and cheese is melted. Cut into wedges.

Per serving: 528 cal., 27 g total fat (14 g sat. fat), 83 mg chol., 870 mg sodium, 41 g carbo., 2 g fiber, 29 g pro.

Beefy CALZONES

This wrapped sandwich is great warm but, like leftover pizza, is also good the next day. Remove chilled calzone from refrigerator and let stand 30 minutes. *Makes 6 calzones*

Prep: **20 minutes**   Bake: **8 minutes**   Stand: **5 minutes**   Oven: **425°F**

8 ounces lean ground beef
½ cup sliced fresh mushrooms
¼ cup chopped green sweet
  pepper
½ cup shredded mozzarella
  cheese (2 ounces)
⅓ cup pizza sauce
1 13.8-ounce package
  refrigerated pizza dough
1 tablespoon milk
  Grated Parmesan cheese
  (optional)
  Pizza sauce, warmed
  (optional)

1. Preheat oven to 425°F. Grease a baking sheet; set aside. In a medium skillet cook ground beef, mushrooms, and green pepper over medium-high heat until meat is brown. Drain off fat. Stir in cheese and the ⅓ cup pizza sauce.

2. On a lightly floured surface, roll or pat pizza dough into a 15×10-inch rectangle. Cut into six 5-inch squares. Divide meat mixture among squares, placing mixture on half of each and spreading to within 1 inch of the edges. Brush edges of dough with water. Fold dough over meat mixture to opposite edge. Press edges with a fork to seal.

3. Place calzones on the prepared baking sheet. Prick tops with the fork to allow steam to escape. Brush with milk. If desired, sprinkle with cheese.

4. Bake for 8 to 10 minutes or until golden brown. Let stand for 5 minutes before serving. If desired, serve with the warmed pizza sauce.

Per calzone: 235 cal., 8 g total fat (3 g sat. fat), 31 mg chol., 358 mg sodium, 26 g carbo., 1 g fiber, 13 g pro.

Skillet
TOSTADAS

Feel free to substitute crisp taco shells for the tostada shells. The only difference is the shape.

Makes 4 servings

Start to Finish: **25 minutes**

8 ounces lean ground beef
½ cup chopped onion
   (1 medium)
1 15-ounce can red kidney
   beans, rinsed and drained
1 11-ounce can condensed
   nacho cheese soup
⅓ cup bottled salsa
8 tostada shells
1 cup shredded taco cheese
   (4 ounces)
Shredded lettuce
Chopped tomato (optional)
Dairy sour cream or
   purchased guacamole
   (optional)

1. In a large skillet cook ground beef and onion over medium-high heat until meat is brown and onion is tender. Drain off fat. Stir in drained beans, soup, and salsa. Heat through.

2. Divide meat mixture among tostada shells. Top with cheese, lettuce, and, if desired, tomato. If desired, serve with sour cream.

Per serving: 576 cal., 33 g total fat (15 g sat. fat), 81 mg chol., 1277 mg sodium, 42 g carbo., 11 g fiber, 26 g pro.

Saucy CHEESEBURGER SANDWICHES

It's no problem to invite the team back for burgers. While you're cheering the team at the game, the meat filling cooks in the slow-cooker. See photo on page 103. *Makes 12 to 15 sandwiches*

Prep: **20 minutes** Cook: Low 6 hours, High 3 hours; plus 5 minutes on Low

2½ pounds lean ground beef
1 10.75-ounce can condensed tomato soup
1 cup finely chopped onion (1 large)
¼ cup water
2 tablespoons tomato paste
1 tablespoon Worcestershire sauce
1 tablespoon yellow mustard
2 teaspoons dried Italian seasoning, crushed
1 teaspoon bottled minced garlic (2 cloves)
¼ teaspoon ground black pepper
6 ounces American cheese, cubed

12 to 15 hamburger buns, split and toasted
12 to 15 American cheese slices (optional)
Assorted pickles (optional)
Pimiento-stuffed olives (optional)

1. In a very large skillet cook ground beef over medium-high heat until brown. Drain off fat. Transfer meat to a 3½- or 4-quart slow cooker. Stir in soup, onion, the water, tomato paste, Worcestershire sauce, mustard, Italian seasoning, garlic, and pepper.

2. Cover and cook on low-heat setting for 6 to 8 hours or on high-heat setting for 3 to 4 hours.

3. If using high-heat setting, turn to low-heat setting. Stir in cubed cheese. Cover and cook for 5 to 10 minutes more or until cheese is melted. Spoon meat mixture in buns. If desired, add a cheese slice to each sandwich and serve with assorted pickles and olives.

Per sandwich: 357 cal., 16 g total fat (7 g sat. fat), 73 mg chol., 664 mg sodium, 28 g carbo., 2 g fiber, 25 g pro.

IN-A-PINCH TIPS!

ITTY BITTY TOMATO PASTE: NEED TO USE JUST A TABLESPOON OR TWO OF TOMATO PASTE? FREEZE THE REMAINING PASTE IN 1 TABLESPOON AMOUNTS IN AN ICE CUBE TRAY. POP CUBES OUT OF THE TRAY WHEN FROZEN AND STORE IN A FREEZER BAG.

*Hot and*

SPICY SLOPPY JOES

These standout "loose-meat" sandwiches gain firepower from a Scotch bonnet chile pepper and ground black pepper. *Makes 12 to 14 sandwiches*

Prep: **25 minutes** Cook: **Low 8 hours, High 4 hours**

- 2 pounds lean ground beef
- 4 medium onions, cut into strips
- 4 medium green sweet peppers, seeded and cut into strips
- 2 medium red sweet peppers, seeded and cut into strips
- 1 cup ketchup
- ¼ cup cider vinegar
- 1 tablespoon chili powder
- 1 fresh Scotch bonnet chile pepper, seeded and finely chopped (see note, page 22), or ¼ teaspoon cayenne pepper
- ½ teaspoon salt
- ½ teaspoon ground black pepper
- 12 to 14 hoagie buns or hot dog buns, split and toasted

1. In a very large skillet cook ground beef and onion over medium-high heat until meat is brown and onion is tender. Drain off fat.

2. Transfer meat mixture to a 5- to 6-quart slow cooker. Stir in sweet peppers, ketchup, vinegar, chili powder, Scotch bonnet pepper, salt, and black pepper.

3. Cover and cook on low-heat setting for 8 to 10 hours or on high-heat setting for 4 to 5 hours. Serve meat mixture in buns.

Per sandwich: 592 cal., 18 g total fat (6 g sat. fat), 48 mg chol., 1,051 mg sodium, 83 g carbo., 6 g fiber, 27 g pro.

Chili-Cheese
HOAGIES

These do-ahead sandwiches are just right for casual get-togethers. Prepare them the day before and heat when ready to serve. *Makes 8 sandwiches*

Start to Finish: **35 minutes**

1 pound lean ground beef
1 cup chopped onion (1 large)
1 cup chopped green and/or red sweet pepper (2 small)
1 teaspoon bottled minced garlic (2 cloves)
1 14.5-ounce can diced tomatoes with chili spices, undrained
½ teaspoon ground cumin (optional)
¼ teaspoon ground black pepper
8 hoagie buns or French-style rolls, split
8 thin slices Monterey Jack cheese or Monterey Jack cheese with jalapeño peppers (8 ounces)
8 thin slices cheddar cheese (8 ounces)
Pickled jalapeño chile peppers (optional)

1. In a large skillet cook ground beef, onion, sweet pepper, and garlic over medium-high heat until meat is brown and onion is tender. Drain off fat.

2. Stir in undrained tomatoes, cumin (if desired), and black pepper. Bring to boiling; reduce heat. Simmer, uncovered, about 15 minutes or until mixture is thickened, stirring occasionally.

3. Meanwhile, using a spoon, hollow out bottoms of buns, leaving ¼-inch shells. Place Monterey Jack cheese on bottoms of buns. Top with meat mixture and cheddar cheese. If desired, sprinkle with pickled jalapeño peppers. Replace tops of buns.

Per sandwich: 738 cal., 31 g total fat (15 g sat. fat), 91 mg chol., 1,274 mg sodium, 79 g carbo., 5 g fiber, 36 g pro.

Meatball
LASAGNA

Using purchased meatballs in this quick-to-assemble recipe results in an easy rendition of the pasta favorite. *Makes 8 servings*

Prep: **25 minutes** Bake: **45 minutes** Stand: **15 minutes** Oven: **375°F**

9 dried lasagna noodles
½ of a 15-ounce carton ricotta cheese
1½ cups shredded mozzarella cheese (6 ounces)
¼ cup grated Parmesan cheese
1 16-ounce package (32) frozen cooked Italian-style meatballs, thawed
1 26- or 28-ounce jar tomato pasta sauce

1. Preheat oven to 375°F. Cook lasagna noodles according to package directions; drain. Rinse with cold water; drain again. Place noodles in a single layer on a piece of foil; set aside.
2. Meanwhile, for filling, in a small bowl stir together ricotta cheese, 1 cup of the mozzarella cheese, and the Parmesan cheese; set aside. In a medium bowl stir together meatballs and about 1 cup of the pasta sauce.
3. To assemble, spread about ½ cup of the remaining pasta sauce over the bottom of an ungreased 2-quart square baking dish. Layer 3 of the cooked noodles in the dish, trimming or overlapping as necessary to fit. Spoon meatball mixture over noodles. Layer 3 more noodles over meatball mixture. Spread half of the remaining pasta sauce and all of the ricotta mixture over noodles. Top with the remaining 3 noodles and the remaining pasta sauce.
4. Bake, covered, for 35 minutes. Sprinkle with the remaining ½ cup mozzarella cheese. Bake, uncovered, about 10 minutes more or until heated through. Let stand for 15 to 20 minutes before serving.

Per serving: 410 cal., 21 g total fat (11 g sat. fat), 66 mg chol., 897 mg sodium, 31 g carbo., 4 g fiber, 23 g pro.

IN-A-PINCH TIPS !

PASTA FIX: IF YOU HAVE A FEW BOIL AND NO-BOIL LASAGNA NOODLES LEFT OVER BUT NOT ENOUGH OF ONE KIND FOR THE RECIPE, COMBINE THEM IN THE SAME DISH. PRECOOK THE REGULAR PASTA BUT NOT THE NO-COOK. ASSEMBLE THE LASAGNA AS DIRECTED IN THE RECIPE, ADDING ½ CUP EXTRA LIQUID, EITHER WATER OR BROTH, FOR THE NON-BOIL NOODLES TO ABSORB.

Cheesy Italian
MEATBALL CASSEROLE

Baked pasta is a surefire crowd pleaser, especially when it is packed with Italian meatballs, tangy pasta sauce, and luscious cheeses. *Makes 8 to 10 servings*

Prep: **30 minutes**   Bake: **45 minutes**   Oven: **350°F**

1 pound dried cut ziti or penne pasta
1 26- or 28-ounce jar tomato pasta sauce
1 16-ounce package (32) frozen cooked Italian-style meatballs, thawed
1 15-ounce can Italian-style tomato sauce
1 15-ounce carton ricotta cheese
½ cup grated Parmesan cheese
2 cups shredded mozzarella cheese (8 ounces)

1. Preheat oven to 350°F. Cook pasta according to package directions; drain. Return to hot pan. Stir in pasta sauce, meatballs, and tomato sauce. Transfer mixture to an ungreased 3-quart rectangular baking dish. Bake, covered, for 30 minutes.

2. Meanwhile, in a small bowl combine ricotta cheese and Parmesan cheese. Spoon ricotta mixture in small mounds on top of pasta mixture.

3. Bake, loosely covered, about 10 minutes or until heated through. Sprinkle with mozzarella cheese. Bake, uncovered, about 5 minutes more or until cheese is melted.

Per serving: 611 cal., 28 g total fat (14 g sat. fat), 86 mg chol., 1441 mg sodium, 57 g carbo., 7 g fiber, 33 g pro.

Sweet and
SOUR MEATBALLS

Pineapple juice and maple syrup combine to make an easy sweet and sour sauce to rival any from a bottle.

Makes 4 servings

Start to Finish: **30 minutes**

1 20-ounce can pineapple
   chunks, undrained
¾ cup maple syrup
½ cup cider vinegar
1 12- or 16-ounce package
   frozen cooked meatballs
2 medium red and/or green
   sweet peppers, seeded and
   cut into ¾-inch pieces
¼ cup cold water
2 tablespoons cornstarch
½ teaspoon salt
2 cups hot cooked Asian
   noodles or rice
   Sliced green onion (optional)

1. Drain pineapple, reserving liquid. Set pineapple aside. In a large saucepan combine the reserved liquid, maple syrup, and vinegar. Stir in meatballs. Bring to boiling; reduce heat. Simmer, covered, for 15 minutes. Stir in sweet pepper. Simmer, covered, for 5 minutes more.

2. In a small bowl combine the cold water, cornstarch, and salt; stir into meatball mixture. Cook and stir over medium heat until thickened and bubbly. Stir in pineapple; heat through.

3. Serve meatball mixture over hot cooked noodles. If desired, sprinkle with green onion.

Per serving: 667 cal., 23 g total fat (9 g sat. fat), 30 mg chol., 972 mg sodium, 107 g carbo., 5 g fiber, 14 g pro.

Saucy Ravioli
WITH MEATBALLS

Three of the all-time, best Italian convenience products—spaghetti sauce, frozen ravioli, and frozen Italian meatballs—make this a super-speedy dish to prepare. *Makes 10 to 12 servings*

Prep: **20 minutes** Cook: Low **4½ hours,** High **2½ hours** Stand: **15 minutes**

Nonstick cooking spray
2 26-ounce jars tomato pasta sauce with mushrooms and onions
2 24-ounce packages frozen ravioli
1 12-ounce package (12) frozen cooked Italian-style meatballs, thawed
2 cups shredded mozzarella cheese (8 ounces)
½ cup finely shredded Parmesan cheese (2 ounces)

1. Lightly coat a 5½- or 6-quart slow cooker with cooking spray. Add 1 cup of the pasta sauce. Add 1 package of the frozen ravioli and the meatballs. Sprinkle with 1 cup of the mozzarella cheese. Top with the remaining pasta sauce from the first jar. Add the remaining package of ravioli and the remaining 1 cup mozzarella cheese. Pour pasta sauce from the second jar over mixture in cooker.

2. Cover and cook on low-heat setting for 4½ to 5 hours or on high-heat setting for 2½ to 3 hours. Remove liner from cooker, if possible, or turn off cooker. Sprinkle with Parmesan cheese. Let stand, covered, for 15 minutes before serving.

Per serving: 510 cal., 18 g total fat (8 g sat. fat), 78 mg chol., 1551 mg sodium, 67 g carbo., 5 g fiber, 26 g pro.

Chili Macaroni

Recipe on page 80

Curried-Cider Pork Stew

Recipe on page 125

Chunky Chipotle Pork Chile

Recipe on page 132

Oven-Barbecued Chicken

Recipe on page 161

Saucy
MEATBALL SANDWICHES

Do you have hungry kids at home who are old enough to work in the kitchen? If so, keep a stock of frozen meatballs, pasta sauce, and preshredded cheese on hand so they can whip up these sandwiches whenever hunger pangs hit. *Makes 6 sandwiches*

Start to Finish: **20 minutes**

18 frozen cooked Italian-style meatballs (18 ounces)
1 26- or 28-ounce jar tomato pasta sauce
½ cup coarsely chopped onion (1 medium)
6 hoagie buns, split and toasted
1 cup shredded Italian cheese blend (4 ounces)

1. In a large saucepan combine frozen meatballs, pasta sauce, and onion. Bring to boiling; reduce heat. Simmer, covered, about 10 minutes or until meatballs are heated through, stirring occasionally.

2. Spoon meatball mixture onto bottoms of buns. Spoon any remaining sauce over meatballs. Sprinkle with cheese. Replace tops of buns. Let stand for 1 to 2 minutes before serving.

Per sandwich: 802 cal., 36 g total fat (14 g sat. fat), 74 mg chol., 2,293 mg sodium, 88 g carbo., 9 g fiber, 32 g pro.

Caliente
POT ROAST

This speedy stew starts with a purchased precooked pot roast. See photo on page 104.

Makes 4 to 6 servings

Start to Finish: **20 minutes**

1 16- or 17-ounce package refrigerated cooked beef pot roast with juices
1½ cups sliced fresh mushrooms
1 8-ounce bottle picante sauce
1 14-ounce can reduced-sodium chicken broth
1 cup couscous
2 tablespoons snipped fresh cilantro or parsley
Chopped tomato (optional)
Sliced avocado (optional)

1. Transfer juices from pot roast package to a large skillet; stir in mushrooms and picante sauce. Cut meat into 1- to 1½-inch pieces; add to mushroom mixture. Bring to boiling; reduce heat. Simmer, covered, for 10 minutes.

2. Meanwhile, in a medium saucepan bring broth to boiling. Stir in couscous; remove from heat. Let stand, covered, for 5 minutes. Fluff with a fork. Stir in cilantro.

3. Serve meat mixture over couscous mixture. If desired, top with tomato, and avocado.

Per serving: 479 cal., 13 g total fat (4 g sat. fat), 120 mg chol., 1,000 mg sodium, 43 g carbo., 3 g fiber, 46 g pro.

Asian-Style
BEEF SOUP

Hurrah for five plus five—a five ingredient soup that cooks in five minutes! *Makes 4 servings*

Start to Finish: 15 minutes

3 14-ounce cans beef broth
1 16-ounce package frozen broccoli stir-fry vegetables
3 tablespoons teriyaki sauce
2 teaspoons grated fresh ginger or ½ teaspoon ground ginger
1 9-ounce package frozen cooked seasoned beef strips, thawed and cut up, or 2 cups chopped cooked beef

1. In a large saucepan bring broth to boiling. Stir in frozen vegetables, teriyaki sauce, and ginger.

2. Return to boiling; reduce heat. Simmer, covered, for 3 to 5 minutes or until vegetables are tender. Stir in cooked beef; heat through.

Per serving: 177 cal., 6 g total fat (2 g sat. fat), 41 mg chol., 1885 mg sodium, 10 g carbo., 2 g fiber, 21 g pro.

Beef and
ROASTED PEPPER CIABATTA SANDWICHES

This sandwich is so easy. Simply layer flat ciabatta rolls with meat, cheese, and tomatoes. It will become a family favorite. *Makes 4 sandwiches*

Start to Finish: 10 minutes

4 ciabatta rolls or individual Italian flatbreads (focaccia)
¼ cup bottled creamy garlic salad dressing
4 ounces thinly sliced deli roast beef, ham, or turkey
8 cherry tomatoes, thinly sliced
4 slices provolone cheese
¼ cup bottled roasted red sweet peppers, drained and chopped
4 romaine lettuce leaves

1. Slice rolls in half horizontally. Spread salad dressing over bottoms of rolls. Layer meat, tomato, cheese, roasted pepper, and lettuce on bottoms of rolls. Replace tops of rolls.

2. If desired, wrap sandwiches individually in plastic wrap and chill for up to 24 hours.

Per sandwich: 461 cal., 19 g total fat (7 g sat. fat), 45 mg chol., 1,235 mg sodium, 54 g carbo., 4 g fiber, 22 g pro.

Reuben
SANDWICH CASSEROLE

Classic Reuben sandwich fixings—sauerkraut, Swiss cheese, and corned beef—are layered with seasonings and croutons in this tasty casserole. *Makes 8 to 10 servings*

Prep: **20 minutes**   Bake: **35 minutes**   Oven: **375°F**

1 32-ounce jar sauerkraut, rinsed and drained
½ cup chopped onion (1 medium)
4 teaspoons dried parsley flakes
2 teaspoons caraway seeds
4 cups shredded Swiss cheese (1 pound)
1⅓ cups bottled Thousand Island salad dressing
12 ounces thinly sliced cooked corned beef, coarsely chopped
6 slices rye bread, cut into ½-inch pieces
¼ cup butter or margarine, melted

1. Preheat oven to 375°F. In a large bowl combine drained sauerkraut, onion, parsley flakes, and caraway seeds. Spread sauerkraut mixture evenly in an ungreased 3-quart rectangular baking dish.
2. Top with half of the cheese, half of the salad dressing, and all of the corned beef. Top with the remaining salad dressing and the remaining cheese.

3. In a large bowl combine bread pieces and melted butter; toss gently to coat. Sprinkle buttered bread pieces over casserole.
4. Bake, uncovered, about 35 minutes or until heated through and bread pieces are browned.

Per serving: 596 cal., 45 g total fat (18 g sat. fat), 120 mg chol., 3,872 mg sodium, 22 g carbo., 10 g fiber, 26 g pro.

LOOK!

MONEY-SAVING TIPS and HINTS

Purchase pork tenderloin when it is on sale. If the marinated tenderloin is cheaper, buy it. If not, make your own marinade for a less costly seasoned pork tenderloin.

CHEAP!

Buy uncooked bacon slices rather than paying extra for precooked bacon. Freeze cooked bacon slices on waxed paper in freezer bags. Pull out as needed for cooked/crumbled bacon. This is a great way to maximize a partially used package of bacon.

Cook a large batch of shredded pork and freeze in 2-cup portions, enough for 4 sandwiches. They are perfect for last-minute dinners.

To average the cost of more expensive Italian seasoned bulk sausage, mix 8 ounces of Italian bulk pork with 8 ounces ground pork or ground beef.

$AVE! $AVE!

Purchase whole pork loins on sale, cut into chops and/or cut the loin into thirds for roasts.

$AVE! $AVE!

Sale! Purchase on sale pork chops, especially the thinner ones, and cut into bite-size slices or pieces for stir-fry.

Purchase ground pork in bulk; freeze in 1-pound amounts.

Buy ham at the holidays when the price is lower. Cut into desired portion. Freeze for use in omelets, casseroles, or sandwiches.

Yes! Make your own breakfast patties by seasoning ground pork with dried sage, brown sugar, ground black pepper, and salt.

CHAPTER 3

Penny-Pinching
PORK

By keeping your eye out for grocery store specials on pork, you can cook up a meal of real comfort. Compared to the meat our parents and grandparents cooked, today's pork is naturally tender and requires shorter cooking. Less than half of all pork sold is fresh; the remainder comes smoked, cured, or salted. The recipes that follow show off pork's ease, versatility, and full flavor while helping you eke out the most savings from your pork purchases.

Herb-Scented Tuscan
PORK LOIN

Seasoned from the inside out, this pork loin roasts with all the seasonings tucked inside the meat.

Makes 12 to 15 servings

Prep: **20 minutes** Marinate: **8 to 24 hours** Roast: **2 hours** Stand: **15 minutes** Oven: **325°F**

3 tablespoons snipped fresh rosemary

4 teaspoons bottled minced garlic (8 cloves)

4 teaspoons finely shredded lemon peel

1 teaspoon kosher salt

1 4½- to 5-pound boneless pork top loin roast (double loin)

4 ounces thinly sliced pancetta

1. In a small bowl combine rosemary, garlic, lemon peel, and salt; set aside.

2. Untie meat; trim fat from meat. Spread rosemary mixture over top of one of the loins. Place pancetta on top of the other loin. Reassemble meat, placing the pancetta-topped loin on top and positioning the rosemary mixture in the middle. Retie with 100-percent-cotton kitchen string. Wrap meat tightly in plastic wrap and marinate in the refrigerator for 8 to 24 hours.

3. Preheat oven to 325°F. Place meat on a roasting rack in a shallow roasting pan. Roast for 2 to 2½ hours or until temperature of the meat reaches 150°F.

4. Cover meat with foil; let stand for 15 minutes before slicing (temperature of the meat will rise 5°F to 10°F while it stands).

Per serving: 286 cal., 12 g total fat (4 g sat. fat), 99 mg chol., 396 mg sodium, 1 g carbo., 0 g fiber, 39 g pro.

IN-A-PINCH TIPS!

HERB ALTERNATES: FOR 1 TABLESPOON OF FRESH HERBS, USE ABOUT 1 TEASPOON DRIED. START WITH 2 TEASPOONS DRIED FOR STRONG HERBS, SUCH AS ROSEMARY, AND TASTE.

Ale-Sauced Pork

RIBS AND VEGETABLES

Country-style pork ribs are the meaty ones that require a knife and fork for eating. A soak in an ale marinade followed by a slow simmer in the slow cooker ensures moist, flavorful meat. Pictured on the cover. *Makes 4 to 6 servings*

Prep: **25 minutes** Marinate: **4 to 24 hours** Cook: **Low 8 hours, High 4 hours**

2½ to 3 pounds bone-in pork country-style ribs
1 12-ounce bottle dark ale or stout or nonalcoholic beer
3 cloves garlic, minced
1 tablespoon finely shredded lemon peel
1 tablespoon dried rosemary, crushed
¼ teaspoon salt
¼ teaspoon freshly ground black pepper
8 small gold or red potatoes (8 ounces total)
12 ounces peeled fresh baby carrots
¼ cup cold water
2 tablespoons cornstarch
Radishes (optional)
Fresh rosemary sprigs (optional)
Shredded lemon peel (optional)

1. Place pork in a large resealable plastic bag set in a shallow bowl. Add ale, garlic, 1 tablespoon lemon peel, the dried rosemary, salt, and pepper. Seal bag; turn to coat. Marinate in the refrigerator for 4 to 24 hours.

2. Place potatoes and carrots in the bottom of a 5- to 6-quart slow cooker. Place pork ribs on top of carrots and potatoes. Pour ale mixture over all.

3. Cover and cook on low-heat setting for 8 to 9 hours or on high-heat setting for 4 to 4½ hours.

4. Remove pork and vegetables from cooker. Cover; keep warm.

5. For sauce, pour cooking juices through a fine-mesh sieve set over a heatproof bowl. Measure 2 cups of cooking juices, adding water to make 2 cups, if necessary. In medium saucepan, stir together the ¼ cup water and the cornstarch. Add the 2 cups strained juices. Cook and stir until thickened and bubbly. Cook and stir for 2 minutes more. Serve sauce with meat, vegetables, and, if desired, radishes. If desired, garnish with rosemary and additional lemon peel.

Per serving: 497 cal., 23 g total fat (8 g sat. fat), 143 mg chol., 342 mg sodium, 25 g carbo., 4 g fiber, 40 g pro.

Pennsylvania
POT ROAST

Teamed with apples, parsnips, sweet potatoes, and onion, this pork shoulder is reminiscent of the home-style pot roasts of Pennsylvania Dutch country. See photo on page 105. *Makes 6 servings*

Prep: 30 minutes   Cook: Low 7 hours, High 3½ hours

1   2½- to 3-pound boneless pork shoulder roast
1   tablespoon cooking oil
6   small parsnips, peeled and quartered
2   small sweet potatoes, peeled and quartered
1   small onion, sliced
1   cup beef broth
½   cup apple cider or apple juice
1   teaspoon dried basil, crushed
1   teaspoon dried marjoram, crushed
½   teaspoon salt
¼   teaspoon ground black pepper
2   small cooking apples, cored and cut into wedges
½   cup cold water
¼   cup all-purpose flour
    Salt and ground black pepper
    Fresh Italian (flat-leaf) parsley (optional)

1. Trim fat from meat. In a large skillet cook meat in hot oil over medium-high heat until brown on all sides. Drain off fat.

2. In a 4½- to 6-quart slow cooker, combine parsnip, sweet potato, and onion. Add meat. In a medium bowl combine broth, cider, basil, marjoram, the ½ teaspoon salt, and the ¼ teaspoon pepper. Pour mixture over meat.

3. Cover and cook on low-heat setting for 7 to 9 hours or on high-heat setting for 3½ to 4½ hours, adding apple during the last 30 minutes of cooking. Using a slotted spoon, transfer meat, vegetables, and apple to a serving platter; cover and keep warm.

4. For gravy, skim fat from cooking liquid; strain liquid through a fine-mesh sieve. Measure 1¾ cups of the liquid; pour into a medium saucepan. In a small bowl stir the cold water into flour; stir into cooking liquid. Cook and stir over medium heat until thickened and bubbly. Cook and stir for 1 minute more. Season to taste with additional salt and pepper.

5. Serve meat, vegetables, and apple with gravy. If desired, garnish with parsley.

Per serving: 485 cal., 16 g total fat (5 g sat. fat), 126 mg chol., 492 mg sodium, 45 g carbo., 8 g fiber, 40 g pro.

IN-A-PINCH TIPS!

PARSNIP POINTER: PARSNIPS, OUT OF SEASON, ARE EXPENSIVE. SUBSTITUTE AN EQUAL AMOUNT OF CARROT, TURNIP, OR SWEET POTATO.

ROAST IN CIDER

This flavor-rich roast with harvest-fresh root vegetables is comfort food at its best. *Makes 4 servings*

Prep: **25 minutes** Cook: **1½ hours**

1 1½- to 2-pound boneless pork blade roast or sirloin roast
2 tablespoons cooking oil
1¼ cups apple cider or apple juice
2 teaspoons instant beef bouillon granules
½ teaspoon dry mustard
¼ teaspoon ground black pepper
3 medium red potatoes or round white potatoes, peeled (if desired) and quartered
3 medium carrots, cut into 2-inch pieces
3 medium parsnips, peeled and cut into 2-inch pieces
1 large onion, cut into wedges
⅓ cup cold water
¼ cup all-purpose flour

1. Trim fat from meat. In a 4- to 6-quart Dutch oven cook meat in hot oil over medium-high heat until brown on all sides. Drain off fat. In a small bowl stir together cider, bouillon granules, dry mustard, and pepper. Pour over meat. Bring to boiling; reduce heat. Simmer, covered, for 1 hour.

2. Add potato, carrot, parsnip, and onion. Return to boiling; reduce heat. Simmer, covered, for 30 to 40 minutes more or until meat and vegetables are tender. Using a slotted spoon, transfer meat and vegetables to a serving platter; cover and keep warm.

3. For gravy, measure cooking liquid; skim off fat. If necessary, add enough water to liquid to equal 1½ cups. Return cooking liquid to Dutch oven. In a small bowl stir the cold water into flour; stir into liquid. Cook and stir over medium heat until thickened and bubbly. Cook and stir for 1 minute more.

4. To serve, remove string from meat, if present. Slice meat and serve with vegetables and gravy.

Slow-Cooker Directions: Trim fat from meat. If necessary, cut meat to fit into a 3½- or 4-quart slow cooker. Brown meat as directed. Place potato, carrot, parsnip, and onion in the cooker. Add meat. Stir together cider, bouillon granules, mustard, and pepper. Pour over meat and vegetables. Cover and cook on low-heat setting for 8 to 10 hours or on high-heat setting for 4 to 5 hours. Transfer meat and vegetables to a serving platter; cover and keep warm. Prepare gravy in a medium saucepan on the range top and serve as directed.

Per serving: 538 cal., 17 g total fat (5 g sat. fat), 110 mg chol., 608 mg sodium, 56 g carbo., 7 g fiber, 39 g pro.

Sweet Potato-
TOPPED PORK STEW

This oven-baked stew is filled with satisfying autumn vegetables and topped with sliced sweet potatoes.

Makes 8 servings

Prep: **20 minutes** Bake: **2 hours** Oven: **350°F**

2½ pounds boneless pork
   shoulder roast
¾ teaspoon salt
¼ teaspoon ground black
   pepper
3 tablespoons olive oil
2 cups frozen small whole
   onions
2 teaspoons bottled minced
   garlic (4 cloves)
1 14.5-ounce can diced
   tomatoes, undrained
1 14-ounce can lower-sodium
   beef broth
½ of a 6-ounce can (⅓ cup)
   tomato paste
8 ounces turnips, peeled and
   cut into 1-inch pieces
8 ounces parsnips, peeled and
   cut into 1-inch pieces
1 pound sweet potatoes,
   peeled and cut crosswise
   into very thin slices
⅛ teaspoon ground black
   pepper
   Fresh Italian (flat-leaf)
   parsley (optional)

1. Preheat oven to 350°F. Trim fat from meat. Cut meat into 1½-inch pieces. Sprinkle meat with ½ teaspoon of the salt and the ¼ teaspoon pepper.

2. In a 5- to 6-quart ovenproof Dutch oven, heat 1 tablespoon of the oil over medium-high heat. Cook meat, half at a time, in hot oil until brown. Remove from Dutch oven. Add onions; cook for 3 to 4 minutes or until light brown, stirring occasionally. Add garlic; cook and stir for 30 seconds.

3. Return all of the meat to Dutch oven. Stir in undrained tomatoes, broth, and tomato paste. Bring to boiling. Cover and transfer to oven. Bake for 1 hour. Carefully stir in turnip and parsnip. Bake, covered, for 30 minutes.

4. Meanwhile, in a medium bowl combine sweet potato and the remaining 2 tablespoons oil; toss gently to coat. Remove stew from oven; carefully spoon off fat. Arrange sweet potato in concentric circles on top of stew. Sprinkle with the remaining ¼ teaspoon salt and the ⅛ teaspoon pepper.

5. Bake, uncovered, for 30 to 35 minutes more or until sweet potato is tender and light brown. If desired, garnish with parsley.

Per serving: 354 cal., 13 g total fat (4 g sat. fat), 92 mg chol., 660 mg sodium, 26 g carbo., 5 g fiber, 31 g pro.

Curried-Cider
PORK STEW

A popular food combo—pork and apples—team up with curry powder, carrots, and butternut squash for a different and delicious stew. See photo on page 106. *Makes 6 servings*

Prep: **35 minutes** Cook: **1 hour**

 4 medium red and/or green tart cooking apples
 2 pounds boneless pork shoulder roast
 1 tablespoon cooking oil
 1 large onion, cut into thin wedges
 2 teaspoons curry powder
 1 14-ounce can chicken broth
 ⅔ cup apple cider or apple juice
 ¼ teaspoon salt
 ¼ teaspoon ground black pepper
12 ounces baby carrots with tops, trimmed, or 2 cups packaged peeled baby carrots
 1 cup sliced celery (2 stalks)
 2 cups peeled and cubed butternut squash (1½ pounds)
    Toppings such as dairy sour cream, finely shredded orange peel, snipped fresh oregano, and/or freshly ground black pepper (optional)

1. Peel, core, and chop 2 of the apples; set aside. Trim fat from meat. Cut meat into 1-inch pieces. In a 4-quart Dutch oven, cook meat, half at a time, in hot oil over medium-high heat until brown. Return all of the meat to Dutch oven.

2. Add the 2 chopped apples, the onion, and curry powder; cook and stir for 2 minutes. Add broth, cider, salt, and pepper. Bring to boiling; reduce heat. Simmer, covered, for 30 minutes, stirring occasionally. Stir in carrots and celery. Return to boiling; reduce heat. Simmer, covered, for 20 minutes, stirring occasionally.

3. Meanwhile, cut the remaining 2 apples into ¼-inch wedges. Add apple wedges and squash to meat mixture.

4. Return to boiling; reduce heat. Simmer, covered, for 10 to 12 minutes more or until meat and vegetables are tender. If desired, serve with toppings.

Per serving: 379 cal., 14 g total fat (4 g sat. fat), 102 mg chol., 526 mg sodium, 31 g carbo., 6 g fiber, 32 g pro.

Pulled Pork
WITH ROOT BEER SAUCE

Root beer gives these pork sandwiches a rich color and pleasant sweetness. Root beer concentrate intensifies the flavor. You'll find it in the spice section of your supermarket. *Makes 8 to 10 sandwiches*

Prep: **25 minutes**   Cook: **Low 8 hours, High 4 hours**

1   2½- to 3-pound boneless
    pork sirloin roast
½   teaspoon salt
½   teaspoon ground black
    pepper
1   tablespoon cooking oil
4   cups root beer (not diet)
2   medium onions, cut into
    thin wedges
1   to 2 tablespoons
    bottled minced garlic
    (6 to 12 cloves)
1   cup chili sauce
¼   teaspoon root beer
    concentrate (optional)
    Several dashes bottled hot
    pepper sauce (optional)
8   to 10 hamburger buns, split
    and toasted
    Lettuce leaves (optional)
    Tomato slices (optional)

1. Trim fat from meat. If necessary, cut meat to fit into a 3½- to 5-quart slow cooker. Sprinkle meat with salt and black pepper. In a large skillet cook meat in hot oil over medium-high heat until brown on all sides. Drain off fat. Transfer meat to cooker. Add 1 cup of the root beer, the onion, and garlic.
2. Cover and cook on low-heat setting for 8 to 10 hours or on high-heat setting for 4 to 5 hours.
3. Meanwhile, for sauce, in a medium saucepan combine the remaining 3 cups root beer and the chili sauce. Bring to boiling; reduce heat. Boil gently, uncovered, about 30 minutes or until mixture is reduced to 2 cups, stirring occasionally. If desired, stir in root beer concentrate and bottled hot pepper sauce.

4. Transfer meat to a cutting board. Using a slotted spoon, remove onion from cooker; discard cooking liquid. Shred meat by pulling two forks through it in opposite directions.
5. If desired, line bottoms of buns with lettuce and tomato. Top with meat, onion, and sauce. Replace tops of buns.

Per sandwich: 356 cal., 10 g total fat (3 g sat. fat), 59 mg chol., 786 mg sodium, 44 g carbo., 1 g fiber, 22 g pro.

Shredded
PORK TACOS

Slow cook the pork during the day. Diners can customize their tacos by choosing from a variety of toppings. See photo on page 107. *Makes 4 servings*

Prep: **30 minutes** Cook: **Low 8 hours, High 4 hours**

1 2½- to 3-pound boneless pork shoulder roast
1 cup chicken broth
½ cup enchilada sauce or bottled salsa
4 8-inch flour tortillas or taco shells, warmed
   Toppers such as shredded lettuce; shredded Mexican cheese blend; chopped tomato; sliced avocado; and/or lime wedges
   Dairy sour cream (optional)

1. Trim fat from meat. If necessary, cut meat to fit into a 3½- or 4-quart slow cooker. Place meat in cooker. Pour broth over meat.

2. Cover and cook on low-heat setting for 8 to 10 hours or on high-heat setting for 4 to 5 hours.

3. Transfer meat to a cutting board; discard cooking liquid. Shred meat by pulling two forks through it in opposite directions. Reserve 2 cups of the meat. (Store the remaining meat in an airtight container in the refrigerator for up to 3 days or in the freezer for up to 3 months.)

4. In a medium saucepan combine the reserved 2 cups meat and the enchilada sauce. Cook, covered, over medium-low heat about 10 minutes or until heated through, stirring occasionally.

5. To serve, spoon meat mixture onto tortillas or into taco shells. Serve with toppers. If using tortillas, fold them over filling. If desired, serve with sour cream.

Per serving: 616 cal., 31 g total fat (10 g sat. fat), 202 mg chol., 846 mg sodium, 20 g carbo., 3 g fiber, 61 g pro.

Cashew Pork
AND VEGETABLES

Prep the meat and veggies ahead for this Asian-inspired stir-fry. Cooking takes less than 10 minutes.

Makes 4 servings

Start to Finish: **40 minutes**

1 pound lean boneless pork
¼ cup orange juice
2 tablespoons hoisin sauce
½ teaspoon ground ginger
⅛ teaspoon crushed red pepper (optional)
1 tablespoon cooking oil
1½ cups bias-sliced carrot (3 medium) or packaged fresh julienned carrot
2 cups fresh pea pods, trimmed, or one 6-ounce package frozen pea pods, thawed
¼ cup sliced green onion (2)
2 cups hot cooked rice
½ cup cashews or peanuts

1. Trim fat from meat. Thinly slice meat across the grain into bite-size strips; set aside. For sauce, in a small bowl stir together orange juice, hoisin sauce, ginger, and, if desired, crushed red pepper; set aside.

2. Pour oil into a wok or large skillet; heat wok over medium-high heat. (Add more oil as necessary during cooking.) Add carrot; cook and stir for 2 minutes. Add pea pods and green onion; cook and stir for 2 to 3 minutes or until vegetables are crisp-tender. Remove vegetables from wok.

3. Add half of the meat to wok. Cook and stir for 2 to 3 minutes or until meat is slightly pink in center. Remove from wok. Repeat with the remaining meat.

4. Return all of the meat and vegetables to wok. Stir sauce; add to wok. Cook and stir until heated through. Stir in hot cooked rice. Sprinkle with cashews.

Per serving: 453 cal., 18 g total fat (4 g sat. fat), 62 mg chol., 189 mg sodium, 41 g carbo., 4 g fiber, 32 g pro.

Sesame
PORK TENDERLOIN

This Asian-influenced pork tenderloin finds its extraordinary flavor from a zesty ginger brush-on sauce.

Makes 4 servings

Prep: **25 minutes**   Roast: **25 minutes**   Stand: **10 minutes**   Oven: **425°F**

2 tablespoons chili sauce or 1 tablespoon Asian chili sauce

1 tablespoon reduced-sodium teriyaki sauce

1 teaspoon bottled minced garlic (2 cloves)

½ teaspoon grated fresh ginger or ⅛ teaspoon ground ginger

1 12- to 16-ounce pork tenderloin

1 teaspoon sesame seeds

2 teaspoons olive oil

⅛ teaspoon salt

⅛ teaspoon ground black pepper

4 cups packaged shredded broccoli (broccoli slaw mix)

1. Preheat oven to 425°F. For sauce, in a small bowl stir together chili sauce, teriyaki sauce, half of the garlic, and the ginger.

2. Trim fat from meat. Place meat on a roasting rack in a shallow roasting pan. Spread half of the sauce over meat. Roast, uncovered, for 15 minutes. Spread the remaining sauce over meat; sprinkle with sesame seeds. Roast, uncovered, for 10 to 20 minutes more or until temperature of the meat reaches 155°F. Remove from oven.

3. Cover meat with foil; let stand for 10 minutes before slicing (temperature of the meat will rise 5°F while it stands).

4. Meanwhile, in a 4-quart Dutch oven heat oil over medium heat. Add the remaining garlic, the salt, and pepper; cook and stir for 15 seconds. Add broccoli. Cook and stir for 1 to 2 minutes or until broccoli is heated through. Slice meat and serve with broccoli.

Per serving: 167 cal., 6 g total fat (1 g sat. fat), 55 mg chol., 365 mg sodium, 8 g carbo., 3 g fiber, 21 g pro.

Chunky Chipotle
PORK CHILI

This quick-to-fix pork stew relies on a flavor boost from the robust chipotle peppers, cumin, and picante sauce. See photo on page 108. *Makes 4 servings*

Start to Finish: **30 minutes**

12 ounces pork tenderloin
2 teaspoons chili powder
2 teaspoons ground cumin
⅓ cup chopped onion (1 small)
2 teaspoons bottled minced garlic (4 cloves)
1 tablespoon cooking oil
1 cup beer or beef broth
¾ cup bite-size pieces yellow or red sweet pepper (1 medium)
½ cup picante sauce or bottled salsa
1 to 2 tablespoons finely chopped canned chipotle chile pepper in adobo sauce (see note, page 22)
1 15-ounce can small red beans or pinto beans, rinsed and drained
½ cup dairy sour cream
Fresh cilantro sprigs or Italian (flat-leaf) parsley sprigs (optional)

1. Trim fat from meat. Cut meat into ¾-inch pieces. In a medium bowl combine meat, chili powder, and cumin; toss gently to coat. Set aside.
2. In a large saucepan cook onion and garlic in hot oil over medium-high heat about 3 minutes or until tender. Add meat; cook and stir until meat is brown. Stir in beer, sweet pepper, picante sauce, and chipotle pepper.

3. Bring to boiling; reduce heat. Simmer, covered, for 5 minutes or until meat is tender. Stir in drained beans; heat through.
4. Top each serving with sour cream and, if desired, garnish with cilantro sprigs.

Per serving: 328 cal., 11 g total fat (4 g sat. fat), 65 mg chol., 625 mg sodium, 29 g carbo., 7 g fiber, 26 g pro.

Peachy
PORK CHILI

Peaches in chili? You bet! They add just the right touch of sweetness to this spicy soup. *Makes 6 servings*

Start to Finish: **30 minutes**

1 pound lean boneless pork
1 tablespoon cooking oil
2 15-ounce cans butter beans, rinsed and drained
2 14.5-ounce cans diced tomatoes, undrained
1½ cups chopped fresh or frozen peaches
¾ cup chopped green sweet pepper (1 medium)
1 5.25-ounce can hot-style vegetable juice
2 to 3 teaspoons finely chopped canned chipotle chile pepper in adobo sauce (see note, page 22)
Salt and ground black pepper

1. Trim fat from meat. Cut meat into bite-size pieces. In a 4-quart Dutch oven cook meat, half at a time, in hot oil over medium-high heat until brown. Drain off fat. Return all of the meat to Dutch oven.

2. Stir in drained beans, undrained tomatoes, peaches, sweet pepper, vegetable juice, and chipotle pepper. Bring to boiling; reduce heat. Simmer, covered, for 15 minutes. Season to taste with salt and black pepper.

Per serving: 279 cal., 6 g total fat (2 g sat. fat), 48 mg chol., 1,130 mg sodium, 30 g carbo., 6 g fiber, 25 g pro.

Tex-Mex Pork
AND CORN SOUP

Tenderloin is the leanest of pork cuts. At first glance, pork tenderloin seems high per pound, but remember, there is no bone and almost no fat. *Makes 5 servings*

Start to Finish: **35 minutes**

12 ounces pork tenderloin or
    other lean boneless pork
1 tablespoon olive oil
1 cup chopped red onion
    (1 large)
2 teaspoons bottled minced
    garlic (4 cloves)
1 10-ounce package frozen
    whole kernel corn
2 14-ounce cans reduced-
    sodium chicken broth
1 cup bottled chipotle salsa or
    other bottled salsa
1 cup chopped red and/or
    yellow sweet pepper
¼ cup snipped fresh cilantro or
    parsley
½ cup chopped tomato
    (1 medium)
    Light dairy sour cream
    (optional)

1. Trim fat from meat. Cut meat into bite-size strips. In a large saucepan cook and stir meat in hot oil over medium-high heat for 3 to 4 minutes or until slightly pink in center. Remove meat from saucepan.

2. Add onion and garlic to saucepan; cook and stir for 3 to 4 minutes or until onion is tender. Add corn; cook and stir for 4 minutes. Stir in broth, salsa, and sweet pepper. Bring to boiling; reduce heat. Simmer, uncovered, for 10 minutes. Return meat to saucepan; heat through.

3. Before serving, stir in cilantro. Top each serving with tomato, and, if desired, sour cream.

Per serving: 199 cal., 6 g total fat (1 g sat. fat), 44 mg chol., 561 mg sodium, 20 g carbo., 3 g fiber, 19 g pro.

Mexican
PORK WRAPS

A takeoff on mole (MOH-lay), a spicy Mexican sauce tinged with chocolate, this quick-fix version starts with bottled barbecue sauce. *Makes 4 wraps*

Prep: 15 minutes   Marinate: 4 to 24 hours   Roast: 25 minutes   Stand: 10 minutes   Oven: 425°F/350°F

1 12-ounce pork tenderloin
⅓ cup bottled hot-style
   barbecue sauce
1 tablespoon unsweetened
   cocoa powder
¼ teaspoon ground cinnamon
2 medium green and/or red
   sweet peppers, seeded and
   cut into ½-inch strips
1 large onion, cut into
   6 wedges
8 7- to 8-inch flour tortillas
   Coarsely chopped avocado
   (optional)

1. Trim fat from meat. For marinade, in a small bowl stir together barbecue sauce, cocoa powder, and cinnamon. Brush half of the marinade evenly over meat. Cover and marinate in the refrigerator for 4 to 24 hours. Cover and chill the remaining marinade for basting.

2. Preheat oven to 425°F. Place meat on a roasting rack in a shallow roasting pan. Arrange sweet pepper and onion around meat. Brush meat and vegetables with the remaining marinade. Roast, uncovered, for 25 to 30 minutes or until temperature of the meat reaches 155°F. Transfer meat to a cutting board. Cover with foil; let meat stand for 10 minutes (temperature of the meat will rise 5°F during standing).

3. Meanwhile, reduce oven temperature to 350°F. Stack tortillas; wrap tightly in foil. Bake about 10 minutes or until heated through.

4. Thinly slice meat into bite-size strips. In a medium bowl toss together meat and vegetables. Spoon meat mixture onto warm tortillas. If desired, sprinkle with avocado. Roll up tortillas.

Per wrap: 344 cal., 7 g total fat (2 g sat. fat), 50 mg chol., 610 mg sodium, 43 g carbo., 3 g fiber, 26 g pro.

Zucchini Pork
CHOP SUPPER

Two layers of herb-seasoned croutons and a layer of creamy zucchini with juicy pork chops on top stack up to a simple but oh-so-good one-dish meal. *Makes 6 servings*

Prep: **30 minutes** Bake: **50 minutes** Oven: **350°F**

1 14-ounce package herb-seasoned stuffing croutons
¼ cup butter or margarine, melted
4 cups coarsely chopped zucchini
1 10.75-ounce can condensed cream of celery soup
1 8-ounce carton light dairy sour cream
¾ cup milk
½ cup shredded carrot (1 medium)
1 tablespoon snipped fresh parsley or 1 teaspoon dried parsley flakes
¼ to ½ teaspoon ground black pepper
6 bone-in pork loin chops, cut ¾ inch thick

1. Preheat oven to 350°F. Grease a 3-quart rectangular baking dish; set aside. In a large bowl combine 7½ cups of the croutons and the melted butter; toss gently to coat. Spread half of the buttered croutons in the prepared baking dish.
2. In another large bowl, combine zucchini, soup, sour cream, ½ cup of the milk, the carrot, parsley, and pepper. Spoon evenly over buttered croutons. Sprinkle with the remaining buttered croutons.
3. Pour the remaining ¼ cup milk into a shallow dish. Coarsely crush the remaining croutons; place in another shallow dish. Trim fat from chops. Dip chops into milk, then into crushed croutons, turning to coat. Place chops on top of layers in baking dish. Sprinkle with any remaining crushed croutons.
4. Bake, uncovered, for 50 to 60 minutes or until chops are slightly pink in center and juices run clear (160°F).

Per serving: 639 cal., 24 g total fat (10 g sat. fat), 130 mg chol., 1,417 mg sodium, 57 g carbo., 4 g fiber, 46 g pro.

Southwest
PORK CHOPS

Seasoned chili beans and bottled salsa are true timesavers. They come spiced, so you don't have to hassle with rounding up and measuring little bits of this and that for a full-flavored dish. *Makes 6 servings*

Prep: 15 minutes   Cook: Low 5 hours, High 2½ hours; plus 30 minutes on High

6 bone-in pork rib chops, cut ¾ inch thick
1 15-ounce can chili beans in chili gravy, undrained
1¼ cups bottled salsa
1 cup fresh or frozen whole kernel corn*
2 cups hot cooked rice
Snipped fresh cilantro or parsley (optional)

1. Trim fat from chops. Place chops in a 3½- or 4-quart slow cooker. Add undrained chili beans in gravy and salsa.
2. Cover and cook on low-heat setting for 5 hours or on high-heat setting for 2½ hours. If using low-heat setting, turn to high-heat setting. Stir in fresh or frozen corn. Cover and cook for 30 minutes more.

3. Serve chops and bean mixture over hot cooked rice. If desired, sprinkle with cilantro.

*Test Kitchen Tip: For fresh corn, cut off kernels from 2 medium ears of fresh corn to equal about 1 cup whole kernel corn.

Per serving: 334 cal., 7 g total fat (2 g sat. fat), 77 mg chol., 716 mg sodium, 34 g carbo., 4 g fiber, 33 g pro.

Spicy Pecan
PORK SANDWICHES

The pecan coating on the meat turns this into one of the best things in a bun. See photo on page 109.

Makes 4 sandwiches

Start to Finish: **30 minutes**

4 boneless pork loin chops,
  cut ½ inch thick (about
  I pound total)
¼ cup all-purpose flour
I egg, lightly beaten
2 tablespoons Dijon-style
  mustard
¼ to ½ teaspoon cayenne
  pepper
½ cup fine dry bread crumbs
½ cup ground toasted pecans
2 tablespoons cooking oil
4 hoagie buns, kaiser rolls, or
  hamburger buns, split and
  toasted, or 8 slices whole
  wheat bread, toasted
  Chipotle chile-flavor light
  mayonnaise
  Lettuce leaves
  Tomato slices

1. Trim fat from chops. Place each chop between 2 pieces of plastic wrap. Working from center to edges, pound lightly with the flat side of a meat mallet to about ¼-inch thickness. Remove plastic wrap.

2. Place flour in a shallow dish. In another shallow dish combine egg, mustard, and cayenne pepper. In a third shallow dish, combine bread crumbs and pecans. Dip meat into flour, then dip into egg mixture and crumb mixture, turning to coat.

3. In a 12-inch skillet heat oil over medium-high heat. Add meat. Cook for 6 to 8 minutes or until meat is slightly pink in center, turning once. If meat browns too quickly, reduce heat to medium.

4. Spread buns or bread with mayonnaise. Serve meat in buns or between 2 slices of bread with lettuce and tomato.

Per sandwich: 634 cal., 31 g total fat (6 g sat. fat), 122 mg chol., 987 mg sodium, 51 g carbo., 4 g fiber, 38 g pro.

Pork Chops
WITH SCALLOPED POTATOES

This old-fashioned duo is easier than ever with refrigerated potatoes and canned soup. It is a sure way to please meat and potato eaters. *Makes 4 servings*

Prep: **20 minutes**   Bake: **40 minutes**   Oven: **350°F**

4 cooked smoked pork chops
  (1½ to 2 pounds total)
1 10.75-ounce can condensed
  cream of celery soup
1 cup milk
⅓ cup sliced green onion (3)
4 slices American cheese
  (4 ounces), torn
1 20-ounce package
  refrigerated diced potatoes
  with onions
⅛ teaspoon ground black
  pepper
2 tablespoons snipped fresh
  chives

1. Preheat oven to 350°F. Trim fat from chops; set aside. In a medium saucepan combine soup, milk, and green onion. Cook and stir over medium heat until heated through. Add cheese, stirring until cheese is melted. Remove from heat.

2. Spread potatoes in a single layer in an ungreased 3-quart rectangular baking dish. Place chops on top of potatoes; sprinkle chops with pepper. Pour soup mixture over chops and potatoes.

3. Bake, covered, about 40 minutes or until heated through. Before serving, sprinkle with chives.

Per serving: 541 cal., 23 g total fat (11 g sat. fat), 123 mg chol., 3,226 mg sodium, 39 g carbo., 4 g fiber, 43 g pro.

Southwest
SPAGHETTI PIE

This pie will be a hit at any potluck where kids are present! Cooked spaghetti serves as the crust and the topping includes cheese, tomato sauce, and ground pork. *Makes 8 servings*

Prep: **40 minutes** Bake: **10 minutes** Stand: **5 minutes** Oven: **425°F**

8 ounces dried spaghetti
1 egg, lightly beaten
½ cup milk
1 pound ground pork
1 cup chopped onion (1 large)
¾ cup chopped green sweet
    pepper (1 medium)
½ teaspoon bottled minced
    garlic (1 clove)
1 tablespoon chili powder
½ teaspoon salt
½ teaspoon ground cumin
½ teaspoon dried oregano,
    crushed
¼ teaspoon ground black
    pepper
1 15-ounce can tomato sauce
1 cup shredded Monterey
    Jack cheese with jalapeño
    peppers (4 ounces)
1 cup shredded cheddar
    cheese (4 ounces)

1. Preheat oven to 425°F. Grease a 3-quart rectangular baking dish; set aside. Cook spaghetti according to package directions; drain. Return to hot pan. In a small bowl combine egg and milk; stir into hot spaghetti. Transfer to prepared baking dish.
2. Meanwhile, in a large skillet cook ground pork, onion, sweet pepper, and garlic over medium-high heat until meat is brown. Drain off fat. Stir in chili powder, salt, cumin, oregano, and black pepper. Cook and stir for 2 minutes. Stir in tomato sauce.
3. Bring to boiling; reduce heat. Simmer, uncovered, for 2 minutes. Spoon over spaghetti. Sprinkle with Monterey Jack cheese and cheddar cheese.
4. Bake, uncovered, about 10 minutes or until bubbly around edges. Let stand for 5 minutes before serving.

Per serving: 330 cal., 15 g total fat (8 g sat. fat), 84 mg chol., 621 mg sodium, 29 g carbo., 2 g fiber, 20 g pro.

Taco
HASH

Chipotle salsa adds a distinct, smoky flavor that complements any Mexican-style dish. *Makes 4 servings*

Start to Finish: **25 minutes**

1 pound ground pork
2 tablespoons cooking oil
½ of a 28-ounce package
    (3 cups) frozen diced hash
    brown potatoes with onions
    and peppers
1 16-ounce jar chipotle salsa or
    other bottled salsa
1 11-ounce can whole kernel
    corn with sweet peppers,
    drained
1 cup shredded Mexican
    cheese blend (4 ounces)
2 cups shredded lettuce
1 cup chopped tomato
    (2 medium)

1. In a large skillet cook ground pork over medium-high heat until brown. Drain off fat, removing meat from skillet.
2. In the same skillet heat oil over medium heat. Add potatoes, spreading in an even layer. Cook, without stirring, for 6 minutes. Stir potatoes; spread in an even layer. Cook, without stirring, for 3 to 4 minutes more or until potatoes are brown.

3. Stir in meat, salsa, and drained corn; heat through. Sprinkle with cheese. Top with lettuce and tomato.

Per serving: 645 cal., 41 g total fat (15 g sat. fat), 107 mg chol., 1,292 mg sodium, 42 g carbo., 7 g fiber, 31 g pro.

Cowboy
BOWLS

Weeknight meals can be a challenge: they have to be fast, easy, and prepared with readily available ingredients. This hearty pork, bean, and potato dinner fills the bill. *Makes 4 servings*

Start to Finish: **20 minutes**

1 24-ounce package refrigerated mashed potatoes
1 17-ounce package refrigerated shredded cooked pork in barbecue sauce
1 15-ounce can chili beans in chili gravy, undrained
1 cup frozen whole kernel corn
½ cup chopped red sweet pepper (1 small)
¼ cup finely chopped onion
½ cup shredded cheddar cheese (2 ounces)

1. Heat mashed potatoes according to package directions.
2. Meanwhile, in a medium saucepan combine pork in barbecue sauce, undrained chili beans in gravy, corn, sweet pepper, and onion; heat through.

3. Transfer mashed potatoes to 4 shallow bowls. Top with pork mixture and sprinkle with cheese.

Per serving: 600 cal., 21 g total fat (7 g sat. fat), 76 mg chol., 1,125 mg sodium, 74 g carbo., 8 g fiber, 31 g pro.

Apple

BUTTER-GLAZED HAM

You save on cooking and cleanup time because the sides—sweet potatoes and Brussels sprouts—cook together in one pan. *Makes 4 servings*

Start to Finish: **20 minutes**

2 medium sweet potatoes, peeled and cut into 1-inch pieces
12 ounces Brussels sprouts, trimmed and halved
1 to 1¼ pounds cooked ham, sliced about ¼ inch thick
2 tablespoons butter or margarine
Salt and ground black pepper
½ cup apple butter
2 tablespoons cider vinegar

1. In a covered large saucepan, cook sweet potato and Brussels sprouts in enough boiling, lightly salted water to cover for 8 to 10 minutes or until tender; drain.
2. Meanwhile, in a 12-inch skillet cook ham in hot butter over medium-high heat for 4 to 5 minutes or until heated through and light brown, turning occasionally. Transfer ham and vegetables to a serving platter. Sprinkle vegetables lightly with salt and pepper. Cover ham and vegetables and keep warm.

3. In the same skillet combine apple butter and vinegar. Cook and stir until heated through, scraping up any crusty browned bits. Serve ham and vegetables with apple butter mixture.

Per serving: 513 cal., 16 g total fat (7 g sat. fat), 80 mg chol., 1,664 mg sodium, 71 g carbo., 8 g fiber, 23 g pro.

Ham Balls
IN BARBECUE SAUCE

Buy ground ham in the supermarket or use leftover ham that has been finely chopped or ground in a food processor. *Makes 6 servings*

Prep: **20 minutes** Bake: **45 minutes** Oven: **350°F**

  2 eggs, lightly beaten
1½ cups soft bread crumbs
      (2 slices bread)
 ½ cup finely chopped onion
      (1 medium)
  2 tablespoons milk
  1 teaspoon dry mustard
 ¼ teaspoon ground black
      pepper
 12 ounces ground cooked ham
 12 ounces ground pork
 ¾ cup packed brown sugar
 ½ cup ketchup
  2 tablespoons vinegar
  1 teaspoon dry mustard

1. Preheat oven to 350°F. Lightly grease a 3-quart rectangular baking dish; set aside. In a large bowl combine eggs, bread crumbs, onion, milk, 1 teaspoon dry mustard, and the pepper. Add ground ham and ground pork; mix well.

2. Using about ⅓ cup of the ham mixture for each ball, shape ham mixture into 12 balls. Place ham balls in the prepared baking dish.

3. In a small bowl combine brown sugar, ketchup, vinegar, and 1 teaspoon dry mustard. Pour mixture over ham balls.

4. Bake, uncovered, about 45 minutes or until ham balls are done (160°F).*

*Test Kitchen Tip: The internal color of a meatball is not a reliable doneness indicator. A pork meatball cooked to 160°F is safe, regardless of color. To measure the doneness of a meatball, insert an instant-read thermometer into the center of the meatball.

Per serving: 428 cal., 19 g total fat (7 g sat. fat), 144 mg chol., 1,107 mg sodium, 42 g carbo., 1 g fiber, 23 g pro.

ONION OPTION: FOR ½ CUP CHOPPED ONION, USE 2 TABLESPOONS INSTANT MINCED ONION.

Ham and
CHEESE MACARONI

This is macaroni and cheese with a twist—ham and broccoli. A little red sweet pepper also adds flavor interest. *Makes 6 servings*

Prep: **30 minutes** Bake: **45 minutes** Oven: **350°F**

1½ cups dried elbow macaroni
3 cups broccoli florets
1½ cups coarsely chopped red sweet pepper (2 medium)
1½ cups cubed cooked ham
1½ cups milk
4½ teaspoons cornstarch
¼ teaspoon ground black pepper
1½ cups cubed American cheese (6 ounces)
1 cup soft bread crumbs
1 tablespoon butter or margarine, melted

1. Preheat oven to 350°F. Cook macaroni according to package directions, adding broccoli and sweet pepper during the last 2 minutes of cooking; drain. Transfer macaroni mixture to an ungreased 3-quart casserole. Stir in ham; set aside.
2. For sauce, in a small saucepan stir together milk, cornstarch, and black pepper. Cook and stir over medium heat until thickened and bubbly. Add cheese, stirring until cheese is melted. Add sauce to macaroni mixture; stir gently to combine. In a small bowl combine bread crumbs and melted butter; toss gently to coat. Sprinkle over casserole.

3. Bake, uncovered, about 45 minutes or until bubbly and bread crumbs are light brown.

Per serving: 373 cal., 16 g total fat (9 g sat. fat), 58 mg chol., 1,036 mg sodium, 35 g carbo., 3 g fiber, 22 g pro.

Hash

BROWN CASSEROLE

A crisp, savory crust tops this tempting meat-and-potato main dish. *Makes 6 servings*

Prep: **20 minutes** Bake: **50 minutes** Stand: **10 minutes** Oven: **350°F**

1 10.75-ounce can reduced-fat and reduced-sodium condensed cream of chicken soup or condensed cream of chicken soup
1 8-ounce carton light dairy sour cream or dairy sour cream
½ of a 30-ounce package (about 4 cups) frozen shredded hash brown potatoes
1 cup cubed cooked ham
1 cup cubed American cheese (4 ounces)
¼ cup chopped onion
⅛ teaspoon ground black pepper
1 cup cornflakes
3 tablespoons butter or margarine, melted

1. Preheat oven to 350°F. In a large bowl stir together soup and sour cream. Stir in frozen potatoes, ham, cheese, onion, and pepper. Transfer mixture to an ungreased 2-quart square baking dish.

2. In a small bowl combine cornflakes and melted butter; toss gently to coat. Sprinkle over ham mixture.

3. Bake, uncovered, for 50 to 55 minutes or until bubbly. Let stand for 10 minutes before serving.

Per serving: 351 cal., 19 g total fat (11 g sat. fat), 63 mg chol., 953 mg sodium, 35 g carbo., 2 g fiber, 13 g pro.

Ham and
BEAN STEW

This homey stew is quick to assemble because little measuring is required. Cream-style corn thickens the broth. *Makes 5 servings*

Prep: 10 minutes   Cook: Low 6 hours, High 3 hours

1 28-ounce can diced
   tomatoes, undrained
2½ cups cubed cooked ham
1 15-ounce can navy beans,
   rinsed and drained
1 14.75-ounce can cream-style
   corn
1 cup chopped onion (1 large)
¼ cup water
¼ teaspoon ground black
   pepper
   Dash bottled hot pepper
   sauce

1. In a 3½- or 4-quart slow cooker, combine undrained tomatoes, ham, drained beans, corn, onion, the water, black pepper, and hot pepper sauce.

2. Cover and cook on low-heat setting for 6 to 8 hours or on high-heat setting for 3 to 4 hours.

Per serving: 368 cal., 8 g total fat (3 g sat. fat), 50 mg chol., 2190 mg sodium, 45 g carbo., 7 g fiber, 29 g pro.

Fettuccine
ALLA CARBONARA

Substitute pancetta for the bacon if you like. Pancetta is cured but not smoked and has a pleasant, mild flavor. *Makes 4 servings*

Start to Finish: **25 minutes**

6 slices bacon, cut into I-inch pieces
6 ounces dried fettuccine or linguine
1 egg, lightly beaten
1 cup half-and-half, light cream, or milk
2 tablespoons butter or margarine
½ cup grated Parmesan or Romano cheese
¼ cup snipped fresh parsley
  Coarsely ground black pepper

1. In a small skillet cook bacon over medium heat until crisp. Using a slotted spoon, remove bacon and drain on paper towels.
2. Meanwhile, cook pasta according to package directions; drain. Return to hot pan; cover and keep warm.
3. For sauce, in a small saucepan combine egg, half-and-half, and butter. Cook and stir over medium heat about 6 minutes or just until egg mixture coats a metal spoon. Do not boil. Immediately pour sauce over cooked pasta; stir gently to coat.

4. Add cooked bacon, cheese, and parsley to pasta mixture; stir gently to combine. Season to taste with pepper. Serve immediately.

Per serving: 422 cal., 23 g total fat (13 g sat. fat), 110 mg chol., 489 mg sodium, 35 g carbo., 1 g fiber, 17 g pro.

Lasagna
BLANCA

With the noodles rolled into spirals, dishing up individual pieces is easy. You also can serve this recipe as a side dish, using half a noodle per serving. *Makes 12 servings*

Prep: **45 minutes** Bake: **35 minutes** Stand: **10 minutes** Oven: **350°F**

12 dried lasagna noodles
1 pound bulk spicy pork sausage
½ cup sliced green onion (4)
½ cup chopped fresh mushrooms
1½ cups shredded Monterey Jack cheese or cheddar cheese (6 ounces)
1 cup cream-style cottage cheese, undrained
½ of an 8-ounce package cream cheese, softened and cut up
½ teaspoon garlic powder
¼ teaspoon ground black pepper
1 tablespoon butter or margarine
1 tablespoon all-purpose flour
⅛ teaspoon dried tarragon, crushed
1 cup milk

1. Preheat oven to 350°F. Grease a 3-quart rectangular baking dish; set aside. Cook lasagna noodles according to package directions; drain. Rinse with cold water; drain again. Place noodles in a single layer on a piece of foil; set aside.

2. Meanwhile, in a large skillet cook sausage, green onion, and mushrooms over medium-high heat until meat is brown. Drain off fat. In a medium bowl combine ½ cup of the Monterey Jack cheese, the undrained cottage cheese, cream cheese, garlic powder, and ⅛ teaspoon of the pepper.

3. Spread cheese mixture evenly over lasagna noodles; sprinkle with meat mixture. Starting from a short end, roll up each noodle into a spiral. Place lasagna rolls, seam sides down, in the prepared baking dish.

4. For sauce, in a small saucepan melt butter over medium heat. Stir in flour, tarragon, and the remaining ⅛ teaspoon pepper. Gradually stir in milk. Cook and stir until slightly thickened and bubbly. Remove from heat. Stir in another ½ cup of the Monterey Jack cheese. Pour sauce over lasagna rolls.

5. Bake lasagna rolls, covered, for 25 minutes. Sprinkle with the remaining ½ cup Monterey Jack cheese. Bake, uncovered, about 10 minutes more or until heated through. Let stand 10 minutes before serving.

Make-Ahead Directions: Prepare as directed through Step 4. Cover tightly with foil; chill for 2 to 24 hours. To serve, preheat oven to 350°F. Bake, covered, for 40 minutes. Sprinkle with the remaining ½ cup Monterey Jack cheese. Bake, uncovered, about 10 minutes more or until heated through.

Per serving: 317 cal., 17 g total fat (9 g sat. fat), 54 mg chol., 378 mg sodium, 21 g carbo., 1 g fiber, 17 g pro.

Easy

SKILLET LASAGNA

Grab a jar of your favorite pasta sauce and create a crowd-pleaser in minutes with this tasty variation of lasagna. *Makes 4 to 6 servings*

Start to Finish: **25 minutes**

1 pound bulk Italian sausage
3 cups sliced fresh mushrooms (8 ounces)
¾ cup chopped green sweet pepper (1 medium)
½ cup chopped onion (1 medium)
8 ounces dried campanelle or mafalda pasta
1 26-ounce jar pasta sauce with mushrooms
1 cup shredded Italian cheese blend (4 ounces)
Snipped fresh parsley (optional)

1. In a very large skillet cook sausage, mushrooms, sweet pepper, and onion over medium-high heat until sausage is brown and vegetables are tender. Drain off fat.

2. Meanwhile, cook pasta according to package directions; drain.

3. Stir cooked pasta and pasta sauce into sausage mixture. Return to simmering. Sprinkle with cheese. Cook, covered, over low heat until cheese is melted. If desired, sprinkle with parsley.

Per serving: 892 cal., 49 g total fat (19 g sat. fat), 106 mg chol., 1881 mg sodium, 78 g carbo., 8 g fiber, 36 g pro.

Sausage and
CAVATELLI SKILLET

Bullet-shaped cavatelli pasta joins Italian sausage, pasta sauce, and mozzarella for a fast-to-fix, hearty meal. *Makes 4 servings*

Start to Finish: **20 minutes**

8 ounces dried cavatelli pasta

1 pound bulk Italian sausage or ground pork

¾ cup chopped green sweet pepper (1 medium)

1 20-ounce jar pasta sauce with mushrooms

1 cup shredded mozzarella cheese (4 ounces)

1. Cook pasta according to package directions; drain.

2. Meanwhile, in a large skillet cook sausage and sweet pepper over medium-high heat until meat is brown. Drain off fat. Stir in pasta sauce; cook about 2 minutes or until heated through, stirring occasionally.

3. Stir in cooked pasta. Sprinkle with cheese. Cook, covered, about 2 minutes more or until cheese is melted.

Per serving: 677 cal., 32 g total fat (13 g sat. fat), 93 mg chol., 1,469 mg sodium, 60 g carbo., 4 g fiber, 32 g pro.

Italian
SAUSAGE GRINDERS

Three ingredients are a must for a sausage grinder: sausage, sweet pepper, and onion. After that, all of the other ingredients are a yummy bonus.

Makes 4 sandwiches

Prep: **25 minutes** Cook: **30 minutes** Broil: **2 minutes**

1 pound bulk hot or mild Italian sausage
1 14.5-ounce can fire-roasted diced tomatoes, undrained
1 14.5-ounce can crushed tomatoes
1 teaspoon dried basil, crushed
1 teaspoon bottled minced garlic (2 cloves)
1 teaspoon balsamic vinegar
½ teaspoon dried oregano, crushed
¼ teaspoon salt
¼ teaspoon crushed red pepper
1 small green sweet pepper, seeded and cut into strips
1 small yellow onion, sliced
2 tablespoons olive oil
4 French-style rolls or hoagie buns, split
4 slices provolone cheese (4 ounces)

1. In a large saucepan cook sausage over medium-high heat until brown. Drain off fat. Stir in undrained diced tomatoes, crushed tomatoes, basil, garlic, vinegar, oregano, salt, and crushed red pepper. Bring to boiling; reduce heat. Simmer, uncovered, about 30 minutes or until mixture is thickened.

2. Meanwhile, in a large skillet cook sweet pepper and onion in hot oil over medium heat until tender. Remove from heat; cover and keep warm.

3. Preheat broiler. Place roll halves on a baking sheet. Spoon meat mixture onto bottoms of rolls; add sweet pepper mixture and cheese. Broil 4 to 5 inches from the heat for 2 to 3 minutes or until cheese is melted and bubbly. Replace tops of rolls.

Per sandwich: 663 cal., 42 g total fat (16 g sat. fat), 96 mg chol., 1,820 mg sodium, 35 g carbo., 4 g fiber, 29 g pro.

Test Kitchen Tip: **To vary the sandwiches, omit the sweet pepper, onion, and olive oil. Top the meat mixture with ½ cup bottled roasted red sweet peppers, drained, and ½ cup bottled sliced banana or pepperoncini peppers, drained, before broiling.**

Sausage and
PEPPER SANDWICHES

Add a slice of mozzarella cheese to top the veggies if you like and broil for a minute or two to melt the cheese. *Makes 4 sandwiches*

Start to Finish: **30 minutes**

4 uncooked mild Italian sausage links (about I pound total)
½ cup water
I tablespoon cooking oil
I cup green sweet pepper strips (I medium)
I cup red sweet pepper strips (I medium)
I large onion, sliced and separated into rings
¼ cup bottled Italian salad dressing
I tablespoon Dijon-style mustard
4 French-style rolls or hoagie buns, split

1. In a large skillet cook sausage over medium heat about 5 minutes or until brown, turning frequently. Carefully add the water. Bring to boiling; reduce heat. Simmer, covered, for 5 minutes. Cook, uncovered, until liquid is evaporated and sausage is done (160°F), turning frequently. Watch carefully so that sausage does not burn. Drain sausage on paper towels. Wipe out skillet, if necessary.

2. In the same skillet heat oil over medium heat. Add sweet peppers and onion. Cook and stir about 5 minutes or until vegetables are crisp-tender. Return sausage to skillet. In a small bowl combine salad dressing and mustard; stir into sausage mixture. Heat through.

3. Using a spoon, slightly hollow out bottoms of rolls. If desired, preheat broiler. Broil roll halves about 4 inches from the heat for 2 to 3 minutes or until toasted. Place sausage on bottoms of rolls. Top with sweet pepper mixture; replace tops of rolls.

Per sandwich: 567 cal., 38 g total fat (12 g sat. fat), 77 mg chol., 993 mg sodium, 29 g carbo., 3 g fiber, 21 g pro.

LOOK!

MONEY-SAVING TIPS and HINTS

Chicken breasts are the priciest cut. Purchase them in bulk (the ones in the large bags) or on sale and freeze in useful portions for you.

When recipes specify meaty chicken, use legs and thighs. Also use these cuts when recipes call for shredded chicken for tacos or other dishes.

Need skinless, boneless chicken breasts? Skinning and boning chicken breasts usually saves money. To double your savings, use the bones to make chicken stock.

Make marinated chicken by placing chicken in a freezer bag, adding desired marinade, and freezing. To use, thaw overnight in the refrigerator. Drain the marinade and grill or cook as you like.

If you love the taste of deli-roasted chicken, buy several on sale. Serve one for dinner; remove the meat from the bones of other chickens; freeze meat. Then you'll have seasoned chicken on hand for sandwiches, soups, salads, and casseroles.

CHEAP! Buy canned chicken in bulk at warehouse or discount stores for last-minute meals, such as salads or sandwiches. **CHEAP!**

Sale! Buy a whole chicken on sale, save the giblets, and cut off the wing tips for making chicken broth. Freeze them until there is time to make broth. Also add any saved chicken bones to the broth.

Make cubed or chopped cooked chicken by purchasing whole chickens and/or chicken pieces on sale. Cook, bone, and cube or chop the meat. Portion into freezer bags and freeze.

Grill extra chicken breasts, slice, and refrigerate or freeze. Add the slices to a salad or cooked pasta, or place them in pitas or tortillas, adding desired toppings for quick-and-easy wraps.

CHAPTER 4

COUNT ON CHICKEN

The popularity of chicken is no secret, thanks to its second name—versatility. Chicken can be cooked whole or cut up, skin on or skinless, bone in or boneless. Whether grilled, simmered, fried, broiled, slow-cooked or stir-fried, chicken always feels right at home on your table. Plus, it is quick to prepare and inexpensive. With these **56** chicken dishes, you can afford, and will enjoy, having a chicken in every pot.

Roasted
ITALIAN CHICKEN

The under-the-skin seasonings in this recipe work like a marinade, adding lots of extra herb flavor to the chicken as it roasts. *Makes 6 servings*

Prep: **20 minutes**   Roast: **1¼ hours**   Stand: **10 minutes**   Oven: **375°F**

2 tablespoons balsamic vinegar
2 tablespoons olive oil
2 tablespoons snipped fresh oregano or 2 teaspoons dried oregano, crushed
2 tablespoons snipped fresh basil or 2 teaspoons dried basil, crushed
1 tablespoon snipped fresh thyme or 1 teaspoon dried thyme, crushed
1 tablespoon lemon juice
2 teaspoons bottled minced garlic (4 cloves)
1 teaspoon salt
1 teaspoon coarsely ground black pepper
1 3- to 3½-pound whole broiler-fryer chicken

1. Preheat oven to 375°F. In a small bowl whisk together vinegar, oil, oregano, basil, thyme, lemon juice, garlic, salt, and pepper. Divide herb mixture in half; set aside.
2. Remove neck and giblets from chicken. Rinse inside of chicken; pat dry with paper towels. On one side of the chicken, slip your fingers between the skin and breast meat of the chicken, forming a pocket; repeat on other side of chicken. Divide one portion of the herb mixture between pockets.
3. Using 100-percent-cotton kitchen string, tie drumsticks to tail. Twist wing tips under back. Place chicken, breast side up, on a roasting rack in a shallow roasting pan.

4. Roast, uncovered, for 1 hour. Cut string between drumsticks. Brush chicken with the remaining herb mixture. Roast, uncovered, for 15 to 30 minutes more or until drumsticks move easily in their sockets and juices run clear (180°F).
5. Transfer chicken to a serving platter. Cover with foil; let stand for 10 minutes before carving.

Per serving: 376 cal., 27 g total fat (7 g sat. fat), 115 mg chol., 476 mg sodium, 3 g carbo., 0 g fiber, 29 g pro.

IN-A-PINCH TIPS!

CHICKEN STOCK: WHEN YOU PREPARE A WHOLE CHICKEN, CUT OFF THE WING TIPS BEFORE COOKING AND FREEZER-STORE THEM IN A HEAVY FREEZER BAG, ADDING MORE TIPS AS YOU GET THEM. WHEN YOU ACCUMULATE ENOUGH, USE THEM TO MAKE CHICKEN STOCK.

Beer
CAN CHICKEN

Before firing up your grill, measure the height from the grid to the lid to see if an almost upright whole chicken will fit under the lid (for a gas grill, remove the upper grill racks if necessary). If so, grill two birds and save the second for another meal. *Makes 4 to 6 servings*

Prep: 30 minutes Grill: 1¼ hours Stand: 10 minutes

2 teaspoons salt
2 teaspoons packed brown sugar
2 teaspoons paprika
1 teaspoon dry mustard
½ teaspoon dried thyme, crushed
½ teaspoon ground black pepper
¼ teaspoon garlic powder
1 12-ounce can beer
1 3½- to 4-pound whole broiler-fryer chicken
2 tablespoons butter or margarine, softened
1 lemon quarter

1. For rub, in a small bowl combine salt, brown sugar, paprika, dry mustard, thyme, pepper, and garlic powder. Discard about half of the beer from the can. Add 1 teaspoon of the rub to the half-empty can (beer will foam).

2. Remove neck and giblets from chicken. Rinse inside of chicken; pat dry with paper towels. Sprinkle 1 teaspoon of the rub inside body cavity. Spread the outside of chicken with butter, then sprinkle with remaining rub.

3. Hold chicken upright with the opening of the body cavity at the bottom and lower it onto the beer can so the can fits into the cavity. Pull chicken legs forward so the bird rests on its legs and the can. Twist wing tips behind back. Stuff lemon quarter into neck cavity to seal in steam.

4. For a charcoal grill, arrange medium-hot coals around a drip pan. Test for medium heat above pan. Stand chicken upright on grill rack over drip pan. Cover and grill for 1¼ to 1¾ hours or until chicken is no longer pink (180°F). If necessary, cover chicken loosely with foil to prevent overbrowning. (For a gas grill, preheat grill. Reduce heat to medium. Adjust for indirect cooking. Grill as above.)

5. Holding chicken by the can, carefully remove it from grill. Cover with foil; let stand for 10 minutes. To pull the can from the chicken, use a hot pad to grasp the can and heavy tongs to grasp the chicken.

Per serving: 635 cal., 45 g total fat (15 g sat. fat), 217 mg chol., 1,180 mg sodium, 3 g carbo., 0 g fiber, 51 g pro.

IN-A-PINCH TIPS!

GIBLET BROTH: WHEN GIBLETS AND OTHER ORGAN MEATS (HEART, GIZZARD) ARE INCLUDED IN A WHOLE TURKEY OR CHICKEN, FREEZE THEM IN A HEAVY FREEZER BAG AND THEN USE THEM TO MAKE THE BROTH FOR GRAVY OR SOUP. COOK THE LIVER SEPARATELY.

Roast

TARRAGON CHICKEN

Tarragon's bold, aniselike flavor complements the sweetness of roasted tomatoes and shallots.
No tarragon? Substitute rosemary, thyme, or basil. *Makes 6 servings*

Prep: 15 minutes   Roast: 45 minutes   Oven: 375°F

3 tablespoons olive oil
2½ teaspoons dried tarragon,
   crushed
1 teaspoon bottled minced
   garlic (2 cloves)
½ teaspoon salt
½ teaspoon coarsely ground
   black pepper
1 pound cherry tomatoes
8 small shallots
2½ to 3 pounds meaty chicken
   pieces (breast halves,
   thighs, and drumsticks)

1. Preheat oven to 375°F. In a medium bowl stir together oil, tarragon, garlic, salt, and pepper. Add tomatoes and shallots; toss gently to coat. Using a slotted spoon, transfer tomatoes and shallots to another medium bowl, reserving oil mixture. Set tomatoes and shallots aside.
2. If desired, remove skin from chicken. Place chicken in a shallow roasting pan. Brush chicken with the oil mixture.

3. Roast, uncovered, for 20 minutes. Add shallots only; roast, uncovered, for 15 minutes. Add tomatoes; roast, uncovered, for 10 to 12 minutes more or until chicken is no longer pink (170°F for breasts; 180°F for thighs and drumsticks) and vegetables are tender.

Per serving: 253 cal., 13 g total fat (3 g sat. fat), 77 mg chol., 173 mg sodium, 8 g carbo., 1 g fiber, 26 g pro.

Oven-Barbecued
CHICKEN

Use any combination of chicken pieces, whatever is on sale at the supermarket. Bone-in chicken with homemade barbecue sauce is a winning combination. See photo on page 110. *Makes 6 servings*

Prep: **10 minutes** Bake: **45 minutes** Oven: **375°F**

2½ to 3 pounds meaty chicken
   pieces (breast halves,
   thighs, and drumsticks)
½ cup chopped onion
   (1 medium)
½ teaspoon bottled minced
   garlic (1 clove)
1 tablespoon cooking oil
¾ cup chili sauce
2 tablespoons honey
2 tablespoons soy sauce
1 tablespoon yellow mustard
½ teaspoon prepared
   horseradish
¼ teaspoon crushed red pepper

1. Preheat oven to 375°F. Remove skin from chicken. Arrange chicken, bone sides up, in an ungreased 15×10×1-inch baking pan. Bake, uncovered, for 25 minutes.
2. Meanwhile, for sauce, in a small saucepan cook onion and garlic in hot oil over medium heat until tender. Stir in chili sauce, honey, soy sauce, mustard, horseradish, and crushed red pepper; heat through.

3. Turn chicken bone sides down. Brush chicken with half of the sauce. Bake, uncovered, for 20 to 30 minutes more or until chicken is no longer pink (170°F for breasts; 180°F for thighs and drumsticks). Bring the remaining sauce to a full boil. Pass with chicken.

Per serving: 244 cal., 9 g total fat (2 g sat. fat), 77 mg chol., 807 mg sodium, 15 g carbo., 2 g fiber, 26 g pro.

IN-A-PINCH TIPS!

MUSTARD MAGIC: FOR A TABLESPOON OF PREPARED MUSTARD, USE 1 TEASPOON DRY MUSTARD STIRRED INTO 1 TABLESPOON WATER.

Sunday
CHICKEN-RICE BAKE

The name says Sunday but enjoy this delectable dish other days too. It's so easy, making it a perfect any-day meal. *Makes 4 to 6 servings*

Prep: **20 minutes** Bake: **55 minutes** Oven: **375°F**

2½ pounds meaty chicken pieces (breast halves, thighs, and drumsticks)
1 10.75-ounce can condensed cream of chicken soup
1 cup milk
½ water
1 4-ounce can (drained weight) sliced mushrooms, drained
1 10-ounce package frozen peas and carrots, thawed
1 6.2-ounce package lemon-and-herb-flavor rice

1. Preheat oven to 375°F. Grease a 3-quart rectangular baking dish or 13×9×2-inch baking pan; set aside. Remove skin from chicken; set chicken aside.

2. In a large bowl combine soup, milk, the water, and drained mushrooms. Reserve ½ cup of the soup mixture. Stir vegetables and uncooked rice into the remaining soup mixture.

3. Transfer rice mixture to the prepared baking dish. Top with chicken. Pour the reserved ½ cup soup mixture over chicken.

4. Bake, covered for 55 to 60 minutes or until chicken is no longer pink (170°F for breasts; 180°F for thighs and drumsticks) and rice is tender.

Per serving: 545 cal., 16 g total fat (5 g sat. fat), 126 mg chol., 1,178 mg sodium, 52 g carbo., 4 g fiber, 47 g pro.

Feta-Topped CHICKEN

An affordable garnish of feta cheese and fresh parsley turns a slow-cooker meal into a Mediterranean-inspired chicken dish. *Makes 6 servings*

Prep: **20 minutes** Cook: **Low 5 hours, High 2½ hours**

3½ to 4 pounds meaty chicken pieces (breast halves, thighs, and drumsticks)
1 teaspoon dried basil, crushed
1 teaspoon dried rosemary, crushed
1 teaspoon finely shredded lemon peel
1 teaspoon bottled minced garlic (2 cloves)
½ teaspoon salt
¼ teaspoon ground black pepper
½ cup reduced-sodium chicken broth
½ cup crumbled feta cheese (2 ounces)
2 tablespoons snipped fresh Italian (flat-leaf) parsley

1. Remove skin from chicken; set chicken aside. For rub, in a small bowl combine basil, rosemary, lemon peel, garlic, salt, and pepper. Sprinkle rub evenly over chicken; rub in with your fingers. Place chicken in a 4- to 5-quart slow cooker. Add broth.

2. Cover and cook on low-heat setting for 5 to 6 hours or on high-heat setting for 2½ to 3 hours.

3. Transfer chicken to a serving platter; discard cooking liquid. Sprinkle chicken with cheese and parsley.

Per serving: 179 cal., 6 g total fat (2 g sat. fat), 97 mg chol., 425 mg sodium, 1 g carbo., 0 g fiber, 29 g pro.

Mu Shu-
STYLE CHICKEN

This slow cooker version of mu shu differs from the classic because it features chicken, not pork, and is served in tortillas instead of thin pancakes. *Makes 4 servings*

Prep: **20 minutes**   Cook: **Low 6 hours, High 3 hours**

2½ to 3 pounds meaty chicken pieces (breast halves, thighs, and drumsticks)
¼ teaspoon salt
⅛ teaspoon ground black pepper
½ cup water
¼ cup soy sauce
2 teaspoons toasted sesame oil
¾ teaspoon ground ginger
8 7- to 8-inch flour tortillas
½ cup hoisin sauce
2 cups packaged shredded broccoli (broccoli slaw mix) or packaged shredded cabbage with carrot (coleslaw mix)

1. Remove skin from chicken. Place chicken in a 3½- or 4-quart slow cooker. Sprinkle chicken with salt and pepper. In a small bowl combine the water, soy sauce, sesame oil, and ginger. Pour over chicken.

2. Cover and cook on low-heat setting for 6 to 7 hours or on high-heat setting for 3 to 3½ hours.

3. Remove chicken from cooker, reserving cooking liquid. When cool enough to handle, remove chicken from bones, discarding bones. Shred chicken by pulling two forks through it in opposite directions. Return chicken to cooker; stir to combine with cooking liquid.

4. To serve, spread each tortilla with 1 tablespoon of the hoisin sauce. Using a slotted spoon, spoon shredded chicken onto tortillas just below the centers. Top with shredded broccoli. Fold bottom edge of each tortilla up and over filling. Fold in opposite sides; roll up tortilla.

Per serving: 520 cal., 18 g total fat (4 g sat. fat), 115 mg chol., 1,315 mg sodium, 44 g carbo., 3 g fiber, 44 g pro.

Old-Fashioned Chicken
NOODLE SOUP

For an authentic old-fashioned soup, use home-style noodles, dried "dumplings," or extra-wide noodles.

Makes 8 servings

Prep: **20 minutes** Cook: **1 hour 40 minutes**

1 3½- to 4-pound broiler-
  fryer chicken, cut up, or
  2½ pounds meaty chicken
  pieces (breast halves,
  thighs, and drumsticks)
8 cups water
½ cup chopped onion
  (1 medium)
1 bay leaf
2 teaspoons salt
¼ teaspoon ground black
  pepper
1 cup chopped carrot
  (2 medium)
1 cup chopped celery
  (2 stalks)
1½ cups dried egg noodles
2 tablespoons snipped fresh
  parsley

1. In a 6- to 8-quart Dutch oven, combine chicken, the water, onion, bay leaf, salt, and pepper. Bring to boiling; reduce heat. Simmer, covered, about 1½ hours or until chicken is very tender.

2. Remove chicken from broth. When cool enough to handle, remove chicken from bones, discarding skin and bones. Cut chicken into bite-size pieces; set aside. Discard bay leaf.

3. Skim fat from broth. Bring broth to boiling. Stir in carrot and celery; reduce heat. Simmer, covered, for 5 minutes. Stir in noodles. Simmer, covered, about 5 minutes more or until noodles are tender but still firm. Stir in chicken and parsley; heat through.

Per serving: 152 cal., 3 g total fat (1 g sat. fat), 73 mg chol., 684 mg sodium, 8 g carbo., 1 g fiber, 22 g pro.

Pesto-Stuffed CHICKEN BREASTS

Purchased pesto makes this recipe a breeze. Serve these flavor-packed chicken breasts on a bed of your favorite pasta. *Makes 4 servings*

Prep: **20 minutes** Bake: **45 minutes** Oven: **375°F**

4 bone-in chicken breast
  halves (about 2½ pounds
  total)
½ cup bottled roasted red
  sweet peppers, drained and
  chopped
⅓ cup refrigerated basil pesto
2 tablespoons finely shredded
  Parmesan cheese
  Salt and ground black pepper
1 tablespoon butter or
  margarine, melted

1. Preheat oven to 375°F. Lightly grease a 2-quart rectangular baking dish; set aside. Using your fingers, gently separate the skin from the meat of each breast half along the rib edge.
2. For stuffing, in a small bowl combine roasted pepper, pesto, and cheese. Spoon a rounded tablespoon of the stuffing between the skin and meat of each chicken half. Sprinkle stuffed chicken with salt and black pepper.

3. Place chicken, bone sides down, in the prepared baking dish. Drizzle with melted butter. Bake, uncovered, for 45 to 55 minutes or until chicken is no longer pink (170°F).

Per serving: 421 cal., 27 g total fat (8 g sat. fat), 124 mg chol., 407 mg sodium, 4 g carbo., 1 g fiber, 39 g pro.

Baked
CHICKEN MARSALA

This classic dish is ideal for company and made easy by roasting in the oven. *Makes 8 servings*

Prep: **30 minutes** Bake: **20 minutes** Oven: **375°F**

8 skinless, boneless chicken breast halves (about 2½ pounds total)

⅓ cup all-purpose flour

6 tablespoons butter or margarine

2 cups sliced fresh mushrooms

1 cup dry Marsala

⅔ cup chicken broth

⅛ teaspoon salt

⅛ teaspoon ground black pepper

1 cup shredded mozzarella cheese or fontina cheese (4 ounces)

⅔ cup grated Parmesan cheese

½ cup thinly sliced green onion (4)

1. Preheat oven to 375°F. Cut each chicken piece in half lengthwise. Place each piece between 2 pieces of plastic wrap. Working from center to edges, pound lightly with the flat side of a meat mallet to ⅛-inch thickness. Remove plastic wrap. Place flour in a shallow dish or on waxed paper. Dip chicken into flour, turning to coat.

2. In a 12-inch skillet melt 1 tablespoon of the butter over medium heat. Add 4 of the chicken pieces; cook about 4 minutes or until brown, turning once. Transfer to an ungreased 3-quart rectangular baking dish. Repeat three more times with the remaining butter and the remaining chicken.

3. In the same skillet melt the remaining 2 tablespoons butter over medium-high heat. Add mushrooms; cook and stir until tender. Stir in Marsala, broth, salt, and pepper. Bring to boiling; reduce heat. Boil gently, uncovered, about 5 minutes or until mixture is reduced to 1 cup (including the mushrooms). Pour mushroom mixture over chicken.

4. In a small bowl combine mozzarella cheese, Parmesan cheese, and green onion; sprinkle over chicken. Bake, uncovered, about 20 minutes or until chicken is no longer pink.

Per serving: 364 cal., 17 g total fat (9 g sat. fat), 121 mg chol., 496 mg sodium, 6 g carbo., 0 g fiber, 42 g pro.

Honey-Glazed
CHICKEN

Double the kick from the honey-mustard mixture by using it as a marinade for the chicken and as the dressing for the greens or pasta. *Makes 4 servings*

Prep: 15 minutes   Marinate: 2 to 4 hours   Bake: 20 minutes   Oven: 400°F

1½ pounds skinless, boneless chicken breasts
½ cup honey
3 tablespoons lemon juice
1 tablespoon reduced-sodium soy sauce
1 tablespoon spicy brown mustard
Torn mixed salad greens or hot cooked pasta (optional)

1. Place chicken in a resealable plastic bag set in a shallow dish. For marinade, in a small bowl whisk together honey, lemon juice, soy sauce, and mustard. Reserve ¼ cup of the marinade for dressing. Pour the remaining marinade over chicken. Seal bag; turn to coat chicken. Marinate in the refrigerator for 2 to 4 hours, turning bag occasionally. Drain chicken, reserving marinade.

2. Preheat oven to 400°F. Place chicken in an ungreased shallow baking pan. Bake, uncovered, about 20 minutes or until chicken is no longer pink (170°F), turning and brushing once with marinade halfway through baking. Discard any remaining marinade.

3. Thinly slice chicken. If desired, serve chicken on salad greens. Drizzle with the reserved ¼ cup marinade.

Per serving: 325 cal., 2 g total fat (1 g sat. fat), 99 mg chol., 299 mg sodium, 36 g carbo., 0 g fiber, 40 g pro.

Baked

PARMESAN CHICKEN

Crushed cereal and cheese enrobe boneless chicken breasts for a short-prep main dish that is long on flavor. *Makes 4 servings*

Prep: 10 minutes   Bake: 30 minutes   Oven: 375°F

3 tablespoons butter or
   margarine, melted
½ cup crushed cornflakes
2 tablespoons grated
   Parmesan cheese
¼ teaspoon dried Italian
   seasoning, crushed
4 skinless, boneless chicken
   breast halves (about
   1¼ pounds total)

1. Preheat oven to 375°F. Pour melted butter into a shallow dish. In another shallow dish combine cornflakes, cheese, and Italian seasoning. Dip chicken into melted butter, then into cornflake mixture, turning to coat.

2. Place chicken on a roasting rack in a shallow baking pan. Bake, uncovered, about 30 minutes or until chicken is no longer pink (170°F).

Per serving: 287 cal., 12 g total fat (7 g sat. fat), 109 mg chol., 318 mg sodium, 9 g carbo., 0 g fiber, 35 g pro.

Creamy
CHICKEN ENCHILADAS

If people ask you for the recipe, don't be surprised. This perfect party dish features spinach and chicken dressed up with a luscious sour cream and yogurt sauce. *Makes 12 enchiladas*

Prep: **40 minutes**   Bake: **40 minutes**   Stand: **5 minutes**   Oven: **350°F**

1 pound skinless, boneless chicken breasts
1 10-ounce package frozen chopped spinach, thawed and well drained
½ cup thinly sliced green onion (4)
2 8-ounce cartons light dairy sour cream
½ cup plain yogurt
¼ cup all-purpose flour
½ teaspoon salt
½ teaspoon ground cumin
1 cup milk
2 4-ounce cans diced green chile peppers, drained
12 7-inch flour tortillas
⅔ cup shredded cheddar cheese or Monterey Jack cheese
Bottled salsa (optional)
Sliced green onion (optional)

1. Preheat oven to 350°F. In a large saucepan combine chicken and enough water to cover. Bring to boiling; reduce heat. Simmer, covered, for 12 to 14 minutes or until chicken is no longer pink (170°F); drain. Shred chicken by pulling two forks through it in opposite directions. In a large bowl combine shredded chicken, spinach, and the ½ cup green onion; set aside.

2. For sauce, in a medium bowl stir together sour cream, yogurt, flour, salt, and cumin. Stir in milk and drained chile peppers. Divide sauce in half. For filling, stir one portion of the sauce into chicken mixture.

3. Spoon filling onto tortillas; roll up tortillas. Place, seam sides down, in an ungreased 3-quart rectangular baking dish. Spoon the remaining sauce over filled tortillas.

4. Bake, uncovered, about 40 minutes or until heated through. Remove from oven; sprinkle with cheese. Let stand for 5 minutes before serving. If desired, serve with salsa and additional green onion.

Per enchilada: 247 cal., 9 g total fat (4 g sat. fat), 44 mg chol., 395 mg sodium, 23 g carbo., 1 g fiber, 18 g pro.

Chicken
PAPRIKASH

In this traditional Hungarian dish, chicken bakes on top of vegetables and noodles flavored with bacon and paprika. The tangy sour cream gravy adds richness and extraordinary flavor. *Makes 6 servings*

Prep: **30 minutes**   Bake: **35 minutes**   Oven: **375°F**

4 cups dried medium noodles
3 slices bacon, chopped
1 cup chopped onion (1 large)
1 cup chopped carrot
    (2 medium)
1 cup chopped celery
    (2 stalks)
1 teaspoon paprika
½ teaspoon finely shredded
    lemon peel
¼ teaspoon salt
⅛ teaspoon ground black
    pepper
1 8-ounce carton dairy sour
    cream
⅓ cup all-purpose flour
1¾ cups milk
6 skinless, boneless chicken
    breast halves (about
    2 pounds total)
    Paprika
    Salt and ground black pepper

1. Preheat oven to 375°F. Cook noodles according to package directions; drain. Meanwhile, in a very large skillet cook bacon over medium heat until crisp. Using a slotted spoon, remove bacon and drain on paper towels, reserving drippings in skillet. Add onion, carrot, and celery to the reserved drippings; cook for 5 minutes, stirring occasionally. Stir in the 1 teaspoon paprika, the lemon peel, the ¼ teaspoon salt, and the ⅛ teaspoon pepper.
2. In a medium bowl combine sour cream and flour. Gradually stir in milk. Stir sour cream mixture into onion mixture. Cook and stir until thickened and bubbly. Stir in cooked noodles and bacon.

3. Transfer noodle mixture to an ungreased 3-quart rectangular baking dish. Arrange chicken on top of noodle mixture. Sprinkle chicken lightly with additional paprika, salt, and pepper.
4. Bake, uncovered, for 35 to 40 minutes or until chicken is no longer pink (170°F).

Per serving: 493 cal., 19 g total fat (9 g sat. fat), 141 mg chol., 389 mg sodium, 33 g carbo., 2 g fiber, 45 g pro.

Sweet-and-Sour
BAKED CHICKEN

Baking makes classic sweet-and-sour chicken easier to make—and more totable. *Makes 8 servings*

Prep: **25 minutes**   Bake: **30 minutes**   Oven: **350°F**

8 skinless, boneless chicken
   breast halves (about
   2½ pounds total)
   Salt and ground black pepper
2 tablespoons cooking oil
1 20-ounce can pineapple
   chunks (juice pack),
   undrained
1 cup canned jellied cranberry
   sauce
¼ cup cornstarch
¼ cup packed brown sugar
¼ cup rice vinegar or cider
   vinegar
¼ cup frozen orange juice
   concentrate, thawed
¼ cup dry sherry, chicken
   broth, or water
¼ cup soy sauce
½ teaspoon ground ginger
2 cups bite-size strips green
   sweet pepper (2 medium)

1. Preheat oven to 350°F. Sprinkle chicken lightly with salt and black pepper. In a very large skillet, heat oil over medium-high heat. Add chicken; cook about 4 minutes or until brown, turning once. (If necessary, brown chicken in batches.) Transfer chicken to an ungreased 3-quart rectangular baking dish or 13×9×2-inch baking pan.

2. Drain pineapple, reserving ⅔ cup juice. Spoon pineapple evenly over chicken; set aside.

3. For sauce, in a medium saucepan whisk together the reserved ⅔ cup pineapple juice, the cranberry sauce, cornstarch, brown sugar, vinegar, juice concentrate, sherry, soy sauce, and ginger. Cook and stir over medium heat until thickened and bubbly. Pour over chicken and pineapple in dish.

4. Bake, covered, for 25 minutes. Add sweet pepper strips, stirring gently to coat with sauce. Bake, uncovered, about 5 minutes more or until chicken is no longer pink (170°F).

Per serving: 354 cal., 5 g total fat (1 g sat. fat), 82 mg chol., 669 mg sodium, 37 g carbo., 2 g fiber, 34 g pro.

Dijon Chicken
AND MUSHROOMS

Dijon-style mustard, containing white wine and seasonings, adds a sharp flavor and a little French refinement to this dish. *Makes 4 servings*

Start to Finish: **30 minutes**

3 tablespoons butter or margarine

2 cups sliced fresh mushrooms

4 skinless, boneless chicken breast halves (about 1¼ pounds total)

1 10.75-ounce can condensed cream of chicken soup

¼ cup dry white wine

¼ cup water

2 tablespoons Dijon-style mustard

½ teaspoon dried thyme or tarragon, crushed

2 cups hot cooked pasta

1. In a large skillet melt 1 tablespoon of the butter over medium-high heat. Add mushrooms; cook for 3 to 4 minutes or until tender. Remove mushrooms from skillet. In the same skillet melt the remaining 2 tablespoons butter. Add chicken; cook for 8 to 10 minutes or until chicken is no longer pink (170°F), turning once.

2. Meanwhile, in a small bowl stir together soup, wine, the water, mustard, and thyme.

3. Return mushrooms to skillet; add soup mixture. Bring to boiling; reduce heat. Simmer, uncovered, for 2 minutes. Serve chicken mixture over hot cooked pasta.

Per serving: 498 cal., 18 g total fat (8 g sat. fat), 112 mg chol., 947 mg sodium, 37 g carbo., 2 g fiber, 41 g pro.

Grilled
CHICKEN SANDWICHES

Think of this as an Italian hero sandwich filled with chicken instead of sausage plus sweet pepper and onion. *Makes 4 sandwiches*

Prep: **35 minutes**   Cook: **16 minutes**   Grill: **8 minutes**   Marinate: **1 to 2 hours**

4 skinless, boneless chicken breast halves (about 1¼ pounds total)

5 tablespoons olive oil

3 tablespoons lemon juice

1 tablespoon dried Greek seasoning or Italian seasoning, crushed

¾ teaspoon salt

½ teaspoon ground black pepper

2 cups bite-size strips red sweet pepper (2 medium)

2 medium onions, cut into ½-inch slices

1½ teaspoons bottled minced garlic (3 cloves)

2 tablespoons balsamic vinegar

3 tablespoons butter or margarine, softened

4 kaiser rolls or French-style rolls, split

4 thin slices provolone cheese

1. Place each chicken half between 2 pieces of plastic wrap. Working from center to edges, pound lightly with the flat side of a meat mallet to ½-inch thickness. Remove plastic wrap. Place chicken in a resealable plastic bag set in a shallow dish.

2. For marinade, in a small bowl combine 3 tablespoons of the oil, the lemon juice, Greek seasoning, ½ teaspoon of the salt, and ¼ teaspoon of the black pepper. Pour marinade over chicken. Seal bag; turn to coat chicken. Marinate in the refrigerator for 1 to 2 hours, turning bag occasionally. Drain chicken, discarding marinade.

3. In a large skillet heat the remaining 2 tablespoons oil over medium-low heat. Add sweet pepper and onion; cook, covered, for 13 to 15 minutes or until tender, stirring occasionally. Increase heat to medium-high. Add 1 teaspoon of the garlic; cook and stir for 3 to 5 minutes or until onion is golden brown. Stir in vinegar, the remaining ¼ teaspoon salt, and the

remaining ¼ teaspoon black pepper. Cook until vinegar is evaporated. Set aside.

4. For a charcoal grill, grill chicken on the rack of an uncovered grill directly over medium coals for 8 to 11 minutes or until chicken is no longer pink, turning once halfway through grilling.

5. Meanwhile, in a small bowl combine butter and the remaining ½ teaspoon garlic. Spread on cut sides of rolls. While chicken is grilling, add rolls, cut sides down, to grill. Grill for 1 to 2 minutes or until golden brown. (For a gas grill, preheat grill. Reduce heat to medium. Place chicken, then rolls on grill rack over heat. Cover and grill as above.)

6. Place cheese on bottoms of rolls. Top with chicken and onion mixture. Replace tops of rolls.

Per sandwich: 627 cal., 33 g total fat (12 g sat. fat), 109 mg chol., 1,007 mg sodium, 42 g carbo., 3 g fiber, 40 g pro.

CHICKEN FAJITAS

Bottled salad dressing mixed with herbs seasons the chicken and veggies in this satisfying one-dish meal. See photo on page III. *Makes 4 servings*

Start to Finish: **25 minutes**

1 tablespoon lime juice or
  lemon juice
½ teaspoon ground cumin
½ teaspoon ground coriander
¼ teaspoon dried oregano,
  crushed
12 ounces skinless, boneless
  chicken breasts, cut into
  bite-size strips
¼ cup bottled Italian salad
  dressing
¾ cup red and/or green sweet
  pepper strips
1 small onion, halved and
  sliced
8 7- to 8-inch flour tortillas,
  warmed
  Purchased guacamole,
  bottled salsa, and/or dairy
  sour cream

1. In a medium bowl combine lime juice, cumin, coriander, and oregano. Stir in chicken; set aside.

2. In a large skillet heat salad dressing over medium-high heat. Add chicken. Cook and stir for 3 to 4 minutes or until chicken is no longer pink. Using a slotted spoon, remove chicken from skillet.

3. Add sweet pepper and onion to skillet. Cook and stir for 2 to 3 minutes or until vegetables are crisp-tender. Return chicken to skillet; heat through.

4. Spoon chicken mixture onto warm tortillas; roll up tortillas. Serve with guacamole, salsa, and/or sour cream.

Per serving: 415 cal., 17 g total fat (2 g sat. fat), 52 mg chol., 469 mg sodium, 33 g carbo., 2 g fiber, 27 g pro.

Chicken
AND BOW TIES

Dried tomatoes add a lot of flavor and a blush of pink to this creamy chicken pasta dish. *Makes 4 servings*

Start to Finish: **30 minutes**

8 ounces dried bow tie pasta
1 teaspoon bottled minced
   garlic (2 cloves)
2 tablespoons olive oil
1 pound skinless, boneless
   chicken breasts, cut into
   thin bite-size strips
1 teaspoon dried basil, crushed
⅛ teaspoon crushed red pepper
¾ cup chicken broth
½ cup oil-packed dried
   tomatoes, drained and cut
   into thin strips
¼ cup dry white wine
½ cup whipping cream
¼ cup grated Parmesan cheese
   Grated Parmesan cheese
   (optional)

1. Cook pasta according to package directions; drain.
2. Meanwhile, in a skillet cook garlic in hot oil over medium-high heat for 30 seconds. Add chicken, basil, and crushed red pepper. Cook and stir for 2 to 3 minutes or until chicken is no longer pink. Stir in broth, dried tomato, and wine.

3. Bring to boiling; reduce heat. Simmer, uncovered, for 10 minutes. Stir in cream and the ¼ cup cheese. Simmer, uncovered, for 2 minutes more. Stir in cooked pasta; heat through. If desired, serve with additional cheese.

Per serving: 574 cal., 24 g total fat (10 g sat. fat), 112 mg chol., 414 mg sodium, 48 g carbo., 2 g fiber, 38 g pro.

IN-A-PINCH TIPS!

WINE WISE: IF YOU DON'T WANT TO COOK WITH WINE, USE CHICKEN OR BEEF BROTH FOR SAVORY DISHES AND FRUIT JUICES FOR SWEET RECIPES.

Creamy
RANCH CHICKEN

Creamed chicken over noodles, but with the tanginess of ranch dressing. What's not to like?

Makes 4 servings

Start to Finish: **30 minutes**

6 slices bacon
1¼ pounds skinless, boneless chicken breasts, cut into bite-size pieces
2 tablespoons all-purpose flour
2 tablespoons ranch dry salad dressing mix
1¼ cups milk
3 cups dried medium noodles
1 tablespoon finely shredded Parmesan cheese

1. Cut bacon into narrow strips. In a large skillet cook bacon over medium heat until crisp. Remove bacon and drain on paper towels, reserving 2 tablespoons drippings in skillet.

2. Add chicken to reserved drippings; cook and stir until chicken is no longer pink. Stir in flour and salad dressing mix. Gradually stir in milk. Cook and stir until thickened and bubbly. Cook and stir for 1 minute more. Stir in bacon.

3. Meanwhile, cook noodles according to package directions; drain. Serve chicken mixture over hot cooked noodles. Sprinkle with cheese.

Per serving: 488 cal., 18 g total fat (7 g sat. fat), 137 mg chol., 574 mg sodium, 27 g carbo., 1 g fiber, 45 g pro.

Ginger-Plum CHICKEN

For convenience, assemble all the ingredients and refrigerate the night before. In the morning, place them in the slow cooker. *Makes 6 servings*

Prep: **20 minutes** Cook: **Low 5 hours, High 2½ hours**

1½ cups thinly sliced carrot (3 medium) or packaged fresh julienned carrot

1⅓ cups thinly sliced leek (4 medium) or 1 cup chopped onion (1 large)

6 skinless, boneless chicken breast halves (about 2 pounds total)

¾ cup plum sauce

2 tablespoons quick-cooking tapioca, crushed

½ teaspoon ground ginger

½ teaspoon dry mustard

3 cups hot cooked white rice or wild rice (optional)

Peanut Topper or sesame seeds, toasted

1. In a 3½- or 4-quart slow cooker, combine carrot and leek. Add chicken. In a small bowl combine plum sauce, tapioca, ginger, and dry mustard. Pour over chicken.

2. Cover and cook on low-heat setting for 5 to 6 hours or on high-heat setting for 2½ to 3 hours.

3. If desired, serve chicken mixture over hot cooked rice. Sprinkle with Peanut Topper.

Peanut Topper: In a small bowl combine ¼ cup chopped honey-roasted peanuts, ¼ cup thinly sliced green onion (2), and 2 tablespoons finely shredded fresh basil.

Per serving: 301 cal., 5 g total fat (1 g sat. fat), 88 mg chol., 309 mg sodium, 26 g carbo., 2 g fiber, 38 g pro.

Chicken
JAMBALAYA

The spicy Cajun flavor of this Louisiana favorite is sure to put a zip in your day. *Makes 6 servings*

Prep: 15 minutes   Cook: Low 5 hours, High 2½ hours; plus 45 minutes on High

8 ounces skinless, boneless chicken breasts

1 16-ounce package frozen sweet pepper stir-fry vegetables

8 ounces cooked smoked turkey sausage, halved lengthwise and cut into ½-inch pieces

2 cups water

1 14.5-ounce can diced tomatoes and green chiles, undrained

1 8-ounce package jambalaya rice mix

1. Cut chicken into ½-inch strips. Place frozen vegetables in a 3½- or 4-quart slow cooker. Top with chicken and sausage. Add the water, undrained tomatoes, and, if present, seasoning packet from rice mix. Set aside rice from mix.

2. Cover and cook on low-heat setting for 5 to 6 hours or on high-heat setting for 2½ to 3 hours.

3. Stir in rice from mix. If using low-heat setting, turn to high-heat setting. Cover and cook about 45 minutes more or until rice is tender and most of the liquid is absorbed.

Per serving: 265 cal., 4 g total fat (1 g sat. fat), 47 mg chol., 1,118 mg sodium, 37 g carbo., 2 g fiber, 19 g pro.

Chicken with
CREAMY CHIVE SAUCE

This creamy chicken is heavenly served over angel hair pasta and just as delightful with fettuccine or rice.

Makes 6 servings

Prep: 15 minutes   Cook: Low 4 hours

6 skinless, boneless chicken breast halves (about 2 pounds total)

1/4 cup butter or margarine, melted

1 0.7-ounce envelope Italian dry salad dressing mix

1 10.75-ounce can condensed golden mushroom soup

1/2 cup dry white wine

1/2 of an 8-ounce tub cream cheese spread with chive and onion

3 cups hot cooked angel hair pasta

Snipped fresh chives (optional)

1. Place chicken in a 3 1/2- or 4-quart slow cooker. In a medium bowl stir together melted butter and dry salad dressing mix. Stir in soup, wine, and cream cheese. Pour soup mixture over chicken.

2. Cover and cook on low-heat setting for 4 to 5 hours. Serve chicken mixture over hot cooked pasta. If desired, sprinkle with chives.

Per serving: 448 cal., 18 g total fat (9 g sat. fat), 132 mg chol., 1,064 mg sodium, 26 g carbo., 1 g fiber, 41 g pro.

Greek Chicken
WITH OLIVES

This dish contains all the best ingredients the countries of the Mediterranean offer, all gently simmered in a slow cooker. Serve with a salad and crusty bread. *Makes 4 servings*

Prep: 15 minutes Cook: Low 6 hours, High 3 hours

3 large tomatoes, coarsely chopped
1 large onion, halved and thinly sliced
¼ cup Greek olives or ripe olives, pitted and sliced
¼ cup dry red wine or reduced-sodium chicken broth
1 tablespoon quick-cooking tapioca*
1 tablespoon capers, drained
1 teaspoon bottled minced garlic (2 cloves)
¼ teaspoon salt
⅛ teaspoon ground black pepper
4 skinless, boneless chicken breast halves (about 1¼ pounds total)
¼ cup snipped fresh basil
2 cups hot cooked couscous

1. In a 3½- or 4-quart slow cooker combine tomato, onion, olives, wine, tapioca, capers, garlic, salt, and pepper. Add chicken, spooning some of the tomato mixture over chicken.
2. Cover and cook on low-heat setting for 6 to 7 hours or on high-heat setting for 3 to 3½ hours.
3. Before serving, stir in basil. Serve chicken mixture over hot cooked couscous.

*Test Kitchen Tip: For a smoother texture, crush or finely grind the tapioca before adding it to the slow cooker.

Per serving: 326 cal., 4 g total fat (1 g sat. fat), 82 mg chol., 373 mg sodium, 32 g carbo., 4 g fiber, 38 g pro.

Chicken
STROGANOFF

Cream of mushroom soup with roasted garlic, chicken, and the slow cooker give a new spin to traditional stroganoff. *Makes 6 to 8 servings*

Prep: **20 minutes**   Cook: **Low 6 hours, High 3 hours**

2 pounds skinless, boneless chicken breasts and/or thighs

I cup chopped onion (I large)

I 4-ounce can (drained weight) sliced mushrooms, drained

2 10.75-ounce cans condensed cream of mushroom soup with roasted garlic

⅓ cup water

12 ounces dried wide egg noodles

I 8-ounce carton dairy sour cream

Freshly ground black pepper (optional)

Fresh thyme sprigs (optional)

I. Cut chicken into I-inch pieces. In a 3½- or 4-quart slow cooker combine chicken, onion, and drained mushrooms. In a medium bowl stir together soup and the water. Pour soup mixture over chicken mixture.

2. Cover and cook on low-heat setting for 6 to 7 hours or on high-heat setting for 3 to 3½ hours.

3. Cook noodles according to package directions; drain. Before serving, stir sour cream into mixture in cooker. Serve over hot cooked noodles. If desired, sprinkle with pepper and garnish with thyme.

Per serving: 539 cal., 14 g total fat (6 g sat. fat), 156 mg chol., 850 mg sodium, 55 g carbo., 3 g fiber, 57 g pro.

Coconut-Chicken
CURRY

This recipe calls for red curry paste, which many large supermarkets stock, often in the Asian food section. If yours does not, ask the store manager to order it for you. *Makes 4 servings*

Prep: **20 minutes**   Marinate: **30 minutes**   Cook: **16 minutes**

1½ pounds skinless, boneless chicken thighs, cut into bite-size pieces
¼ cup red curry paste
1 tablespoon olive oil
1 cup coarsely chopped onion (1 large)
1¼ cups fresh coconut milk* or one 14-ounce can unsweetened coconut milk
1½ cups thinly sliced carrot (3 medium)
1 teaspoon finely shredded lime peel
2 cups hot cooked rice
Snipped fresh cilantro or parsley

1. In a medium bowl combine chicken and curry paste. Cover and marinate at room temperature for 30 minutes.
2. In a 12-inch skillet heat oil over medium heat. Add chicken and onion. Cook for 8 to 10 minutes or until chicken is no longer pink, stirring occasionally. Remove from skillet.
3. Carefully add coconut milk to skillet, scraping up crusty browned bits. Add carrot and lime peel. Bring to boiling; reduce heat. Simmer, uncovered, about 5 minutes or until carrot is crisp-tender. Return chicken mixture to skillet. Simmer, uncovered, for 3 to 5 minutes or until slightly thickened.
4. Serve chicken mixture with hot cooked rice. Sprinkle with cilantro.

*Test Kitchen Tip: To make fresh coconut milk, cut the tip from a young coconut. Pour out coconut liquid; scoop out coconut meat. In a blender combine coconut liquid and coconut meat; cover and blend until nearly smooth. Add enough chicken broth or vegetable broth to make 1¼ cups.

Per serving: 561 cal., 28 g total fat (18 g sat. fat), 136 mg chol., 433 mg sodium, 36 g carbo., 2 g fiber, 39 g pro.

Spanish
CHICKEN STEW

Chicken thighs are not only tasty but a great buy. If you have a 6-quart slow cooker, double this recipe and invite the neighbors for dinner. *Makes 4 servings*

Prep: **20 minutes** Cook: **Low 10 hours, High 5 hours; plus 15 minutes on High**

1¼ pounds skinless, boneless chicken thighs, cut into 1½-inch pieces
1 14.5-ounce can diced tomatoes, undrained
12 ounces red potatoes, cut into ½-inch wedges
1 cup chicken broth
1 cup red sweet pepper strips (1 medium)
1 medium onion, thinly sliced
1 teaspoon bottled minced garlic (2 cloves)
½ teaspoon dried thyme, crushed
¼ teaspoon salt
¼ teaspoon ground black pepper
⅓ cup pimiento-stuffed green olives, cut up

1. In a 3½- or 4-quart slow cooker combine chicken, undrained tomatoes, potato, broth, sweet pepper, onion, garlic, thyme, salt, and black pepper.

2. Cover and cook on low-heat setting for 10 to 11 hours or on high-heat setting for 5 to 5½ hours.

3. If using low-heat setting, turn to high-heat setting. Stir in olives. Cover and cook for 15 minutes more.

Per serving: 286 cal., 31 g total fat (2 g sat. fat), 118 mg chol., 856 mg sodium, 24 g carbo., 4 g fiber, 31 g pro.

Quick Thai
CHICKEN PASTA

Thai seasoning varies from brand to brand, but most include a great variety of herbs and spices, such as coriander, ginger, lemon peel, and chile peppers. The product makes it easy to bring a windfall of flavor to a recipe—without a lengthy ingredient list. *Makes 4 servings*

Start to Finish: **20 minutes**

8 ounces dried angel hair pasta
1 cup sliced carrot (2 medium)
1 cup fresh pea pods, trimmed and halved
12 ounces skinless, boneless chicken thighs, cut into strips
1 tablespoon cooking oil
1 14-ounce can unsweetened coconut milk
1 10.75-ounce can condensed cream of chicken soup
1½ to 2 teaspoons Thai seasoning
½ cup chopped peanuts

1. Cook pasta and carrot according to the pasta package directions, adding pea pods during the last 1 minute of cooking; drain. Return pasta mixture to hot pan; cover and keep warm.

2. Meanwhile, in a large skillet cook chicken in hot oil over medium-high heat for 3 to 4 minutes or until no longer pink. Drain off fat. Stir in coconut milk, soup, and Thai seasoning. Cook over medium heat until heated through, stirring frequently.

3. Pour hot chicken mixture over cooked pasta mixture; toss gently to coat. Transfer to a serving platter or bowl. Sprinkle with peanuts.

Per serving: 727 cal., 39 g total fat (21 g sat. fat), 74 mg chol., 858 mg sodium, 60 g carbo., 5 g fiber, 33 g pro.

Spiced Chicken
THIGHS AND BEAN SALAD

The spice rub is hot and the bean salad is cool and creamy—a great yin-yang combination.

Makes 4 servings

Start to Finish: **30 minutes**

2 tablespoons olive oil

1 teaspoon ground coriander

1 teaspoon ground cumin

½ teaspoon salt

½ teaspoon ground cinnamon

¼ teaspoon cayenne pepper

1¼ pounds skinless, boneless chicken thighs

1 cup fresh or frozen green and/or wax beans

1 cup frozen shelled sweet soybeans (edamame) or lima beans

1 medium avocado, seeded, peeled, and sliced

¾ cup crumbled blue cheese (3 ounces)

¼ cup bottled creamy garlic, cucumber ranch, or Italian salad dressing

1. In a small bowl combine oil, coriander, cumin, salt, cinnamon, and cayenne pepper. Brush chicken with oil mixture.

2. Heat a nonstick or well-seasoned grill pan over medium heat. Add chicken; cook about 12 minutes or until chicken is no longer pink (180°F), turning once. Transfer chicken to a cutting board. Cut each thigh into 3 pieces.

3. Meanwhile, in a covered large saucepan cook fresh green and/or wax beans in enough boiling water to cover for 10 to 12 minutes or until crisp-tender. (If using frozen beans, cook about 5 minutes or until crisp-tender.) Using a slotted spoon,* remove beans. Add soybeans to boiling water. Cook, covered, for 4 to 6 minutes or until tender; drain.

4. Arrange chicken, beans, soybeans, avocado, and cheese on 4 salad plates or a serving platter. Drizzle with dressing.

*Test Kitchen Tip: If you do not have a slotted spoon, place green and/or wax beans in a heat-proof strainer. Lower strainer into boiling water and cook as directed. Lift strainer out of water to drain.

Per serving: 543 cal., 35 g total fat (9 g sat. fat), 129 mg chol., 880 mg sodium, 15 g carbo., 7 g fiber, 43 g pro.

Indoor Grilling Directions: Preheat an indoor electric grill. Brush chicken with oil mixture as directed. Place chicken on the grill rack. If using a covered grill, close lid. Grill until chicken is no longer pink (180°F). (For a covered grill, allow 4 to 6 minutes. For an uncovered grill, allow 14 to 18 minutes, turning once halfway through grilling.)

Nutty CHICKEN

Slow cooker to the rescue! A quick-to-assemble dish, featuring good-value chicken thighs, cooks while you work or play. *Makes 6 servings*

Prep: **20 minutes**   Cook: **Low 6 hours, High 3 hours**

1 10.75-ounce can condensed golden mushroom soup
¼ cup reduced-sodium soy sauce
3 tablespoons quick-cooking tapioca, crushed
¼ to ½ teaspoon crushed red pepper
1½ pounds skinless, boneless chicken thighs, cut into ½-inch pieces
1 16-ounce package frozen French-cut green beans
1½ cups thinly sliced celery (3 stalks)
1 8-ounce can sliced water chestnuts, drained
1 2-ounce jar sliced pimiento, drained, or ¼ cup bottled roasted red sweet peppers, drained and chopped
1 cup slivered almonds, cashew halves, or toasted broken walnuts
3 cups hot cooked rice

1. In a 4- to 5-quart slow cooker combine soup, soy sauce, tapioca, and crushed red pepper. Stir in chicken, frozen beans, celery, drained water chestnuts, and drained pimiento.

2. Cover and cook on low-heat setting for 6 to 7 hours or on high-heat setting for 3 to 3½ hours.

3. Before serving, stir in nuts. Serve chicken mixture over hot cooked rice.

Per serving: 513 cal., 20 g total fat (3 g sat. fat), 93 mg chol., 862 mg sodium, 54 g carbo., 6 g fiber, 34 g pro.

Creole
CHICKEN

French, Spanish, and African cuisine are the foundations of Creole cooking. With such varied origins, the cooking style appeals to a wide range of people. Cooking it gently in a slow cooker enhances all the wonderful flavors. *Makes 6 servings*

Prep: **25 minutes**   Cook: **Low 5 hours, High 2½ hours**   Stand: **10 minutes**

1 pound skinless, boneless chicken thighs, cut into ¾-inch pieces
1 14.5-ounce can diced tomatoes, undrained
1 14-ounce can chicken broth
8 ounces cooked smoked Polish sausage, coarsely chopped
1 cup diced cooked ham
¾ cup chopped onion
1 6-ounce can tomato paste
½ cup water
1½ teaspoons Cajun seasoning
Several dashes bottled hot pepper sauce
2 cups uncooked instant rice
1 cup chopped green sweet pepper
Bottled hot pepper sauce

1. In a 3½- or 4-quart slow cooker stir together chicken, undrained tomatoes, broth, sausage, ham, onion, tomato paste, the water, Cajun seasoning, and the several dashes hot pepper sauce.

2. Cover and cook on low-heat setting for 5 to 6 hours or on high-heat setting for 2½ to 3 hours.

3. Remove liner from cooker, if present, or turn off cooker. Stir in rice and sweet pepper. Cover and let stand for 10 to 15 minutes or until rice is tender and most of the liquid is absorbed. Pass additional hot pepper sauce.

Per serving: 439 cal., 18 g total fat (6 g sat. fat), 99 mg chol., 1,362 mg sodium, 41 g carbo., 2 g fiber, 28 g pro.

Chicken
TACO PASTA

Mexican meets Italian with a little bit of something to please everyone. Substitute a Mexican cheese blend for the cheddar cheese, if you like. *Makes 12 servings*

Prep: **25 minutes** Bake: **45 minutes** Oven: **350°F**

8 ounces dried penne pasta
2 pounds uncooked ground chicken
1 cup chopped onion (1 large)
1½ cups water
1 1.25-ounce envelope taco seasoning mix
2 11-ounce cans whole kernel corn with sweet peppers, drained
2 cups shredded cheddar cheese (8 ounces)
1½ cups sliced, pitted ripe olives
1 cup bottled salsa
2 4-ounce cans diced green chile peppers, drained
8 cups shredded lettuce
2 medium tomatoes, cut into thin wedges
Dairy sour cream (optional)
Tortilla chips (optional)

1. Preheat oven to 350°F. Lightly grease a 3-quart rectangular baking dish; set aside. Cook pasta according to package directions; drain.
2. Meanwhile, in a 12-inch skillet cook ground chicken and onion, half at a time, over medium heat until chicken is brown. Drain off any fat. Return all of the chicken mixture to skillet. Stir in the water and taco seasoning mix.
3. Bring to boiling; reduce heat. Simmer, uncovered, for 2 minutes, stirring occasionally. Stir in cooked pasta, drained corn, half of the cheese, the olives, salsa, and drained chile peppers. Transfer chicken mixture to prepared baking dish.

4. Bake, covered, about 45 minutes or until heated through. Sprinkle with the remaining cheese.
5. Serve with lettuce, tomato, and, if desired, sour cream and tortilla chips.

Per serving: 365 cal., 20 g total fat (4 g sat. fat), 77 mg chol., 926 mg sodium, 27 g carbo., 4 g fiber, 23 g pro.

Sloppy Chicken
PIZZA JOES

Sloppy joes don't have to be made with ground beef; chicken can get sloppy too! Sneak some veggies in for great flavor. *Makes 8 sandwiches*

Prep: **20 minutes** Cook: **Low 6 hours, High 3 hours**

Nonstick cooking spray
3 pounds uncooked ground chicken
2 14-ounce jars pizza sauce
2 cups frozen sweet pepper stir-fry vegetables, thawed and chopped
8 hoagie buns, split and toasted
8 slices mozzarella cheese or provolone cheese (8 ounces)

1. Coat a very large skillet with cooking spray; heat skillet over medium heat. Cook ground chicken in hot skillet until brown. Drain off any fat.
2. In a 3½- or 4-quart slow cooker, stir together pizza sauce and chopped vegetables. Stir in chicken.

3. Cover and cook on low-heat setting for 6 to 8 hours or on high-heat setting for 3 to 4 hours. Serve chicken mixture in buns with cheese.

Per sandwich: 641 cal., 24 g total fat (3 g sat. fat), 16 mg chol., 1,132 mg sodium, 58 g carbo., 2 g fiber, 47 g pro.

Tandoori-Style
CHICKEN BURGERS

Look for garam masala in the supermarket's ethnic foods section or at an East Indian market.

Makes 4 servings

Prep: **30 minutes** Grill: **14 minutes**

¼ cup fine dry bread crumbs
2 teaspoons garam masala
¼ teaspoon salt
¼ teaspoon cayenne pepper
1 pound uncooked ground chicken
2 tablespoons plain yogurt
4 seeded hamburger buns or kaiser rolls, split and toasted
Minty Cucumbers
Kale leaves or lettuce leaves

1. In a large bowl combine bread crumbs, garam masala, salt, and cayenne pepper. Add ground chicken and yogurt; mix well. Shape chicken mixture into four ¾-inch-thick patties.

2. For a charcoal grill, grill patties on the rack of an uncovered grill directly over medium coals for 14 to 18 minutes or until no longer pink (165°F), turning once halfway through grilling. (For a gas grill, preheat grill. Reduce heat to medium. Place patties on grill rack over heat. Cover and grill as above.)

3. Serve burgers in buns with Minty Cucumbers and kale.

Minty Cucumbers: In a small bowl combine 1 cup thinly sliced cucumber, ½ cup thinly sliced red onion, ¼ cup snipped fresh mint, 1 tablespoon bottled balsamic vinaigrette salad dressing, and ¼ teaspoon salt.

Per serving: 383 cal., 13 g total fat 36 mg chol., 841 mg sodium, 37 g carbo.,

Southwest
CHICKEN BURGERS

Jazzed up with Southwestern-inspired ingredients, chicken burgers are a tasty alternative to traditional beef burgers. See photo on page 112. *Makes 4 servings*

Prep: **20 minutes**   Grill: **15 minutes**

3 tablespoons finely chopped green sweet pepper

¾ teaspoon chili powder

¼ teaspoon salt

¼ teaspoon ground black pepper

1 pound uncooked ground chicken

1 cup shredded Monterey Jack cheese with jalapeño peppers (4 ounces)

4 Cheesy Corn Bread Slices or 4 kaiser rolls, split and toasted

Chopped, peeled avocado; chopped red onion; and chopped, seeded jalapeño chile pepper (see note, page 22) (optional)

1. In a large bowl combine sweet pepper, chili powder, salt, and black pepper. Add ground chicken; mix well. Shape chicken mixture into four ¾-inch-thick patties.

2. For a charcoal grill, grill patties on the rack of an uncovered grill directly over medium coals for 14 to 18 minutes or until no longer pink (165°F), turning once halfway through grilling. Sprinkle with cheese. Grill for 1 to 2 minutes more or until cheese is melted. (For a gas grill, preheat grill. Reduce heat to medium. Place patties on grill rack over heat. Cover and grill as above.) If using Cheesy Corn Bread Slices, add them for the last 2 minutes of grilling.

3. Serve burgers on Cheesy Corn Bread Slices or rolls. If desired, top with avocado, onion, and jalapeño chile pepper.

Cheesy Corn Bread Squares: Preheat oven to 400°F. In a large bowl combine 1 ½ cups all-purpose flour, 1 cup yellow cornmeal, ¼ cup sugar, 4 teaspoons baking powder, and 1 teaspoon salt. In a small bowl whisk together 3 eggs, 1 ½ cups milk, and ⅓ cup cooking oil; add all at once to flour mixture. Stir just until moistened. Fold in 1 cup shredded cheddar cheese (4 ounces). Pour batter into well-greased 8×8×2-inch baking pan. Bake about 30 minutes or until toothpick inserted in center comes out clean. Cool in pan on wire rack for 10 minutes. Remove from pan; cool completely. Wrap and store corn bread overnight before slicing. Cut corn bread in half crosswise. Reserve half of the corn bread for another use. Cut remaining half of the corn bread into four slices.

Per serving: 801 cal., 50 g total fat (12 g sat. fat), 176 mg chol., 1,056 mg sodium, 48 g carbo., 6 g fiber, 41 g pro.

Chuck Wagon
CHICKEN SHEPHERD'S PIE

Classic shepherd's pie is made with lamb and spuds. Chicken stands in for the more classic lamb and is mixed with economical baked beans, then topped with mashed potatoes. *Makes 6 servings*

Prep: **30 minutes**   Bake: **30 minutes**   Oven: **350°F**

2¼ cups milk
1 22-ounce package frozen
   mashed potatoes
¼ cup snipped fresh parsley
½ teaspoon salt
1 2- to 2½-pound purchased
   roasted chicken
1 28-ounce can baked beans,
   undrained
1 11-ounce can whole kernel
   corn with sweet peppers,
   drained
½ cup bottled salsa

1. Preheat oven to 350°F. In a large saucepan bring milk to simmering over medium heat. Stir in frozen mashed potatoes; reduce heat to medium-low. Cook for 5 to 8 minutes or until heated through and smooth, stirring frequently. Stir in 2 tablespoons of the parsley and the salt; set aside.

2. Remove meat from chicken, discarding skin and bones. Shred chicken by pulling two forks through it in opposite directions. In a large bowl combine shredded chicken, the remaining 2 tablespoons parsley, the undrained baked beans, drained corn, and salsa. Transfer mixture to an ungreased 3-quart rectangular baking dish. Spread mashed potatoes evenly over chicken mixture.

3. Bake, uncovered, for 30 to 35 minutes or until heated through.

Per serving: 536 cal., 19 g total fat (7 g sat. fat), 97 mg chol., 1,796 mg sodium, 70 g carbo., 10 g fiber, 32 g pro.

Easy Chicken
AND DUMPLINGS

Rotisserie roasted chicken is both economical and a time saver. For this quick-to-prepare dish, add frozen veggies and condensed soup to the chicken. See photo on page 273. *Makes 4 to 6 servings*

Prep: **25 minutes** Cook: **15 minutes** Oven: **Per package directions**

1 2- to 2½-pound purchased roasted chicken

1 16-ounce package frozen mixed vegetables

1 10.75-ounce can reduced-fat and reduced-sodium condensed cream of chicken soup

1¼ cups reduced-sodium chicken broth or water

½ teaspoon dried Italian seasoning, crushed

⅛ teaspoon ground black pepper

1 11-ounce package (12) refrigerated breadsticks

1. Remove meat from chicken, discarding skin and bones. Chop or shred chicken. In a large saucepan stir together chicken, frozen vegetables, soup, broth, Italian seasoning, and pepper. Bring to boiling; reduce heat. Simmer, covered, about 15 minutes or until vegetables are tender.

2. Meanwhile, cut breadsticks along perforations. Press 2 breadsticks together to make 1 strip of dough; roll the strip into a spiral. Place on an ungreased baking sheet. Repeat with the remaining breadsticks. Bake according to package directions.

3. Serve chicken mixture with corn bread.

Per serving: 650 cal., 30 g total fat (8 g sat. fat), 107 mg chol., 1,399 mg sodium, 57 g carbo., 5 g fiber, 42 g pro.

Chicken Linguine
WITH PESTO SAUCE

A satisfying pasta dish that is long on flavor when you are short on time. *Makes 4 servings*

Start to Finish: **20 minutes**

8 ounces dried linguine
1 10-ounce package frozen broccoli, cauliflower, and carrots
1 10-ounce container refrigerated Alfredo pasta sauce or 1 cup bottled Alfredo pasta sauce
⅓ cup refrigerated basil pesto
¼ cup milk
½ of a 2- to 2¼-pound purchased roasted chicken
  Milk (optional)
  Grated Parmesan cheese

1. In a 4- to 5-quart Dutch oven, cook pasta according to package directions, adding frozen vegetables during the last 5 minutes of cooking; drain. Return pasta mixture to Dutch oven.

2. Meanwhile, in a small bowl combine pasta sauce, pesto, and the ¼ cup milk; set aside. Remove meat from chicken, discarding skin and bones. Chop or shred chicken. Add pesto mixture and chicken to pasta mixture; toss gently to coat.

3. Cook over medium-low heat until heated through, stirring occasionally. If desired, stir in enough additional milk to reach desired consistency. Sprinkle each serving with cheese.

Per serving: 801 cal., 48 g total fat (4 g sat. fat), 109 mg chol., 546 mg sodium, 54 g carbo., 3 g fiber, 37 g pro.

 *Pulled*

CHICKEN SANDWICHES

This sandwich is great any time, but for best flavor, make the filling a day ahead, chill, and reheat. See photo on page 274. *Makes 6 sandwiches*

Start to Finish: **30 minutes**

1 2- to 2¼-pound purchased roasted chicken
1 medium onion, cut into ¼-inch slices
1 tablespoon olive oil
⅓ cup cider vinegar or white wine vinegar
½ cup tomato sauce
3 to 4 tablespoons seeded and finely chopped fresh red and/or green chile pepper (see note, page 22)
2 tablespoons snipped fresh thyme
2 tablespoons molasses
2 tablespoons water
½ teaspoon salt
4 ciabatta buns or kaiser rolls, split
Bread-and-butter pickle slices (optional)

1. Remove meat from chicken, discarding skin and bones. Shred chicken by pulling two forks through it in opposite directions; set aside.

2. In a large skillet cook onion in hot oil over medium heat about 5 minutes or until tender, stirring occasionally to separate into rings. Add vinegar; cook and stir for 1 minute more.

3. Stir in tomato sauce, chile pepper, thyme, molasses, the water, and salt. Bring to boiling. Stir in shredded chicken; heat through. Serve chicken mixture on buns. If desired, serve with pickle slices.

Per sandwich: 445 cal., 12 g total fat (3 g sat. fat), 84 mg chol., 990 mg sodium, 51 g carbo., 2 g fiber, 33 g pro.

Chicken
SUPREME CASSEROLE

Remember this chicken dish when you have all ages and all kinds of tastes to please. *Makes 6 to 8 servings*

Prep: **25 minutes** Bake: **30 minutes** Stand: **10 minutes** Oven: **350°F**

8 ounces dried rotini pasta

1 16-ounce package frozen broccoli stir-fry vegetables

2 10.75-ounce cans condensed cream of chicken soup

2 cups milk

¼ cup mayonnaise or salad dressing

¼ teaspoon ground black pepper

2 cups chopped cooked chicken

2 cups cubed French bread

2 tablespoons butter or margarine, melted

¼ teaspoon garlic powder

1 tablespoon snipped fresh parsley

1. Preheat oven to 350°F. Cook pasta according to package directions, adding frozen vegetables during the last 5 minutes of cooking; drain.

2. Meanwhile, in a large bowl combine soup, milk, mayonnaise, and pepper. Stir in pasta mixture and chicken.

3. Transfer chicken mixture to an ungreased 3-quart rectangular baking dish. In a medium bowl combine bread cubes, melted butter, and garlic powder; toss gently to coat. Sprinkle over chicken mixture.

4. Bake, uncovered, for 30 to 35 minutes or until heated through and bread cubes are golden brown. Let stand for 10 minutes before serving. Sprinkle with parsley.

Per serving: 584 cal., 25 g total fat (8 g sat. fat), 71 mg chol., 1,123 mg sodium, 60 g carbo., 4 g fiber, 28 g pro.

IN-A-PINCH TIPS!

QUICK COOKED CHICKEN: PURCHASE A ROTISSERIE CHICKEN WHEN ON SALE AND REMOVE THE MEAT FROM THE BONES. THIS MAKES ABOUT 4 CUPS OF SHREDDED OR CHOPPED COOKED CHICKEN.

Chicken
TETRAZZINI

This clever way to use leftover cooked chicken is so loved that no one thinks of it as a "leftover."

Makes 6 servings

Prep: **30 minutes**   Bake: **15 minutes**   Oven: **350°F**

8 ounces dried spaghetti or
   linguine
2 cups sliced fresh mushrooms
½ cup sliced green onion (4)
2 tablespoons butter or
   margarine
¼ cup all-purpose flour
⅛ teaspoon ground nutmeg
⅛ teaspoon ground black
   pepper
1¼ cups chicken broth
1¼ cups half-and-half, light
   cream, or milk
2 cups chopped cooked
   chicken
¼ cup grated Parmesan cheese
2 tablespoons dry sherry
   (optional)
¼ cup sliced almonds, toasted
2 tablespoons snipped fresh
   parsley

1. Preheat oven to 350°F. Cook pasta according to package directions; drain.

2. Meanwhile, in a large saucepan cook mushrooms and green onion in hot butter over medium heat until tender. Stir in flour, nutmeg, and pepper. Gradually stir in broth and half-and-half. Cook and stir until thickened and bubbly. Stir in chicken, half of the cheese, and, if desired, sherry. Add cooked pasta; stir gently to coat.

3. Transfer pasta mixture to an ungreased 2-quart rectangular baking dish. Sprinkle with the remaining cheese and the almonds.

4. Bake, uncovered, about 15 minutes or until heated through. Before serving, sprinkle with parsley.

Per serving: 404 cal., 18 g total fat (8 g sat. fat), 74 mg chol., 342 mg sodium, 37 g carbo., 2 g fiber, 24 g pro.

Deep-Dish
CHICKEN POT PIE

Loaded with flavorful vegetables and chicken baked under a flaky crust, this pot pie is what soothing and satisfying food is all about. See photo on page 275. *Makes 9 servings*

Prep: **50 minutes** Bake: **35 minutes** Stand: **20 minutes** Oven: **400°F**

1 recipe Pastry Topper
3 tablespoons butter or margarine
1½ cups chopped leek or onion
1½ cups sliced fresh mushrooms
1¼ cups sliced celery
¾ cup chopped red sweet pepper (1 medium)
½ cup all-purpose flour
1½ teaspoons poultry seasoning
¼ teaspoon salt
¼ teaspoon ground black pepper
2¼ cups chicken broth
1½ cups half-and-half, light cream, or milk
3¾ cups chopped cooked chicken
1½ cups frozen peas and carrots
1 egg, lightly beaten

1. Prepare Pastry Topper; set aside.
2. Preheat oven to 400°F. In a large saucepan melt butter over medium heat. Add leek, mushrooms, celery, and sweet pepper. Cook and stir for 5 to 8 minutes or until vegetables are tender. Stir in flour, poultry seasoning, salt, and black pepper. Gradually stir in broth and half-and-half. Cook and stir until thickened and bubbly. Stir in chicken and peas and carrots.
3. Transfer chicken mixture to an ungreased 3-quart rectangular baking dish or 13×9×2-inch baking pan. Place Pastry Topper on top of chicken mixture. Brush pastry with egg.
4. Bake, uncovered, for 35 to 40 minutes or until pastry is golden brown. Let stand for 20 minutes before serving.

Pastry Topper: In a medium bowl stir together 2¼ cups all-purpose flour and ¾ teaspoon salt. Using a pastry blender, cut in ⅔ cup shortening until pieces are pea-size. Sprinkle 1 tablespoon cold water over part of the flour mixture; toss gently with a fork. Push moistened dough to side of bowl. Repeat with additional cold water, 1 tablespoon at a time (7 to 9 tablespoons total), until all of the flour mixture is moistened. Shape into a ball. On a lightly floured surface, roll dough into a 13×9-inch rectangle. Cut slits in pastry or use a small cookie cutter to cut shapes from pastry to allow steam to escape.

Per serving: 520 cal., 30 g total fat (11 g sat. fat), 101 mg chol., 644 mg sodium, 38 g carbo., 3 g fiber, 22 g pro.

IN-A-PINCH TIPS!

FOR HOMEMADE POULTRY SEASONING COMBINE 1¼ TEASPOONS DRIED SAGE, CRUSHED, PLUS ¼ TEASPOON DRIED THYME OR MARJORAM, CRUSHED.

Chicken
ALFREDO POT PIES

Homemade pot pies for a weeknight meal—what a treat! Chicken and vegetables mixed with purchased sauce makes this possible. *Makes 4 servings*

Prep: **20 minutes**   Bake: **12 minutes**   Oven: **450°F**

½ of a 15-ounce package (1 crust) rolled refrigerated unbaked piecrust

1 16-ounce package frozen broccoli, cauliflower, and carrots

3 cups cubed cooked chicken

1 10-ounce container refrigerated alfredo pasta sauce

½ teaspoon dried sage, marjoram, or thyme, crushed

1. Preheat oven to 450°F. Let piecrust stand according to package directions. Line a shallow baking pan with foil; set aside.

2. In a large skillet cook frozen vegetables in a small amount of boiling water for 5 minutes; drain. Stir in chicken, pasta sauce, and sage. Cook until bubbly, stirring occasionally. Remove from heat; cover and keep warm.

3. Meanwhile, on a lightly floured surface, roll piecrust into a 12½- to 13-inch circle. Cut into four 5-inch circles.

4. Divide hot chicken mixture among 4 ungreased 10-ounce casseroles or custard cups. Place pastry on top of casseroles. Press edges of pastry firmly against sides of casseroles. Cut slits in pastry to allow steam to escape.

5. Place casseroles in the prepared baking pan. Bake for 12 to 15 minutes or until pastry is golden brown.

Per serving: 709 cal., 41 g total fat (19 g sat. fat), 143 mg chol., 596 mg sodium, 45 g carbo., 4 g fiber, 38 g pro.

Cheesy
CHICKEN BUNDLES

These chicken- and cheese-filled rolls fall somewhere between lasagna and stuffed manicotti. Warm crusty bread and steamed asparagus or broccoli complete the menu. *Makes 8 servings*

Prep: **30 minutes** Bake: **30 minutes** Stand: **10 minutes** Oven: **375°F**

8 dried lasagna noodles
1 egg, lightly beaten
1 15-ounce carton ricotta cheese
1½ cups finely chopped cooked chicken
½ teaspoon dried basil, crushed
2 tablespoons butter or margarine
2 tablespoons all-purpose flour
½ teaspoon dry mustard
¼ teaspoon salt
⅛ teaspoon ground black pepper
1½ cups milk
1½ cups shredded process Swiss cheese (6 ounces)

1. Preheat oven to 375°F. Cook lasagna noodles according to package directions; drain. Rinse with cold water; drain again. Place noodles in a single layer on a piece of foil.

2. Meanwhile, for filling, in a medium bowl combine egg, ricotta cheese, chicken, and basil.

3. Spread about ⅓ cup of the filling evenly over each lasagna noodle. Starting from a short end, roll up each noodle into a spiral. Place lasagna rolls, seam sides down, in an ungreased 2-quart rectangular baking dish.

4. For sauce, in a medium saucepan melt butter over medium heat. Stir in flour, dry mustard, salt, and pepper. Gradually stir in milk. Cook and stir until thickened and bubbly. Gradually add Swiss cheese, stirring until cheese is melted. Pour sauce over lasagna rolls.

5. Bake, covered, for 30 to 35 minutes or until heated through. Let stand for 10 minutes before serving.

Per serving: 369 cal., 19 g total fat (10 g sat. fat), 106 mg chol., 522 mg sodium, 25 g carbo., 1 g fiber, 24 g pro.

Chipotle
CHICKEN ENCHILADAS

Simple, sassy, and satisfying, this enchilada dish comes together quickly and bakes less than an hour. Take the baking time to unwind, walk the dog, or play a game of catch. *Makes 4 servings*

Prep: **25 minutes** Bake: **40 minutes** Oven: **350°F**

2½ cups chopped cooked
    chicken
 1 to 2 teaspoons chipotle chili
    pepper
 1 10.75-ounce can condensed
    cream of chicken soup
 1 8-ounce carton dairy sour
    cream
 1 4-ounce can diced green
    chile peppers, undrained
 8 7- to 8-inch flour tortillas
 2 cups shredded cheddar
    cheese (8 ounces)
 ¼ cup sliced green onion (2)

1. Preheat oven to 350°F. Grease a 3-quart rectangular baking dish; set aside. In a medium bowl combine chicken and chipotle chili pepper; set aside.

2. For sauce, in a large bowl combine soup, sour cream, and undrained chile peppers. Stir ½ cup of the sauce into chicken mixture.

3. Divide chicken mixture among tortillas. Sprinkle with 1½ cups of the cheese and the green onion. Roll up tortillas. Place, seam sides down, in the prepared baking dish. Pour the remaining sauce over filled tortillas.

4. Bake, covered, about 35 minutes or until heated through and edges are bubbly. Sprinkle with the remaining ½ cup cheese. Bake, uncovered, about 5 minutes more or until cheese is melted.

Per serving: 786 cal., 47 g total fat (24 g sat. fat), 169 mg chol., 1,376 mg sodium, 42 g carbo., 2 g fiber, 47 g pro.

Chicken
MUSHROOM STRATA

Stratas can hardly be beat for entertaining! Make them oven-ready up to 24 hours in advance, easing the last-minute time crunch when serving a crowd. *Makes 10 to 12 servings*

Prep: **25 minutes**   Chill: **2 to 24 hours**   Bake: **45 minutes**   Stand: **10 minutes**   Oven: **325°F**

2 5.5-ounce packages large croutons

2½ cups chopped cooked chicken

1 4-ounce can (drained weight) sliced mushrooms, drained

½ cup sliced green onion (4)

1½ cups shredded Colby Jack cheese or cheddar cheese (6 ounces)

5 eggs, lightly beaten

1 10.75-ounce can condensed cream of chicken soup or cream of mushroom soup

1 tablespoon Dijon-style mustard

¼ teaspoon ground black pepper

1½ cups milk

1. Grease a 3-quart rectangular baking dish or 13×9×2-inch baking pan. Place croutons in the prepared baking dish. Layer chicken, mushrooms, and green onion over croutons; sprinkle with cheese.

2. In a large bowl combine eggs, soup, mustard, and pepper; gradually stir in milk. Pour soup mixture evenly over layers in dish. Press down lightly with a rubber spatula or the back of a large spoon to moisten all of the croutons. Cover and chill for 2 to 24 hours.

3. Preheat oven to 325°F. Bake, uncovered, about 45 minutes or until a knife inserted near the center comes out clean (170°F). Let stand for 10 minutes before serving.

Per serving: 355 cal., 15 g total fat (7 g sat. fat), 158 mg chol., 722 mg sodium, 29 g carbo., 2 g fiber, 23 g pro.

Peanut-Chicken
BOWLS

This is a popular Asian-style chicken noodle dish. Frugal amounts of peanut butter, soy sauce, and cooked chicken pack a flavor punch served over noodles. *Makes 4 servings*

Start to Finish: **25 minutes**

2 3-ounce packages Oriental-
   flavor ramen noodles
3 cups assorted cut-up
   vegetables such as broccoli
   florets, red sweet pepper
   strips, halved pea pods,
   and/or thinly sliced carrot
1¼ cups water
¼ cup peanut butter
¼ cup soy sauce
2 tablespoons packed brown
   sugar
1 tablespoon cornstarch
½ teaspoon crushed red pepper
2 cups chopped cooked
   chicken
1 8-ounce can sliced water
   chestnuts, drained
1 8-ounce can bamboo shoots,
   drained
¼ cup chopped peanuts
¼ cup sliced green onion (2)

1. Set aside 1 seasoning packet from noodles to use in recipe; reserve the remaining packet for another use. Break up noodles slightly. In a large saucepan cook noodles and vegetables in a large amount of boiling water for 3 minutes; drain. Return noodle mixture to saucepan; cover and keep warm.

2. Meanwhile, for sauce, in a medium saucepan whisk together seasoning packet, the 1¼ cups water, the peanut butter, soy sauce, brown sugar, cornstarch, and crushed red pepper until smooth. Cook and stir over medium heat until thickened and bubbly. Cook and stir for 2 minutes more. Stir in chicken, drained water chestnuts, and drained bamboo shoots; heat through.

3. Add chicken mixture to noodle mixture; toss gently to combine. Top each serving with peanuts and green onion.

Per serving: 646 cal., 30 g total fat (4 g sat. fat), 82 mg chol., 1,511 mg sodium, 64 g carbo., 6 g fiber, 38 g pro.

Chicken
WITH NOODLES

Chicken with noodles—a classic comfort dish—receives a colorful update with olives, roasted red pepper, and peas. *Makes 4 servings*

Start to Finish: **20 minutes**

8 ounces dried egg noodles

1 10.75-ounce can condensed cream of chicken soup

½ cup milk

1 2.25-ounce can sliced, pitted ripe olives, drained

2 tablespoons bottled roasted red sweet peppers, drained and chopped

¼ teaspoon dried marjoram, crushed

⅛ teaspoon ground black pepper

2 cups chopped cooked chicken

1 cup frozen peas

¼ cup dry white wine or chicken broth

1. Cook noodles according to package directions; drain. Return to hot pan; cover and keep warm.

2. Meanwhile, in a large saucepan combine soup and milk. Stir in drained olives, roasted pepper, marjoram, and black pepper. Bring to boiling, stirring occasionally. Stir in chicken, peas, and wine; heat through. Stir in cooked noodles.

Per serving: 506 cal., 15 g total fat (4 g sat. fat), 125 mg chol., 827 mg sodium, 55 g carbo., 5 g fiber, 33 g pro.

Great Northern
WHITE CHILI

White chili is growing in popularity because it packs the same wallop as a bowl of red. *Makes 4 servings*

Prep: **20 minutes** Cook: **15 minutes**

½ cup chopped onion
 (I medium)
I teaspoon bottled minced
 garlic (2 cloves)
I tablespoon cooking oil
2 teaspoons chili powder
I teaspoon ground cumin
2 15-ounce cans Great
 Northern beans, navy
 beans, or cannellini (white
 kidney) beans, rinsed and
 drained
2 14-ounce cans reduced-
 sodium chicken broth
I 4-ounce can diced green
 chile peppers, undrained
I cup chopped cooked chicken
 Dairy sour cream
 Shredded Monterey Jack
 cheese with jalapeño
 peppers
 Snipped fresh cilantro or
 parsley (optional)

1. In a large saucepan cook onion and garlic in hot oil over medium heat about 4 minutes or until onion is tender, stirring occasionally. Stir in chili powder and cumin; cook and stir for I minute more.

2. Stir in drained beans, broth, and undrained chile peppers. Bring to boiling; reduce heat. Simmer, uncovered, for 10 minutes, stirring occasionally. Stir in chicken; heat through.

3. Top each serving with sour cream, cheese, and, if desired, cilantro.

Per serving: 445 cal., 12 g total fat (4 g sat. fat), 43 mg chol., 689 mg sodium, 53 g carbo., 12 g fiber, 33 g pro.

Easy Chicken
TORTILLA SOUP

Serve tortilla chips on the side or break up a few in the bottom of the bowls and ladle the soup over them. See photo on page 276. *Makes 4 servings*

Start to Finish: **25 minutes**

2 14-ounce cans chicken broth with roasted garlic

2 cups chopped cooked chicken

2 cups frozen sweet pepper stir-fry vegetables

1 14.5-ounce can Mexican-style stewed tomatoes, undrained

Tortilla chips

Sliced fresh jalapeño chile pepper (see note, page 22) (optional)

Lime wedges (optional)

1. In a large saucepan combine broth, chicken, frozen vegetables, and undrained tomatoes. Bring to boiling; reduce heat. Simmer, covered, for 5 minutes.

2. Serve with tortilla chips and, if desired, jalapeño pepper and lime wedges.

Per serving: 266 cal., 9 g total fat (2 g sat. fat), 65 mg chol., 1,260 mg sodium, 22 g carbo., 1 g fiber, 24 g pro.

Chicken
BURRITOS

This favorite is the choice of Mexican food lovers everywhere. Preparation is so easy, your children can help. *Makes 8 burritos*

Prep: **25 minutes**   Bake: **30 minutes**   Oven: **350°F**

8 8- to 10-inch flour tortillas
1½ cups shredded cooked chicken
1 cup bottled salsa
1 3.1-ounce can jalapeño-flavor bean dip
1 teaspoon fajita seasoning
8 ounces Monterey Jack cheese or cheddar cheese, cut into eight 5×½-inch sticks
   Shredded lettuce, dairy sour cream, and/or bottled salsa (optional)

1. Preheat oven to 350°F. Grease a 3-quart rectangular baking dish; set aside. Stack tortillas; wrap tightly in foil. Bake about 10 minutes or until heated through.

2. Meanwhile, in a large bowl stir together chicken, the 1 cup salsa, the bean dip, and fajita seasoning.

3. Spoon about ⅓ cup of the chicken mixture onto each tortilla just below the center. Top with cheese. Fold bottom edge of each tortilla up and over filling. Fold in opposite sides; roll up tortilla. Place filled tortillas, seam sides down, in the prepared baking dish.

4. Bake, uncovered, about 30 minutes or until heated through. If desired, serve with lettuce, sour cream, and additional salsa.

Per burrito: 261 cal., 13 g total fat (6 g sat. fat), 48 mg chol., 441 mg sodium, 18 g carbo., 1 g fiber, 17 g pro.

IN-A-PINCH TIPS !

FAJITA FLAVOR: MAKE YOUR OWN FAJITA SEASONING BY COMBINING 1½ TEASPOONS GROUND CUMIN, ½ TEASPOON DRIED OREGANO, CRUSHED, ¼ TEASPOON SALT, ¼ TEASPOON CAYENNE PEPPER, ¼ TEASPOON BLACK PEPPER, ⅛ TEASPOON GARLIC POWDER, AND ⅛ TEASPOON ONION POWDER IN A BOWL. COVER AND STORE IN A COOL, DRY PLACE FOR UP TO 1 MONTH.

Basil

CHICKEN WRAPS

When fresh basil season ends, you can still enjoy this chicken wrap. Just combine ½ teaspoon dried basil with I tablespoon snipped fresh parsley. *Makes 4 wraps*

Start to Finish: 15 minutes

Basil Mayonnaise
4 8- to 9-inch plain, tomato, or spinach flour tortillas, warmed
12 ounces thinly sliced cooked chicken, cut into thin strips
½ cup bottled roasted red sweet peppers, drained and cut into thin strips
Fresh basil leaves

I. Spread Basil Mayonnaise over warm tortillas. Top with chicken, roasted pepper, and basil. Roll up tortillas.

Basil Mayonnaise: In a small bowl stir together ½ cup low-fat mayonnaise dressing, I tablespoon snipped fresh basil, ¼ teaspoon bottled minced garlic (I small clove), and, if desired, ⅛ teaspoon cayenne pepper. Makes about ½ cup.

Per wrap: 366 cal., 15 g total fat (3 g sat. fat), 44 mg chol., 1,330 mg sodium, 37 g carbo., 2 g fiber, 21 g pro.

Chipotle Chicken
TOSTADAS WITH AVOCADO-CORN SALSA

Substitute leftover cooked chicken for the precooked chicken strips in this Mexican open-face sandwich.

Makes 6 servings

Start to Finish: **30 minutes**

1½ cups bottled mild salsa
1 medium avocado, seeded, peeled, and chopped
¼ cup frozen whole kernel corn, thawed
2 tablespoons finely chopped green onion (1)
2 tablespoons sliced, pitted ripe olives
6 tostada shells
1 16-ounce can refried beans
1 canned chipotle chile pepper in adobo sauce, finely chopped (see note, page 22)
1 6-ounce package refrigerated cooked Southwestern-style chicken breast strips, chopped
1½ cups shredded Colby Jack cheese (6 ounces)
2 to 3 tablespoons snipped fresh cilantro or parsley

1. For salsa, in a medium bowl combine the bottled salsa, avocado, corn, green onion, and olives; set aside.

2. Preheat broiler. Line a very large baking sheet with foil. Place tostada shells on the prepared baking sheet; set aside.

3. In a small saucepan combine refried beans and chipotle pepper. Cook and stir over medium heat until heated through. Spread bean mixture over tostada shells. Top with chicken and cheese.

4. Broil 4 to 5 inches from the heat for 2 to 3 minutes or until cheese is melted. Sprinkle tostadas with cilantro. Serve with salsa.

Per serving: 307 cal., 16 g total fat (8 g sat. fat), 49 mg chol., 1,125 mg sodium, 25 g carbo., 6 g fiber, 19 g pro.

Crunchy Curried
CHICKEN SALAD WRAPS

The apple and the mint cool the heat of the curry in this wrap. To mellow the curry powder, toast it in a dry small skillet over medium-high heat for 30 to 60 seconds until it is aromatic. Cool. *Makes 4 wraps*

Start to Finish: **20 minutes**

- ⅓ cup mayonnaise or salad dressing
- 1½ teaspoons curry powder
- ⅛ teaspoon ground black pepper
- 1½ cups shredded cabbage with carrot (coleslaw mix)
- ⅔ cup chopped apple (1 medium)
- ½ cup pine nuts or slivered almonds, toasted (optional)
- ⅓ cup fresh mint leaves, finely shredded
- 1 9-ounce package frozen cooked chicken breast strips, thawed
- 4 10-inch flour tortillas

1. In a large bowl combine mayonnaise, curry powder, and pepper. Add cabbage, apple, pine nuts (if desired), and mint; toss gently to combine.
2. Place chicken on tortillas just below the centers. Top with cabbage mixture. Roll up tortillas; secure with toothpicks, if necessary.

Make-Ahead Directions: **Prepare as directed. Wrap individually in plastic wrap and chill for up to 24 hours.**

Per wrap: 366 cal., 19 g total fat (4 g sat. fat), 44 mg chol., 329 mg sodium, 29 g carbo., 2 g fiber, 18 g pro.

Smoky Chicken
AND CHEESY POTATO CASSEROLE

Smoked chicken and smoked cheddar cheese highlight this comforting casserole. Frozen hash browns, croutons, and canned soup make preparation super easy. *Makes 6 servings*

Prep: **20 minutes** Bake: **40 minutes** Oven: **350°F**

1 10.75-ounce can condensed cream of chicken with herbs soup
1 8-ounce carton dairy sour cream
1 28-ounce package frozen diced hash brown potatoes with onions and peppers, thawed
1 pound smoked or roasted chicken, cut into bite-size strips
1½ cups shredded smoked cheddar cheese (6 ounces)
1 cup crushed croutons
1 tablespoon butter or margarine, melted

1. Preheat oven to 350°F. Lightly grease a 3-quart rectangular baking dish; set aside. In a large bowl combine soup and sour cream. Stir in potatoes, chicken, and cheese. Transfer mixture to the prepared baking dish.

2. In a small bowl combine croutons and melted butter; toss gently to coat. Sprinkle over chicken mixture.

3. Bake, uncovered, for 40 to 50 minutes or until heated through.

Per serving: 461 cal., 24 g total fat (13 g sat. fat), 89 mg chol., 1,468 mg sodium, 36 g carbo., 3 g fiber, 27 g pro.

Barbecue Chicken
AND CHEDDAR QUESADILLAS

Dip quesadilla wedges into salsa and green onion-topped sour cream. Or, top the quesadillas and eat them with a knife and fork. *Makes 4 servings*

Prep: **20 minutes** Cook: **4 minutes per batch**

4 7- to 8-inch flour tortillas
  Nonstick cooking spray
1 cup shredded sharp cheddar
  cheese or Mexican cheese
  blend (4 ounces)
1 18-ounce tub refrigerated
  shredded cooked chicken in
  barbecue sauce
1 4-ounce can diced green
  chile peppers, drained
1 cup bottled salsa
¼ cup dairy sour cream
¼ cup sliced green onion (2)

1. Coat one side of each tortilla with cooking spray. Place tortillas, coated sides down, on a piece of waxed paper. Divide cheese among tortillas, placing cheese on half of each tortilla. Top with chicken in barbecue sauce and drained chile peppers. Fold each tortilla over filling to opposite edge, pressing gently.
2. Heat a 10-inch nonstick skillet over medium heat. Add 2 of the quesadillas; cook for 4 to 6 minutes or until light brown, turning once. Keep warm in a 300°F oven while cooking the remaining quesadillas.

3. Cut each quesadilla into 3 wedges. Serve with salsa, sour cream, and green onion.

Per serving: 469 cal., 21 g total fat (10 g sat. fat), 86 mg chol., 1,629 mg sodium, 46 g carbo., 1 g fiber, 25 g pro.

Turkey
SALTIMBOCCA

This version of the venerable Italian dish takes advantage of less expensive turkey in place of veal. More good news—there's no compromise in flavor. *Makes 4 servings*

Start to Finish: **25 minutes**

1 pound turkey breast
   tenderloin
¼ teaspoon coarsely ground
   black pepper
2 tablespoons butter or
   margarine
2 ounces thinly sliced cooked
   ham, cut into bite-size
   strips
½ cup orange juice
2 9- to 10-ounce packages
   fresh spinach
   Salt and ground black pepper
   Orange wedges (optional)

1. Split turkey tenderloin in half horizontally. Sprinkle with the ¼ teaspoon pepper. In a very large skillet, melt butter over medium-high heat. Add turkey; cook about 12 minutes or until turkey is no longer pink (170°F), turning once. Remove turkey from skillet. Slice turkey; cover and keep warm.

2. Add ham to skillet. Cook and stir for 1 to 2 minutes or until ham is heated through and starts to crisp. Remove ham from skillet. Add orange juice to skillet; bring to boiling.

3. Add spinach, half at a time, and cook about 1 minute or just until spinach starts to wilt. Using tongs, remove spinach from skillet and divide among 4 dinner plates. Sprinkle with salt and pepper.

4. Arrange turkey and ham on top of spinach. Drizzle with any remaining orange juice from skillet. If desired, serve with orange wedges.

Per serving: 244 cal., 8 g total fat (4 g sat. fat), 94 mg chol., 528 mg sodium, 9 g carbo., 3 g fiber, 34 g pro.

Herb-Butter

TURKEY TENDERLOINS

Turkey tenderloins can vary in thickness so always test doneness with an instant-read thermometer.

Makes 4 servings

Prep: 20 minutes Broil: 8 minutes

¼ cup snipped fresh parsley
¼ cup chopped pistachio nuts
   or toasted sliced almonds
¾ teaspoon finely shredded
   orange peel
⅓ cup butter or margarine,
   softened
1 teaspoon dried Italian
   seasoning, crushed
1 teaspoon lemon-pepper
   seasoning
1 teaspoon bottled minced
   garlic (2 cloves)
2 turkey breast tenderloins
   (about 1 pound total)
   Salt and ground black pepper

1. Preheat broiler. For gremolata, in a small bowl stir together parsley, nuts, and orange peel. Set aside.

2. In another small bowl stir together butter, Italian seasoning, lemon-pepper seasoning, and garlic. Set aside.

3. Split turkey tenderloins in half horizontally. Sprinkle with salt and pepper. Place turkey on the greased unheated rack of a broiler pan. Broil 4 to 5 inches from the heat for 8 to 10 minutes or until turkey is no longer pink (170°F), turning once halfway through broiling.

4. Transfer turkey to a serving platter. Top with butter mixture and sprinkle with gremolata.

Per serving: 309 cal., 20 g total fat (10 g sat. fat), 111 mg chol., 584 mg sodium, 3 g carbo., 1 g fiber, 30 g pro.

Buffalo-Style
TURKEY WRAPS

The hot pepper sauce and cayenne pepper that give the turkey a kick also can cause irritating fumes as they cook. Grill the tenderloins on an outdoor grill to avoid inhaling the fumes. *Makes 6 wraps*

Prep: **35 minutes** Marinate: **2 to 3 hours** Grill: **12 minutes**

1 to 1½ pounds turkey breast
    tenderloin
3 tablespoons bottled hot
    pepper sauce
2 tablespoons cooking oil
2 teaspoons paprika
¼ teaspoon salt
¼ teaspoon cayenne pepper
6 10-inch flour tortillas
3 cups shredded lettuce
1½ cups thin bite-size strips
    carrot (3 medium)
1½ cups thinly bias-sliced celery
    (3 stalks)
1 cup bottled blue cheese
    salad dressing

1. Split turkey tenderloin in half horizontally. Place turkey in a resealable plastic bag set in a shallow dish. For marinade, in a small bowl combine hot pepper sauce, oil, paprika, salt, and cayenne pepper. Pour marinade over turkey in bag. Seal bag; turn to coat turkey. Marinate in the refrigerator for 2 to 3 hours, turning bag occasionally. Drain turkey, discarding marinade.

2. For a charcoal grill, grill turkey on the rack of an uncovered grill directly over medium coals for 12 to 15 minutes or until turkey is no longer pink (170°), turning once halfway through grilling. While turkey is grilling, stack tortillas and wrap tightly in foil. Add tortillas to grill. Grill about 10 minutes or until heated through, turning once halfway through grilling. (For a gas grill, preheat grill. Reduce heat to medium. Place turkey, then tortillas on grill rack over heat. Cover and grill as above.)

3. Thinly slice turkey across the grain. Divide turkey, lettuce, carrot, and celery among warm tortillas. Top with salad dressing. Roll up tortillas.

Per wrap: 461 cal., 27 g total fat (5 g sat. fat), 54 mg chol., 738 mg sodium, 30 g carbo., 3 g fiber, 24 g pro.

Creamy Turkey
AND ORZO

If you prefer pasta topped with the sauce, don't stir in the orzo. Add the peas to the creamy sauce and then ladle the sauce over the pasta. *Makes 4 servings*

Start to Finish: **25 minutes**

⅔ cup dried orzo pasta
12 ounces turkey breast
    tenderloin, cut into bite-size
    strips
3 cups sliced fresh mushrooms
    (8 ounces)
¼ cup sliced green onion (2)
2 tablespoons olive oil or
    cooking oil
½ cup bottled blue cheese
    salad dressing or buttermilk
    ranch salad dressing
3 tablespoons all-purpose flour
1½ cups milk
1 cup frozen peas
    Salt and ground black pepper

1. Cook pasta according to package directions; drain.

2. Meanwhile, in a large skillet cook and stir turkey, mushrooms, and green onion in hot oil over medium-high heat for 3 to 4 minutes or until turkey is no longer pink.

3. In a small bowl combine salad dressing and flour; gradually stir in milk. Stir cooked pasta and dressing mixture into turkey mixture. Cook and stir until thickened and bubbly. Stir in peas. Cook and stir for 2 minutes more. Season to taste with salt and pepper.

Per serving: 520 cal., 26 g total fat (5 g sat. fat), 65 mg chol., 515 mg sodium, 39 g carbo., 3 g fiber, 33 g pro.

Turkey and
PASTA PRIMAVERA

Great for the family, this recipe serves many and takes only a short time to make. Serve it with a sprinkling of Parmesan cheese. *Makes 8 servings*

Prep: 15 minutes Cook: Low 4 hours, High 2 hours

2 pounds turkey breast tenderloin, cut into 1-inch pieces

1 16-ounce package frozen sugar snap pea stir-fry vegetables

2 teaspoons dried basil, oregano, or Italian seasoning, crushed

1 16-ounce jar Alfredo pasta sauce

12 ounces dried spaghetti or linguine, broken
   Shredded Parmesan cheese (optional)

1. In a 4½- to 6-quart slow cooker, combine turkey, frozen vegetables, and basil. Stir in pasta sauce.

2. Cover and cook on low-heat setting for 4 to 5 hours or on high-heat setting for 2 to 2½ hours.

3. Cook pasta according to package directions; drain. Stir cooked pasta into turkey mixture. If desired, sprinkle each serving with cheese.

Per serving: 407 cal., 11 g total fat (5 g sat. fat), 103 mg chol., 447 mg sodium, 39 g carbo., 2 g fiber, 36 g pro.

Sassy
TURKEY BURGERS

Together, ground turkey and pork sausage flavor and moisten these juicy burgers. *Makes 6 servings*

Prep: **25 minutes** Grill: **14 minutes**

1 cup chopped tomato
  (2 medium)
½ cup finely chopped onion
  (1 medium)
¼ cup seeded and finely
  chopped fresh jalapeño
  chile pepper (see note,
  page 22)
¼ cup bottled salsa
2 tablespoons Worcestershire
  sauce
½ teaspoon ground cumin
¼ teaspoon salt
¼ teaspoon ground black
  pepper
1½ pounds uncooked ground
  turkey
8 ounces bulk pork sausage
6 hamburger buns, split and
  toasted (if desired)

1. For salsa, in a small bowl combine tomato, ¼ cup of the onion, the jalapeño pepper, and bottled salsa. Cover and chill until ready to serve.

2. In a large bowl combine the remaining ¼ cup onion, the Worcestershire sauce, cumin, salt, and black pepper. Add ground turkey and sausage; mix well. Shape turkey mixture into six ¾-inch-thick patties.

3. For a charcoal grill, grill patties on the rack of an uncovered grill directly over medium coals for 14 to 18 minutes or until no longer pink (165°F), turning once halfway through grilling. (For a gas grill, preheat grill. Reduce heat to medium. Place patties on grill rack over heat. Cover and grill as above.)

4. Serve the burgers in buns with salsa.

Per serving: 430 cal., 21 g total fat (6 g sat. fat), 117 mg chol., 772 mg sodium, 27 g carbo., 2 g fiber, 30 g pro.

Italian-Style
TURKEY BURGERS

The key to any good tender burger is to handle the meat gently and not to overmix it. *Makes 4 servings*

Start to Finish: **30 minutes**

1 egg, lightly beaten
¼ cup seasoned fine dry bread
   crumbs
¼ teaspoon salt
1 pound uncooked ground
   turkey
4 slices provolone cheese or
   mozzarella cheese
   (4 ounces)
4 kaiser rolls or hamburger
   buns, split and toasted
   Fresh basil leaves or
   shredded lettuce
¼ cup light mayonnaise or
   salad dressing
2 tablespoons refrigerated
   pesto

1. Preheat broiler. In a bowl combine egg, bread crumbs, and salt. Add ground turkey; mix well. Shape turkey mixture into four ¾-inch-thick patties.

2. Place patties on the unheated rack of a broiler pan. Broil 4 to 5 inches from the heat for 14 to 18 minutes or until no longer pink (165°F), turning once halfway through broiling. Top with cheese; broil about 30 seconds more or until cheese is melted.

3. To serve, place burgers on bottoms of rolls; add basil. In a small bowl combine mayonnaise and pesto. Spread mayonnaise mixture on tops of buns; place on burgers.

Per serving: 559 cal., 28 g total fat (10 g sat. fat), 168 mg chol., 1,117 mg sodium, 39 g carbo., 2 g fiber, 36 g pro.

Tamale

PIE

No-salt-added tomatoes reduce the sodium in this turkey and cornmeal pie. If you like, turn up the heat by opting for hot chili powder. See photo on page 277. *Makes 6 servings*

Prep: **35 minutes** Bake: **25 minutes** Oven: **350°F**

1⅓ cups water
½ cup yellow cornmeal
½ cup cold water
½ teaspoon salt
8 ounces uncooked ground turkey breast
½ cup chopped onion (1 medium)
½ cup chopped green or red sweet pepper (1 small)
½ teaspoon bottled minced garlic (1 clove)
1 tablespoon chili powder
1 14.5-ounce can no-salt-added diced tomatoes, drained
1 11-ounce can whole kernel corn, drained
2 tablespoons snipped fresh cilantro or parsley
2 tablespoons tomato paste
½ cup shredded reduced-fat cheddar cheese or Monterey Jack cheese (2 ounces)
Snipped fresh cilantro or parsley (optional)

1. Preheat oven to 350°F. Lightly grease a 2-quart square baking dish; set aside. In a small saucepan bring the 1⅓ cups water to boiling. Meanwhile, in a small bowl combine cornmeal, the ½ cup cold water, and ¼ teaspoon of the salt.

2. Slowly add cornmeal mixture to boiling water, stirring constantly. Cook and stir until mixture returns to boiling; reduce heat to low. Cook about 10 minutes or until mixture is very thick, stirring occasionally. Pour into the prepared baking dish. Cover and chill while preparing filling.

3. For filling, in a large skillet cook ground turkey, onion, sweet pepper, and garlic over medium heat until meat is brown. Drain off any fat. Stir in the remaining ¼ teaspoon salt and the chili powder; cook and stir for 1 minute. Stir in drained tomatoes, drained corn, the 2 tablespoons cilantro, and the tomato paste. Spoon filling evenly over cornmeal mixture.

4. Bake, uncovered, about 25 minutes or until heated through. Sprinkle with cheese and, if desired, cilantro.

Per serving: 182 cal., 3 g total fat (1 g sat. fat), 22 mg chol., 546 mg sodium, 25 g carbo., 4 g fiber, 14 g pro.

Turkey Cranberry
FRIED RICE

Yearning for the holidays? Stir together all the wonderful flavors of Thanksgiving in this quick-to-prepare one-pot meal. *Makes 4 servings*

Start to Finish: **25 minutes**

1 pound uncooked ground
    turkey
½ cup chopped celery (1 stalk)
½ cup chopped onion
    (1 medium)
1 8.8-ounce pouch cooked
    long grain and wild rice
½ cup apple cider or apple juice
⅓ cup dried cranberries
½ teaspoon dried thyme,
    crushed
⅓ cup chopped pecans, toasted
    Salt and ground black pepper

1. In a very large skillet, cook ground turkey, celery, and onion over medium heat until meat is brown and vegetables are tender. Drain off any fat.

2. Meanwhile, prepare rice according to package directions.

3. Stir rice, cider, dried cranberries, and thyme into turkey mixture. Cook and stir until liquid is absorbed. Stir in pecans. Season to taste with salt and pepper.

Per serving: 385 cal., 18 g total fat (3 g sat. fat), 90 mg chol., 395 mg sodium, 34 g carbo., 2 g fiber, 23 g pro.

Turkey and
WILD RICE AMANDINE

The wild and brown rice add extra nuttiness and satisfaction to this slow cooker casserole.

Makes 10 servings

Prep: 15 minutes   Cook: Low 6 hours, High 3 hours

1 10.75-ounce can condensed cream of mushroom with roasted garlic soup

1 cup uncooked wild rice, rinsed and drained

1 cup uncooked regular brown rice

1 8-ounce can sliced water chestnuts, drained

1 4-ounce can (drained weight) whole mushrooms, drained

½ cup chopped onion (1 medium)

¼ teaspoon ground black pepper

3 14-ounce cans reduced-sodium chicken broth

½ cup water

3 cups shredded or chopped cooked turkey

1 cup dairy sour cream

½ cup sliced almonds, toasted

1. In a 4- or 5-quart slow cooker combine soup, wild rice, brown rice, drained water chestnuts, drained mushrooms, onion, and pepper. Stir in broth and the water.

2. Cover and cook on low-heat setting for 6 to 7 hours or on high-heat setting for 3 to 3½ hours. Stir in turkey.

3. Top each serving with sour cream and sprinkle with almonds.

Per serving: 340 cal., 12 g total fat (4 g sat. fat), 42 mg chol., 604 mg sodium, 40 g carbo., 3 g fiber, 21 g pro.

Turkey
TORTILLA SOUP

The contrasting crisp and soft textures are what make this soup so satisfying. *Makes 4 servings*

Start to Finish: **20 minutes**

3 6-inch corn tortillas, cut into strips
2 tablespoons cooking oil
2 14-ounce cans reduced-sodium chicken broth
1 cup bottled red or green salsa
2 cups cubed cooked turkey
1 large zucchini, coarsely chopped
  Dairy sour cream (optional)
  Lime wedges (optional)

1. In a large skillet cook tortilla strips in hot oil over medium-high heat until crisp. Using a slotted spoon, remove tortilla strips and drain on paper towels.
2. In a large saucepan combine broth and salsa. Bring to boiling over medium-high heat. Stir in turkey and zucchini. Cook until heated through, stirring occasionally.

3. Top each serving with tortilla strips. If desired, serve with sour cream and lime wedges.

Per serving: 262 cal., 11 g total fat (2 g sat. fat), 53 mg chol., 920 mg sodium, 16 g carbo., 3 g fiber, 26 g pro.

Mexican-Style
TURKEY SOUP

Chock-full of nutritious vegetables, this spicy soup makes smart use of cooked turkey.

Makes 5 or 6 servings

Prep: **20 minutes** Cook: **20 minutes**

1¼ cups chopped red sweet
pepper (I large)

1 cup chopped onion (I large)

1 tablespoon cooking oil

1 teaspoon ground cumin

1 teaspoon chili powder

½ teaspoon paprika

5 cups reduced-sodium
chicken broth

1½ cups peeled and cubed
winter squash

1 large tomato, chopped

¼ teaspoon salt

¼ teaspoon ground black
pepper

2 cups chopped cooked turkey

1 cup frozen whole kernel corn

2 tablespoons snipped fresh
cilantro or parsley

1. In a Dutch oven cook sweet pepper and onion in hot oil over medium heat about 5 minutes or until tender, stirring occasionally. Stir in cumin, chili powder, and paprika; cook and stir for 30 seconds.

2. Add broth, squash, tomato, salt, and black pepper. Bring to boiling; reduce heat. Simmer, covered, about 20 minutes or until squash is tender, stirring occasionally. Stir in turkey, corn, and cilantro; heat through.

Per serving: 205 cal., 6 g total fat (I g sat. fat), 43 mg chol., 790 mg sodium, 17 g carbo., 3 g fiber, 22 g pro.

IN-A-PINCH TIPS!

WINTER TOMATOES: NEED FRESH TOMATOES IN WINTER?
USE AN EQUAL AMOUNT OF SMALL CHERRY TOMATOES, CUT UP.

Turkey-Stuffed
MANICOTTI

Stop racking your brain for ideas to use leftover turkey and ham. Instead, try this creamy main dish.

Makes 8 servings

Prep: **40 minutes** Bake: **20 minutes** Stand: **5 minutes** Oven: **400°F**

8 dried manicotti shells
¼ cup finely chopped onion
¼ cup butter or margarine
3 tablespoons all-purpose flour
¼ teaspoon salt
2 cups whole milk
1 15-ounce carton ricotta cheese
1¼ cups grated Parmesan cheese
1 cup shredded cooked turkey
½ cup diced cooked ham
1 egg yolk
½ teaspoon ground nutmeg
Ground nutmeg (optional)
Fresh Italian (flat-leaf) parsley sprigs (optional)

1. Preheat oven to 400°F. Grease a 2-quart rectangular baking dish; set aside. Cook manicotti shells according to package directions; drain. Rinse with cold water; drain again.

2. Meanwhile, for sauce, in a medium saucepan cook onion in hot butter over medium heat about 4 minutes or until tender. Stir in flour and salt. Gradually stir in milk. Cook and stir until thickened and bubbly. Set aside.

3. For filling, in a medium bowl combine ricotta cheese, 1 cup of the Parmesan cheese, the turkey, ham, egg yolk, and the ½ teaspoon nutmeg.

4. Spread about ½ cup of the sauce in the bottom of the prepared baking dish. Gently spoon about ⅓ cup of the filling into each manicotti shell. Arrange stuffed shells in a single layer in the baking dish. Pour the remaining sauce over the stuffed shells. Sprinkle with the remaining ¼ cup Parmesan cheese.

5. Bake, uncovered, about 20 minutes or until heated through. Let stand for 5 to 10 minutes before serving. If desired, sprinkle with additional nutmeg and garnish with parsley.

Make-Ahead Directions: **Prepare as directed through Step 4. Cover and chill for 2 to 24 hours. To serve, preheat oven to 400°F. Bake, uncovered, for 25 to 30 minutes or until heated through.**

Per serving: 370 cal., 22 g total fat (13 g sat. fat), 108 mg chol., 572 mg sodium, 20 g carbo., 1 g fiber, 23 g pro.

Turkey
AND WILD RICE BAKE

Two cheeses, a packaged rice mix, and cream of chicken soup transform leftover roasted turkey into a rich, oven meal. *Makes 6 servings*

Prep: **35 minutes** Bake: **15 minutes** Oven: **350°F**

- 1 6-ounce package long grain and wild rice mix
- 1 tablespoon butter or margarine
- 1 cup chopped onion (1 large)
- 1½ teaspoons bottled minced garlic (3 cloves)
- 1 10.75-ounce can condensed cream of chicken soup
- 1 cup milk
- 1½ teaspoons dried basil, crushed
- 2 cups shredded Swiss cheese (8 ounces)
- 3 cups chopped cooked turkey
- 1 4-ounce can (drained weight) sliced mushrooms, drained
- ½ cup finely shredded Parmesan cheese (2 ounces)
- ⅓ cup sliced almonds, toasted

1. Prepare rice mix according to package directions, except discard the seasoning packet.

2. Meanwhile, preheat oven to 350°F. In a 12-inch skillet melt butter over medium heat. Add onion and garlic; cook until onion is tender, stirring occasionally. Stir in soup, milk, and basil; heat through. Gradually add Swiss cheese, stirring until cheese is melted. Stir in cooked rice, turkey, and drained mushrooms.

3. Transfer mixture to an ungreased 3-quart rectangular baking dish. Sprinkle with Parmesan cheese. Bake, uncovered, for 15 to 20 minutes or until heated through. Before serving, sprinkle with almonds.

Per serving: 700 cal., 36 g total fat (19 g sat. fat), 132 mg chol., 1,400 mg sodium, 37 g carbo., 4 g fiber, 56 g pro.

Mexican

TURKEY CASSEROLE

Stash away some holiday turkey in the freezer—in 1½-cup portions—so that you'll have the meat on hand for this casserole. Freeze cooked turkey meat in freezer containers for up to 4 months.

Makes 4 to 6 servings

Prep: **20 minutes**   Bake: **35 minutes**   Oven: **375°F**

1½ cups chopped cooked turkey

1 10.75-ounce can condensed cream of chicken soup or cream of mushroom soup

½ cup dairy sour cream

1 4-ounce can diced green chile peppers, undrained

1 2.25-ounce can sliced, pitted ripe olives, undrained

¼ cup sliced green onion (2)

1½ cups coarsely crushed tortilla chips or corn chips

1½ cups shredded Monterey Jack cheese with jalapeño peppers or Monterey Jack cheese (6 ounces)

1 cup chopped tomato (2 medium)

1. Preheat oven to 375°F. Grease a 2-quart square baking dish; set aside. In a large bowl combine turkey, soup, sour cream, undrained chile peppers, undrained olives, and green onion.

2. Sprinkle one-third of the chips in the bottom of the prepared baking dish. Top with half of the turkey mixture and half of the cheese. Repeat layers, ending with a layer of chips.

3. Bake, uncovered, about 35 minutes or until heated through. Before serving, sprinkle with tomato.

Per serving: 487 cal., 32 g total fat (15 g sat. fat), 87 mg chol., 1,413 mg sodium, 26 g carbo., 3 g fiber, 27 g pro.

Roasted Turkey,
BACON, AND AVOCADO WRAPS

Creamy avocado, satisfying turkey, and crispy bacon are wrapped in an easy-to-eat sandwich.

Makes 4 wraps

Start to Finish: **20 minutes**

8 slices bacon

1 ripe medium avocado,
  seeded, peeled, and sliced

2 tablespoons lime juice

10 ounces cooked turkey breast,
  cut into bite-size strips
  Salt and ground black pepper

6 tablespoons light mayonnaise
  or chipotle chile-flavor light
  mayonnaise

4 9- to 10-inch flour tortillas

1. Cook bacon in a large skillet until crisp and golden. Drain on paper towels. Set aside.

2. Place avocado in a small bowl; drizzle with 1 tablespoon of the lime juice. Set aside.

3. In a medium bowl combine turkey and the remaining 1 tablespoon lime juice; toss gently to coat. Season to taste with salt and pepper.

4. To assemble, spread mayonnaise on one side of each tortilla, leaving a 1-inch border. Top with avocado, turkey, and bacon. Fold in opposite sides of each tortilla; roll up tortilla.

Per wrap: 400 cal., 22 g total fat (5 g sat. fat), 49 mg chol., 1,430 mg sodium, 31 g carbo., 4 g fiber, 20 g pro.

Turkey
SALAD SANDWICHES

This quick-to-fix sandwich provides so many choices for change. Vary the flavor by using thyme or basil instead of tarragon. Serve on a croissant or your favorite bread. Add lettuce, red onion, and/or tomato for crunch and color. *Makes 6 sandwiches*

Start to Finish: **20 minutes**

3 cups finely chopped cooked turkey

½ cup mayonnaise or salad dressing

¼ cup thinly sliced green onion (2)

2 tablespoons Dijon-style mustard

1 teaspoon dried tarragon, thyme, or basil, crushed

6 croissants, split, or 12 slices rye or whole wheat bread, toasted

6 slices provolone cheese (6 ounces)

Lettuce leaves, red onion slices, and/or tomato slices (optional)

1. In a large bowl combine turkey, mayonnaise, green onion, mustard, and tarragon.

2. Divide turkey mixture among bottoms of croissants. Top with cheese. If desired, add lettuce, red onion, and/or tomato. Replace tops of croissants.

Per sandwich: 553 cal., 34 g total fat (11 g sat. fat), 96 mg chol., 733 mg sodium, 22 g carbo., 1 g fiber, 37 g pro.

Broccoli
AND TURKEY CHEESE SOUP

Use frozen chopped broccoli in place of the fresh broccoli in this soup if preparation time is short.

Makes 4 servings

Start to Finish: **25 minutes**

3 slices bacon, chopped
½ cup chopped onion
 (1 medium)
2 tablespoons all-purpose flour
¼ teaspoon ground black
 pepper
2¾ cups chicken broth
2 cups bite-size broccoli florets
⅔ cup beer
1½ cups chopped smoked turkey
6 ounces process Swiss
 cheese, torn
⅓ cup half-and-half or
 light cream

1. In a large saucepan cook bacon and onion over medium heat until bacon is crisp and onion is tender, stirring occasionally. Stir in flour and pepper.

2. Add broth, broccoli, and beer to bacon mixture. Bring to boiling; reduce heat. Simmer, uncovered, for 3 to 5 minutes or until broccoli is nearly tender.

3. Stir in turkey, cheese, and half-and-half. Cook and stir until cheese is melted.

Per serving: 386 cal., 22 g total fat (11 g sat. fat), 97 mg chol., 2,048 mg sodium, 13 g carbo., 2 g fiber, 31 g pro.

Smoked
TURKEY JAMBALAYA

Guests will feel treated to something special when they taste this Cajun-inspired masterpiece loaded with crisp-tender veggies. *Makes 6 servings*

Prep: 30 minutes   Bake: 55 minutes   Oven: 350°F

2 cups water
1 cup uncooked long grain rice
1 16-ounce package frozen sweet pepper stir-fry vegetables
1 14.5-ounce can diced tomatoes with green pepper, celery, and onions, undrained
1 10-ounce can diced tomatoes and green chiles, undrained
8 ounces cooked turkey kielbasa or smoked turkey sausage, sliced ¼ inch thick
½ cup sliced green onion (4)
½ teaspoon Cajun seasoning
½ teaspoon bottled minced garlic (1 clove)
Bottled hot pepper sauce

1. In a medium saucepan combine the water and rice. Bring to boiling; reduce heat. Simmer, covered, for 15 to 18 minutes or until rice is tender and water is absorbed.

2. Meanwhile, preheat oven to 350°F. In a large bowl combine frozen vegetables, undrained tomatoes, kielbasa, green onion, Cajun seasoning, and garlic. Stir in cooked rice. Transfer mixture to an ungreased 2-quart square baking dish.

3. Bake, uncovered, about 55 minutes or until heated through, stirring once. Pass hot pepper sauce.

Per serving: 219 cal., 3 g total fat (0 g sat. fat), 0 mg chol., 842 mg sodium, 35 g carbo., 3 g fiber, 12 g pro.

Breakfast
BURRITOS

Yes, this is great for breakfast and brunch, but don't let the name stop you. It is good for a light supper as well. *Makes 6 servings*

Prep: **20 minutes** Cook: **10 minutes**

2 cups refrigerated or frozen egg product, thawed, or 8 eggs, lightly beaten
1/3 cup fat-free milk
1/2 teaspoon garlic salt
8 ounces uncooked bulk turkey sausage
1/2 cup chopped green sweet pepper (1 small)
1/2 cup chopped fresh mushrooms
1/4 cup chopped onion
3/4 cup bottled chunky salsa
1/2 cup chopped romaine lettuce
2 tablespoons finely chopped fresh jalapeño chile pepper (see note, page 22) (optional)
6 8- to 10-inch whole wheat flour tortillas, warmed
3/4 cup shredded reduced-fat cheddar cheese (3 ounces)
Bottled chunky salsa (optional)

1. In a medium bowl combine egg product, milk, and garlic salt. Set aside.
2. In a large skillet cook sausage, sweet pepper, mushrooms, and onion over medium heat until meat is brown and vegetables are tender. Drain off fat. Add egg mixture to skillet. Cook, without stirring, until mixture starts to set on the bottom and around the edges.
3. Using a spatula or large spoon, lift and fold the partially cooked egg mixture so that the uncooked portion flows underneath. Continue cooking over medium heat for 2 to 3 minutes or until egg mixture is cooked through, but is still glossy and moist. Immediately remove from heat. Stir in the 3/4 cup salsa, the lettuce, and, if desired, jalapeño pepper.

4. Divide egg mixture among warm tortillas; sprinkle with cheese. Roll up tortillas. If desired, serve with additional salsa.

Per serving: 325 cal., 11 g total fat (3 g sat. fat), 37 mg chol., 1,038 mg sodium, 30 g carbo., 3 g fiber, 26 g pro.

LOOK!
MONEY-SAVING TIPS and HINTS

Take advantage of specials on large pieces of fish at warehouse or discount stores. Cut them into serving-sized pieces, freeze on trays, then store in freezer bags.

Buy frozen shrimp, fish fillets, and frozen breaded or battered fillets in bulk at a super store. Repackage into smaller portions.

Opt for shrimp in the shell, then peel and remove the vein yourself.

Be flexible. If you find a fish variety at the store that is <u>cheaper</u> than the one specified in your recipe, use the less-expensive fish.

Check the discount area at the supermarket for marked-down fish and seafood. You may have to prepare it that night, but you may be able to afford your favorite variety that way.

Stock up on canned salmon during the holidays when it is typically on sale. Mark the purchase date on the top of the can, using the oldest can first.

If available, sign up at your local fish market to be on a monthly mailing that offers special prices or coupons for regular customers.

Yes! Buy Alaska salmon in season and watch for store specials. Purchase a whole fish and cut into steaks and freeze. Or cook the whole fish then shred and package it in user-friendly portions.

Canned tuna and salmon are usually more economical than foil-packed.

CHAPTER 6

Affordable FISH AND SEAFOOD

For nights when time is of the essence, fish and seafood are terrific solutions. Fish by its very nature is a fast food and should be cooked quickly. Granted, fish can be more costly than other protein-rich sources. But with wise buying and noting supermarket specials, you can serve fish to your family weekly. Here are great seafood dishes, some familiar, others new, and **ALL** with satisfying tastes.

Cajun
FISH SOUP

Jazz up the mild fish in this soup with peppery Cajun seasoning. *Makes 4 servings*

Start to Finish: **20 minutes**

12 ounces fresh or frozen skinless sea bass, cod, or orange roughy fillets

1 16-ounce package frozen stir-fry vegetables

4 cups reduced-sodium chicken broth

2 teaspoons Cajun seasoning

1 14.5-ounce can diced tomatoes, undrained

1. Thaw fish, if frozen. Rinse fish; pat dry with paper towels. Cut fish into 1-inch pieces; set aside.

2. In a large saucepan combine frozen vegetables, broth, and Cajun seasoning. Bring to boiling; reduce heat. Simmer, covered, for 3 to 5 minutes or until vegetables are crisp-tender.

3. Stir in fish and undrained tomatoes. Return to boiling; reduce heat. Simmer, covered, for 2 to 3 minutes or until fish flakes easily when tested with a fork.

Per serving: 157 cal., 2 g total fat (0 g sat. fat), 35 mg chol., 968 mg sodium, 12 g carbo., 3 g fiber, 21 g pro.

Fish TACOS

Seafood tacos first originated in Southern California. Now they are gaining in popularity nationwide as a delicious way to stretch fish. See photo on page 278. *Makes 4 servings*

Prep: **20 minutes** Bake: **4 minutes** Oven: **450°F**

12 ounces fresh or frozen skinless fish fillets
 1 tablespoon olive oil
 ¼ teaspoon ground cumin
 ⅛ teaspoon garlic powder
 3 tablespoons mayonnaise or salad dressing
 1 teaspoon lime juice
 1½ cups packaged shredded cabbage with carrot (coleslaw mix) or shredded cabbage
 8 taco shells, warmed according to package directions
 Purchased mango or pineapple salsa

1. Thaw fish, if frozen. Preheat oven to 450°F. Grease a shallow baking pan; set aside. Rinse fish; pat dry with paper towels. Cut fish crosswise into ¾-inch slices.
2. Place fish in a single layer in the prepared baking pan. In a small bowl combine oil, cumin, and garlic powder; brush over fish. Bake for 4 to 6 minutes or until fish flakes easily when tested with a fork.

3. Meanwhile, in a medium bowl stir together mayonnaise and lime juice. Add cabbage; toss gently to coat.
4. To serve, spoon cabbage mixture into taco shells. Top with fish and salsa.

Per serving: 322 cal., 19 g total fat (3 g sat. fat), 44 mg chol., 353 mg sodium, 21 g carbo., 3 g fiber, 17 g pro.

Hearty
FISH CHOWDER

Thick and chunky, this chowder measures up to a full-meal deal. Halibut or haddock are fine substitutes for the cod. *Makes 6 servings*

Prep: 15 minutes   Cook: Low 6 hours, High 3 hours; plus 1 hour on High

2 cups chopped potato
   (2 large)
1 cup chopped onion (1 large)
1 teaspoon bottled minced
   garlic (2 cloves)
1 10.75-ounce can condensed
   cream of celery soup
1 10-ounce package frozen
   whole kernel corn
1 10-ounce package frozen
   baby lima beans
1½ cups chicken broth
⅓ cup dry white wine or
   chicken broth
1 teaspoon lemon-pepper
   seasoning
1 pound fresh or frozen
   skinless cod or other white
   fish fillets
1 14.5-ounce can stewed
   tomatoes, undrained
⅓ cup nonfat dry milk powder

1. In a 3½- or 4-quart slow cooker, combine potato, onion, and garlic. Stir in soup, frozen corn, frozen lima beans, broth, wine, and lemon-pepper seasoning.

2. Cover and cook on low-heat setting for 6 to 7 hours or on high-heat setting for 3 to 3½ hours.

3. Meanwhile, thaw fish, if frozen. Rinse fish; pat dry with paper towels. Place fish on top of vegetable mixture. If using low-heat setting, turn to high-heat setting. Cover and cook for 1 hour more.

4. Add undrained tomatoes and milk powder, stirring gently to break up fish.

Per serving: 317 cal., 4 g total fat (1 g sat. fat), 40 mg chol., 1,034 mg sodium, 45 g carbo., 6 g fiber, 24 g pro.

IN-A-PINCH TIPS !

LEMON PEPPER OPTION: USE FRESHLY GROUND PEPPER AND
FRESH GRATED LEMON PEEL INSTEAD; SALT IS OPTIONAL.

Catfish
WITH BLACK BEAN AND AVOCADO RELISH

A squeeze of fresh lime brightens the flavor of this black bean and avocado relish. Here it is paired with grilled catfish. See photo on page 279. *Makes 4 servings*

Prep: 15 minutes Grill: 4 minutes

4 6-ounce fresh or frozen skinless catfish fillets, about ½ inch thick
2 tablespoons snipped fresh cilantro or parsley
2 tablespoons snipped fresh oregano
½ teaspoon finely shredded lime peel
2 tablespoons lime juice
1 tablespoon olive oil
½ to 1 teaspoon bottled minced garlic (1 to 2 cloves)
¼ to ½ teaspoon bottled hot pepper sauce
1 15-ounce can black beans, rinsed and drained
1 medium avocado, seeded, peeled, and chopped

1. Thaw fish, if frozen. In a small bowl combine cilantro, oregano, lime peel, lime juice, oil, garlic, and hot pepper sauce. For relish, in a medium bowl combine drained beans and avocado; stir in half of the cilantro mixture. Cover and chill until ready to serve.

2. Rinse fish; pat dry with paper towels. Brush 2 tablespoons of the remaining cilantro mixture over both sides of fish.

3. For a charcoal grill, grill fish on the greased rack of an uncovered grill directly over medium coals for 4 to 6 minutes or until fish flakes easily when tested with a fork, carefully turning and brushing once with the remaining cilantro mixture halfway through grilling. (For a gas grill, preheat grill. Reduce heat to medium. Place fish on greased grill rack over heat. Cover and grill as above.)

4. To serve, divide three-fourths of the relish among 4 dinner plates. Arrange fish on top of relish; spoon the remaining relish over fish.

Per serving: 416 cal., 23 g total fat (5 g sat. fat), 79 mg chol., 360 mg sodium, 22 g carbo., 9 g fiber, 35 g pro.

Crunchy Catfish
AND ZUCCHINI STICKS

Tasty, economical cornflake crumbs add pleasing crisp texture to fish and veggies. *Makes 4 servings*

Prep: 15 minutes   Bake: 12 minutes   Oven: 425°F

1 pound fresh or frozen
  skinless catfish fillets
1 medium zucchini or yellow
  summer squash
4 cups cornflakes
1 cup bottled ranch salad
  dressing
2 teaspoons bottled hot pepper
  sauce

1. Thaw fish, if frozen. Preheat oven to 425°F. Grease a 15×10×1-inch baking pan; set aside. Rinse fish; pat dry with paper towels. Bias-slice fish into 1-inch strips. Cut zucchini in half crosswise; cut each half lengthwise into 6 wedges.
2. Place cornflakes in a large resealable plastic bag. Seal and crush slightly; set aside. In a large bowl combine ranch dressing and hot pepper sauce. Reserve half of the dressing mixture for dipping sauce.
3. Add fish and zucchini to the remaining dressing mixture; stir gently to coat. Add fish and zucchini, a few pieces at a time, to crushed cornflakes, shaking to coat. Place fish and zucchini in a single layer in the prepared baking pan.

4. Bake, uncovered, for 12 to 15 minutes or until fish flakes easily when tested with a fork and crumbs are golden brown. Serve fish and zucchini with the reserved dipping sauce.

Per serving: 545 cal., 40 g total fat (7 g sat. fat), 58 mg chol., 779 mg sodium, 24 g carbo., 0 g fiber, 20 g pro.

Spicy CATFISH

Acids like lime juice and vinegar used in a marinade can add an abundance of flavor in 20 minutes. But leave them on the fish any longer and they'll toughen instead of tenderize. *Makes 4 servings*

Prep: **10 minutes** Grill: **4 minutes per ½-inch thickness** Marinate: **20 minutes**

4 6-ounce fresh or frozen
   skinless catfish fillets,
   ½ to 1 inch thick
2 tablespoons lime juice
2 tablespoons red wine vinegar
1 tablespoon cooking oil
1 teaspoon dry mustard
1 teaspoon ground cumin
1 teaspoon chili powder
½ teaspoon cayenne pepper
⅛ teaspoon salt
   Lime wedges (optional)

1. Thaw fish, if frozen. Rinse fish; pat dry with paper towels. Place fish in a resealable plastic bag.

2. For marinade, in a small bowl combine lime juice, vinegar, oil, mustard, cumin, chili powder, cayenne pepper, and salt. Pour marinade over fish. Seal bag; turn to coat fish. Marinate in the refrigerator for 20 minutes, turning bag once. Drain fish, discarding marinade. Measure thickness of fish.

3. For a charcoal grill, grill fish on the greased rack of an uncovered grill directly over medium coals for 4 to 6 minutes per ½-inch thickness or until fish flakes easily when tested with a fork, carefully turning once halfway through grilling. (For a gas grill, preheat grill. Reduce heat to medium. Place fish on greased grill rack over heat. Cover and grill as above.) If desired, serve fish with lime wedges.

Per serving: 271 cal., 17 g total fat (4 g sat. fat), 79 mg chol., 171 mg sodium, 2 g carbo., 1 g fiber, 27 g pro.

Cajun Catfish
WITH COLESLAW

Oven-frying the catfish is a healthy and easy way to prepare this freshwater fish. *Makes 4 servings*

Prep: 10 minutes Bake: 15 minutes Oven: 350°F

1 pound fresh or frozen skinless catfish fillets, about ½ inch thick
2½ teaspoons salt-free Cajun seasoning
¼ teaspoon salt
2 cups shredded cabbage with carrot (coleslaw mix)
3 tablespoons mayonnaise or salad dressing
Salt and ground black pepper
Bottled hot pepper sauce (optional)

1. Thaw fish, if frozen. Preheat oven to 350°F. Grease a 3-quart rectangular baking dish; set aside. Rinse fish; pat dry with paper towels. Cut fish into 4 serving-size pieces. In a small bowl combine 2 teaspoons of the Cajun seasoning and the ¼ teaspoon salt. Sprinkle both sides of fish with seasoning mixture. Arrange fish in the prepared baking dish, tucking under any thin edges to make fish of uniform thickness.

2. Bake, uncovered, for 15 to 20 minutes or until fish flakes easily when tested with a fork.

3. Meanwhile, for coleslaw, in a medium bowl stir together cabbage, mayonnaise, and the remaining ½ teaspoon Cajun seasoning. Season to taste with salt and black pepper. Cover and chill until ready to serve.

4. Serve fish with coleslaw and, if desired, hot pepper sauce.

Per serving: 241 cal., 17 g total fat (3 g sat. fat), 57 mg chol., 127 mg sodium, 3 g carbo., 1 g fiber, 18 g pro.

Sesame-Coated
TILAPIA SALAD

A mustard and sesame coating contrasts deliciously with tilapia, a mild whitefish. *Makes 4 servings*

Start to Finish: **20 minutes**

1 pound fresh or frozen
   skinless tilapia fillets
⅔ cup bottled honey-Dijon
   salad dressing
¼ cup all-purpose flour
¼ cup sesame seeds
½ teaspoon ground
   black pepper
2 tablespoons cooking oil
1 5-ounce package baby
   spinach with red leaf
   lettuce or baby spinach
   with radicchio

1. Thaw fish, if frozen. Rinse the fish; pat dry with paper towels. Cut fish into 4 serving-size pieces.
2. Transfer 2 tablespoons of the salad dressing to a small bowl. In a shallow dish combine flour, sesame seeds, and pepper. Brush both sides of fish with the 2 tablespoons salad dressing. Dip fish into flour mixture, turning and pressing to coat.
3. In a 12-inch skillet heat oil over medium heat. Add fish; cook about 6 minutes or until fish flakes easily when tested with a fork, carefully turning once.
4. To serve, divide spinach mixture among 4 dinner plates; top with fish. Drizzle with the remaining salad dressing.

Per serving: 418 cal., 30 g total fat (3 g sat. fat), 0 mg chol., 247 mg sodium, 16 g carbo., 4 g fiber, 22 g pro.

Tilapia with
CHILI CREAM SAUCE

Originally from the waters surrounding Africa, tilapia is raised commercially everywhere from North America to Asia. In this recipe, the sweet, mild fish—sometimes called Hawaiian sun fish—fries up crisp and tender and soaks up all the glorious flavor of the sassy sauce. *Makes 4 servings*

Start to Finish: **25 minutes**

1 pound fresh or frozen skinless tilapia or other firm-flesh fish fillets, ½ to 1 inch thick
2 tablespoons cornmeal
2 tablespoons all-purpose flour
Nonstick cooking spray
1 teaspoon cooking oil
2 teaspoons butter or margarine
2 teaspoons all-purpose flour
1 teaspoon chili powder
¼ teaspoon salt
¼ teaspoon ground cumin
¾ cup fat-free half-and-half
2 tablespoons snipped fresh parsley or cilantro (optional)
Lime slices (optional)

1. Thaw fish, if frozen. Rinse fish; pat dry with paper towels. Cut fish into 4 serving-size pieces. In a shallow dish combine cornmeal and the 2 tablespoons flour. Dip fish into cornmeal mixture, turning to coat.

2. Lightly coat a 12-inch nonstick skillet with cooking spray. Add oil; heat skillet over medium-high heat. Add fish; cook for 4 to 6 minutes or until fish flakes easily when tested with a fork, carefully turning once. If fish browns too quickly, reduce heat to medium. Remove fish from skillet; cover and keep warm.

3. For sauce, in the same skillet melt butter over medium heat. Stir in the 2 teaspoons flour, the chili powder, salt, and cumin. Gradually stir in half-and-half. Cook and stir until thickened and bubbly. Cook and stir for 1 minute more.

4. Serve fish with sauce. If desired, sprinkle with parsley and garnish with lime slices.

Per serving: 187 cal., 4 g total fat (2 g sat. fat), 60 mg chol., 258 mg sodium, 12 g carbo., 1 g fiber, 23 g pro.

# *Browned*

BUTTER SALMON

Browning the butter gives it a subtle nutty flavor that complements the maple syrup and orange peel, giving the salmon a sweet richness. *Makes 4 servings*

Prep: **20 minutes** Broil: **8 minutes**

4 6-ounce fresh or frozen
  salmon or halibut steaks,
  cut 1 inch thick
  Salt and ground black pepper
2 tablespoons butter or
  margarine
2 tablespoons maple syrup
1 teaspoon finely shredded
  orange peel

1. Thaw fish, if frozen. Preheat broiler. Rinse fish; pat dry with paper towels. Sprinkle both sides of fish with salt and pepper; set aside.

2. In a small saucepan cook butter over medium heat about 3 minutes or until golden brown, stirring occasionally. Cool for 10 minutes. Stir in syrup and orange peel (mixture may thicken).

3. Meanwhile, line a broiler pan with foil; set aside. Spread both sides of fish with butter mixture. Place fish on the greased unheated rack of the prepared broiler pan. Broil about 4 inches from the heat for 8 to 12 minutes or until fish flakes easily when tested with a fork, carefully turning once halfway through broiling.

Per serving: 277 cal., 12 g total fat (5 g sat. fat), 105 mg chol., 322 mg sodium, 7 g carbo., 0 g fiber, 34 g pro.

Oven-Roasted
SALMON

Save energy by baking potatoes at the same time the salmon roasts in the oven. *Makes 4 servings*

Prep: **10 minutes** Roast: **4 minutes per ½-inch thickness** Oven: **450°F**

4 5- to 6-ounce fresh or frozen
   skinless salmon fillets
1 tablespoon olive oil or
   flavored oil
1 teaspoon seasoned salt
¼ teaspoon ground
   black pepper

1. Thaw fish, if frozen. Preheat oven to 450°F. Line a shallow baking pan with parchment paper or foil; set aside.
2. Rinse fish; pat dry with paper towels. Measure thickness of fish. Brush both sides of fish with oil and sprinkle with seasoned salt and pepper. Place fish in the prepared baking pan.

3. Bake, uncovered, for 4 to 6 minutes per ½-inch thickness of fish or until fish flakes easily when tested with a fork.

Per serving: 195 cal., 8 g total fat (1 g sat. fat), 74 mg chol., 475 mg sodium, 0 g carbo., 0 g fiber, 28 g pro.

Teriyaki-Glazed
SALMON

Balsamic vinegar is naturally sweeter than most other vinegars. When cooked down on the stove, it thickens into a syrupy glaze that tastes awesome with grilled salmon. *Makes 4 servings*

Prep: **15 minutes** Cook: **5 minutes** Grill: **4 minutes per ½-inch thickness**

4 6-ounce fresh or frozen
   skinless, boneless salmon
   fillets, ½ to 1 inch thick
½ cup balsamic vinegar
1 tablespoon packed brown
   sugar or full-flavor molasses
1 teaspoon soy sauce
⅛ teaspoon ground ginger

1. Thaw fish, if frozen. Rinse fish; pat dry with paper towels. Measure thickness of fish; set aside.

2. For glaze, in a small saucepan bring vinegar to boiling over medium heat. Boil gently, uncovered, about 5 minutes or until reduced by about half. Stir in brown sugar, soy sauce, and ginger. Brush both sides of fish with glaze.

3. For a charcoal grill, grill fish on the greased rack of an uncovered grill directly over medium coals for 4 to 6 minutes per ½-inch thickness of fish or until fish flakes easily when tested with a fork; carefully turning once halfway through grilling. (For a gas grill, preheat grill. Reduce heat to medium. Place fish on greased grill rack over heat. Cover and grill as above.)

Per serving: 336 cal., 15 g total fat (4 g sat.. fat), 105 mg chol., 171 mg sodium, 11 g carbo., 0 g fiber, 36 g pro.

IN-A-PINCH TIPS!

BALSAMIC VINEGAR ALTERNATE: USE 1 TABLESPOON CIDER OR RED WINE VINEGAR PLUS ½ TEASPOON SUGAR. (FLAVOR WILL NOT BE THE SAME.)

Basil-Buttered
SALMON

Use the leftover basil-and-butter mixture to season your favorite cooked vegetables. *Makes 4 servings*

Start to Finish: **25 minutes**

4 5-ounce fresh or frozen
   skinless salmon, halibut,
   or sea bass fillets, about
   I inch thick
½ teaspoon salt-free lemon-
   pepper seasoning
 I tablespoon butter or
   margarine, softened
 I teaspoon snipped fresh basil
   or dill or ¼ teaspoon dried
   basil, crushed, or dried dill
 I teaspoon snipped fresh
   parsley or cilantro
¼ teaspoon finely shredded
   lemon peel or lime peel

I. Thaw fish, if frozen. Preheat broiler. Rinse fish; pat dry with paper towels. Sprinkle with lemon-pepper seasoning.
2. Place fish on the greased unheated rack of a broiler pan, tucking under any thin edges to make fish of uniform thickness. Broil about 4 inches from the heat for 8 to 12 minutes or until fish flakes easily when tested with a fork, carefully turning once halfway through broiling.
3. Meanwhile, in a small bowl combine butter, basil, parsley, and lemon peel. To serve, spoon butter mixture on top of fish.

Grilling Directions: **For a charcoal grill, grill fish on the greased rack of an uncovered grill directly over medium coals for 8 to 12 minutes or until fish flakes easily when tested with a fork, carefully turning once halfway through grilling. (For a gas grill, preheat grill. Reduce heat to medium. Place fish on greased grill rack over heat. Cover and grill as above.**

Per serving: 284 cal., 18 g total fat (5 g sat. fat), 91 mg chol., 104 mg sodium, 0 g carbo., 0 g fiber, 28 g pro.

Salmon
POTATO SCRAMBLE

Farm-raised salmon is usually more economical and available than wild salmon. Serve this dish either for a brunch with a fresh fruit salad or as supper fare with a crisp green salad. *Makes 6 servings*

Start to Finish: **25 minutes**

I pound fresh or frozen skinless salmon fillets, about ¾ inch thick

2 tablespoons butter or margarine

2 cups frozen diced hash brown potatoes, thawed

¾ cup chopped green sweet pepper (I medium)

2 to 3 teaspoons Old Bay® seasoning

6 eggs, lightly beaten

⅓ cup water

I. Thaw fish, if frozen. Rinse fish; pat dry with paper towels. In a covered 12-inch skillet cook fish in a small amount of boiling water for 6 to 9 minutes or until fish flakes easily when tested with a fork. Remove fish from skillet; discard liquid. Using a fork, break fish into large chunks.

2. Wipe skillet with paper towels. In the skillet melt butter over medium-high heat. Add potatoes, sweet pepper, and Old Bay seasoning. Cook for 5 to 10 minutes or until potatoes start to brown, stirring occasionally.

3. In a medium bowl combine eggs and the water; add to potato mixture. Cook over medium heat, without stirring, until mixture starts to set on the bottom and around edges. Using a spatula or large spoon, lift and fold the partially cooked egg mixture so that the uncooked portion flows underneath. Continue cooking over medium heat for 2 to 3 minutes or until egg mixture is cooked through, but is still glossy and moist. Gently stir in fish; heat through.

Per serving: 294 cal., 17 g total fat (6 g sat. fat), 266 mg chol., 396 mg sodium, 12 g carbo., 1 g fiber, 23 g pro.

Salmon
CONFETTI CHOWDER

Canned salmon is a true economic value—low in cost, highly nutritious, and oh, did we mention? ever so delicious. See photo on page 280. *Makes 4 servings*

Start to Finish: **25 minutes**

2 cups frozen vegetables (such as broccoli, sweet peppers, and corn)

2 tablespoons seeded and finely chopped fresh jalapeño chile pepper (see note, page 22)

1 tablespoon butter or margarine

2 tablespoons all-purpose flour

2 cups fat-free milk

1 cup fat-free half-and-half

2 cups refrigerated diced potatoes with onions

1 15-ounce can salmon, drained, flaked, and skin and bones removed

¼ cup snipped watercress

2 tablespoons lemon juice

½ teaspoon salt

½ teaspoon ground black pepper

1. In a large saucepan cook frozen vegetables and jalapeño pepper in hot butter over medium heat for 3 to 5 minutes or until tender, stirring occasionally. Stir in flour. Gradually stir in milk and half-and-half. Cook and stir until slightly thickened. Cook and stir for 2 minutes more.

2. Stir in potatoes, salmon, watercress, lemon juice, salt, and black pepper; heat through.

Per serving: 349 cal., 10 g total fat (3 g sat. fat), 68 mg chol., 1,174 mg sodium, 33 g carbo., 3 g fiber, 29 g pro.

Mediterranean-Style
TUNA CASSEROLE

With tomatoes, raisins, black olives, and Parmesan in this tuna casserole it is a far cry, and welcome change, from the one you probably enjoyed as a child. *Makes 4 servings*

Prep: **25 minutes**   Bake: **30 minutes**   Oven: **350°F**

2 cups dried bow tie pasta
1 small onion, thinly sliced
2 cloves garlic, minced
1 tablespoon olive oil
1 12-ounce can tuna, drained and broken into chunks
¾ cup water
½ cup raisins
½ cup dried tomatoes (not oil-packed), thinly sliced
¼ cup oil-cured black olives or kalamata olives, pitted and halved
2 tablespoons pine nuts (optional)
1 tablespoon snipped fresh parsley
½ cup finely shredded Parmesan cheese (2 ounces)
½ cup coarsely torn fresh basil

1. Preheat oven to 350°F. Cook pasta according to package directions; drain. Meanwhile, in a large ovenproof skillet, cook onion and garlic in hot oil over medium heat until onion is tender, stirring occasionally.
2. Stir tuna, the water, raisins, dried tomato, olives, pine nuts (if desired), and parsley into onion mixture. Stir in cooked pasta.

3. Bake, covered, for 25 minutes. Sprinkle with cheese. Bake, uncovered, about 5 minutes more or until heated through and cheese is melted. Before serving, sprinkle with basil.

Per serving: 401 cal., 15 g total fat (4 g sat. fat), 23 mg chol., 691 mg sodium, 35 g carbo., 3 g fiber, 33 g pro.

IN-A-PINCH TIPS!

RAISIN COUSINS: DARK AND GOLDEN RAISINS CAN BE USED INTERCHANGEABLY. THEY ARE THE SAME GRAPE VARIETY. GOLDEN ARE OFTEN A BIT MORE EXPENSIVE.

Tuna
NOODLE CASSEROLE

Most everyone has sampled a version of this revered comfort food. This rendition is updated with a creamier texture and the addition of mushrooms and green beans. *Makes 12 servings*

Prep: **30 minutes**   Bake: **30 minutes**   Oven: **350°F**

8   ounces dried medium
     noodles
1   16-ounce package frozen
     whole or cut green beans
½   cup fine dry bread crumbs
2   tablespoons butter or
     margarine, melted
2   tablespoons butter or
     margarine
2   cups sliced fresh mushrooms
1½ cups chopped red and/or
     green sweet pepper
     (2 medium)
1   cup sliced celery (2 stalks)
1   cup chopped onion (1 large)
1   teaspoon bottled minced
     garlic (2 cloves)
2   10.75-ounce cans condensed
     cream of mushroom or
     cream of celery soup
1   cup milk
1   cup shredded process Swiss
     cheese or American cheese
     (4 ounces)
2   9- or 9.25-ounce cans tuna
     (water pack), drained
     and flaked

1. Preheat oven to 350°F. Cook noodles according to package directions, adding green beans during the last 3 minutes of cooking; drain. Meanwhile, in a small bowl combine bread crumbs and the 2 tablespoons melted butter; toss gently to coat. Set aside.

2. In a 12-inch skillet melt the 2 tablespoons butter over medium heat. Add mushrooms, sweet pepper, celery, onion, and garlic. Cook until vegetables are tender, stirring occasionally. Add soup, milk, and cheese, stirring until cheese is melted. Stir in cooked noodle mixture and tuna.

3. Transfer tuna mixture to an ungreased 3-quart rectangular baking dish. Sprinkle buttered bread crumbs around outside edges of dish. Bake, uncovered, for 30 to 35 minutes or until heated through and bread crumbs are golden brown.

Per serving: 306 cal., 13 g total fat (6 g sat. fat), 57 mg chol., 746 mg sodium, 28 g carbo., 3 g fiber, 19 g pro.

IN-A-PINCH TIPS!

DRY CRUMB OPTION: MAKE YOUR OWN CRUMBS FROM DAY-OLD BREAD. CUBE THE BREAD AND PLACE ON A BAKING SHEET. BAKE IN A 300°F OVEN FOR 10 MINUTES; COOL. PROCESS IN A FOOD PROCESSOR OR BLENDER UNTIL FINE CRUMBS. ONE SLICE BREAD YIELDS ABOUT ¼ CUP FINE BREAD CRUMBS.

Curried
TUNA CUPS

To mellow the curry powder, heat it in a dry skillet for 30 seconds before adding to the coleslaw.

Makes 4 servings

Start to Finish: 15 minutes

1½ cups deli creamy coleslaw
⅓ cup seeded and chopped
    tomato (1 small)
1 teaspoon curry powder
1 7- to 7.1-ounce pouch chunk
    white tuna (water pack),
    drained
4 large butterhead (Boston or
    bibb) lettuce leaves
¼ cup chopped peanuts
    Dairy sour cream chive-flavor
    dip (optional)

1. In a small bowl stir together coleslaw, tomato, and curry powder. Gently fold in tuna.

2. Spoon tuna mixture onto lettuce leaves. Sprinkle with peanuts. If desired, spoon dip on top of tuna mixture.

Per serving: 148 cal., 7 g total fat (1 g sat. fat), 21 mg chol., 213 mg sodium, 9 g carbo., 2 g fiber, 14 g pro.

Hot

TUNA HOAGIES

This open-face sandwich is otherwise known as a tuna melt. *Makes 4 open-face sandwiches*

Start to Finish: **25 minutes**

1½ cups packaged shredded cabbage with carrot (coleslaw mix)

1 9.25-ounce can chunk white tuna (water pack), drained and broken into small chunks

2 tablespoons mayonnaise or salad dressing

2 tablespoons bottled buttermilk ranch, creamy cucumber, or creamy Parmesan salad dressing

2 hoagie buns, split and toasted

2 ounces cheddar or Swiss cheese, thinly sliced

1. Preheat broiler. In a medium bowl combine cabbage and tuna. In a small bowl stir together mayonnaise and ranch salad dressing. Pour mayonnaise mixture over tuna mixture; toss gently to coat.

2. Spoon tuna mixture onto bun halves. Place on the unheated rack of a broiler pan or on a baking sheet. Broil 4 to 5 inches from the heat for 2 to 3 minutes or until heated through. Top with cheese. Broil for 30 to 60 seconds more or until cheese is melted.

Per open-face sandwich: 406 cal., 19 g total fat (6 g sat. fat), 39 mg chol., 704 mg sodium, 38 g carbo., 2 g fiber, 20 g pro.

Thai TUNA WRAPS

With the same light and fresh flavors of traditional spring rolls, these "sandwiches" are wrapped up in easy-to-find, easy-to-roll tortillas instead of rice paper. *Makes 6 wraps*

Start to Finish: **30 minutes**

4 ounces dried thin spaghetti, broken
²⁄₃ cup lime juice
¹⁄₃ cup fish sauce
2 tablespoons sugar
2 tablespoons rice vinegar
2 tablespoons soy sauce
¹⁄₂ cup snipped fresh cilantro or parsley
2 fresh Thai chile peppers or jalapeño chile peppers, seeded and finely chopped (see note, page 22)
1 12- or 12.25-ounce can solid white tuna, drained and broken into chunks
¹⁄₃ cup shredded carrot (1 small)
2 cups coarsely chopped romaine lettuce
6 9- to 10-inch flour tortillas, warmed

1. Cook pasta according to package directions; drain. Rinse with cold water; drain again.
2. Meanwhile, in a small bowl combine lime juice, fish sauce, sugar, vinegar, and soy sauce. Stir in cilantro and chile pepper.
3. In a large bowl combine cooked pasta, ¹⁄₄ cup of the lime juice mixture, tuna, and carrot; toss gently to moisten.

4. To assemble, place ¹⁄₃ cup of the lettuce on each tortilla just below the center. Top each with ¹⁄₂ cup of the tuna mixture. Fold bottom edge of each tortilla up and over filling. Fold in opposite sides; roll up tortilla. Cut each in half crosswise. Serve with the remaining lime juice mixture for dipping.

Per wrap: 319 cal., 6 g total fat (1 g sat. fat), 24 mg chol., 1,930 mg sodium, 45 g carbo., 2 g fiber, 21 g pro.

Asian-Style Noodles
WITH CLAMS

Clams acquire an Asian flair when teamed with sweet peppers, fresh ginger, garlic, crushed red pepper, and soy sauce. *Makes 4 servings*

Start to Finish: **30 minutes**

8 ounces dried linguine

½ cup shredded fresh spinach

1 teaspoon toasted sesame oil or olive oil

2 6.5-ounce cans chopped or minced clams, undrained

2 teaspoons cornstarch

1 tablespoon olive oil

2 cups thin bite-size strips red and/or yellow sweet pepper (2 medium)

1 tablespoon grated fresh ginger

½ teaspoon bottled minced garlic (1 clove)

¼ teaspoon crushed red pepper

1 tablespoon soy sauce

1. Cook linguine according to package directions; drain. Return to hot pan. Stir in spinach and sesame oil. Cover and keep warm.

2. Meanwhile, drain clams, reserving liquid. Measure ¾ cup of the clam liquid (if necessary, add enough water to clam liquid to equal ¾ cup). In a small bowl stir clam liquid into cornstarch; set aside.

3. In a large skillet heat olive oil over medium-high heat. Add sweet pepper, ginger, garlic, and crushed red pepper; cook and stir for 3 minutes. Stir in clam liquid mixture and soy sauce. Cook and stir over medium heat until thickened and bubbly. Cook and stir for 1 minute more. Stir in clams. Cook and stir about 1 minute or until clams are heated through.

4. Serve clam mixture over linguine mixture.

Per serving: 414 cal., 7 g total fat (1 g sat. fat), 62 mg chol., 340 mg sodium, 53 g carbo., 3 g fiber, 32 g pro.

IN-A-PINCH **TIPS!**

SAUCE AND GRAVY THICKENER: SUBSTITUTE 1 TEASPOON CORNSTARCH FOR EVERY 2 TEASPOONS FLOUR OR VICE VERSA.

Shrimp
ALFREDO

Watch for specials on frozen shrimp and stock up. It is a good seafood to have in reserve for "special treat" nights. *Makes 4 servings*

Start to Finish: **25 minutes**

3 cups water
1 cup milk
¼ cup butter or margarine
2 4.4-ounce packages noodles
    with Alfredo-style sauce
3 cups thinly sliced zucchini
    (3 small)
1 10- to 12-ounce package
    frozen peeled, cooked
    shrimp, thawed, or
    12 ounces chunk-style
    imitation crabmeat

1. In a large saucepan combine water, milk, and butter. Bring to boiling. Stir in noodle mixes. Return to boiling; reduce heat. Simmer, uncovered, for 5 minutes.

2. Stir in zucchini. Return to a gentle boil. Cook, uncovered, about 3 minutes or until noodles are tender.

3. Gently stir in shrimp; heat through. Remove from heat. Let stand, covered, for 3 to 5 minutes or until slightly thickened.

Per serving: 486 cal., 21 g total fat (12 g sat. fat), 264 mg chol., 1,279 mg sodium, 44 g carbo., 2 g fiber, 30 g pro.

Spicy Jalapeño
SHRIMP PASTA

This is an economical dish to serve during fresh tomato season especially if you grow your own. The juicy, vine-ripened tomatoes help to moisten the pasta. *Makes 4 servings*

Start to Finish: **30 minutes**

12 ounces fresh or frozen large shrimp in shells

8 ounces dried linguine

2 tablespoons olive oil

1 to 2 tablespoons finely chopped fresh jalapeño chile pepper (see note, page 22)

1 teaspoon bottled minced garlic (2 cloves)

½ teaspoon salt

⅛ teaspoon ground black pepper

2 cups chopped tomato and/or halved or quartered cherry tomato

Finely shredded Parmesan cheese (optional)

1. Thaw shrimp, if frozen. Peel and devein shrimp. Rinse shrimp; pat dry with paper towels. Set aside. Cook linguine according to package directions; drain. Return linguine to hot pan. Cover and keep warm.

2. Meanwhile, in a large skillet heat oil over medium-high heat. Add jalapeño pepper, garlic, salt, and black pepper; cook and stir for 1 minute. Add shrimp; cook and stir about 3 minutes or until shrimp are opaque. Stir in tomato; heat through.

3. Add shrimp mixture to cooked linguine; toss gently to combine. If desired, sprinkle each serving with cheese.

Per serving: 363 cal., 9 g total fat (1 g sat. fat), 97 mg chol., 396 mg sodium, 48 g carbo., 3 g fiber, 21 g pro.

Spanish-Style Rice
WITH SEAFOOD

A package of Spanish rice is the base for this quick skillet meal. *Makes 4 servings*

Start to Finish: **25 minutes**

1 5.6- to 6.2-ounce package Spanish rice mix
1¾ cups water
1 tablespoon butter or margarine
    Several dashes bottled hot pepper sauce
1 12-ounce package frozen peeled and deveined shrimp
1 cup frozen peas
½ cup chopped tomato (1 medium)

1. In a large skillet combine rice mix, the water, butter, and hot pepper sauce. Bring to boiling; reduce heat. Simmer, covered, for 5 minutes.

2. Stir in shrimp. Return to boiling; reduce heat. Simmer, covered, for 2 to 3 minutes or until shrimp are opaque. Remove from heat. Stir in peas. Let stand, covered, for 10 minutes. Before serving, sprinkle with tomato.

Per serving: 197 cal., 6 g total fat (2 g sat. fat), 137 mg chol., 414 mg sodium, 15 g carbo., 2 g fiber, 21 g pro.

Spinach and
PASTA SALAD WITH SHRIMP

Fresh dill flavors this satisfying pasta shrimp salad. No fresh dill? Use a combination of dried dill and 2 tablespoons snipped fresh parsley. *Makes 6 servings*

Start to Finish: **25 minutes**

1 cup dried medium shell pasta or elbow macaroni
1 10- to 12-ounce package frozen peeled, cooked shrimp, thawed
1 cup chopped red sweet pepper
⅓ cup bottled creamy onion or Caesar salad dressing
2 tablespoons snipped fresh dill (optional)
Salt and ground black pepper
1 6-ounce package fresh baby spinach
4 ounces goat cheese (chèvre), sliced, or feta cheese, crumbled

1. Cook pasta according to package directions; drain. Rinse with cold water; drain again.

2. In a very large bowl, combine cooked pasta, shrimp, and sweet pepper. Drizzle with salad dressing and, if desired, sprinkle with dill; toss gently to coat. Season to taste with salt and black pepper.

3. Divide spinach among 6 salad plates or bowls. Top with shrimp mixture and cheese.

Per serving: 247 cal., 10 g total fat (4 g sat. fat), 156 mg chol., 435 mg sodium, 17 g carbo., 2 g fiber, 23 g pro.

Shrimp-Avocado
HOAGIES

Think of this as a Maine lobster roll made affordable by using shrimp. *Makes 4 sandwiches*

Start to Finish: 15 minutes

1 10- to 12-ounce package
   frozen peeled, cooked
   shrimp, thawed and
   coarsely chopped
2 large avocados, seeded,
   peeled, and chopped
½ cup shredded carrot
   (1 medium)
⅓ cup bottled coleslaw salad
   dressing
4 hoagie buns, split
   Lemon wedges (optional)

1. In a large bowl combine shrimp, avocado, carrot, and salad dressing.

2. Using a spoon, hollow out tops and bottoms of buns, leaving ½-inch shells. Toast buns.

3. Serve shrimp mixture in buns. If desired, serve with lemon wedges.

Per sandwich: 560 cal., 24 g total fat (4 g sat. fat), 144 mg chol., 825 mg sodium, 63 g carbo., 8 g fiber, 25 g pro.

LOOK!

MONEY-SAVING TIPS and HINTS

Need a use for the partial can of chicken broth and/or tomato paste? Transfer the remainder to ice cube trays and freeze. Once frozen, pop the cubes into freezer bags. Label, date, and store in the freezer. Do the same for leftover wine.

CHEAP!

Purchase flour tortillas in bulk for less at your local Mexican market.

Before juicing a lemon, shred all of the peel off the lemon and freeze in a freezer bag.

SAVE! Check uncooked rice, grains, and tofu at bulk prices at local health food markets. **SAVE!**

To stretch milk and thereby cut its price, purchase dry milk powder. Add I quart of the reconstituted milk powder to I quart of fresh milk.

Compare prices for a dozen eggs. Eggs vary in sizes and egg prices change according to the time of the year. In some markets, brown-shelled eggs cost more than white shells or vice versa yet the nutritional value is the same regardless of the color of the eggshell.

Save remaining chipotle peppers in adobo sauce, one or two per container, in the freezer.

Use vegetable recipes that feature in-season vegetables. For example, prepare stuffed peppers in August.

Specialty items such as olives and cheeses are available at attractive prices when purchased in bulk at local import markets, delis, or grocery stores.

CHAPTER 7

Money-Smart MEATLESS

When a bad economy squeezes your budget, stock up on foods from the produce, grains, and nuts sections of your supermarket and your local farmer's market to ease your food spending. This chapter offers a whole world of tasty meatless dishes, so dig in. Served as the main event, meatless meals mean dinner is served in season and in style and with lots of savings.

Vegetable
CHILI

This hearty chili for two features black beans and a multitude of vegetables. *Makes 2 servings*

Prep: **20 minutes** Cook: **Low 6 hours, High 3 hours**

1 15-ounce can black beans, rinsed and drained
1½ cups reduced-sodium tomato juice
1 cup frozen whole kernel corn
¾ cup coarsely chopped zucchini or yellow summer squash
⅓ cup coarsely chopped red or yellow sweet pepper
¼ cup chopped onion
1 teaspoon chili powder
½ teaspoon bottled minced garlic (1 clove)
¼ teaspoon dried oregano, crushed
⅛ teaspoon salt

1. In a 1½-quart slow cooker, combine drained beans, tomato juice, frozen corn, zucchini, sweet pepper, onion, chili powder, garlic, oregano, and salt.

2. Cover and cook on low-heat setting for 6 to 8 hours or on high-heat setting for 3 to 4 hours. If no heat setting is available, cook for 5 to 6 hours.

Per serving: 271 cal., 2 g total fat (0 g sat. fat), 0 mg chol., 790 mg sodium, 59 g carbo., 14 g fiber, 19 g pro.

Two-Bean Chili
WITH AVOCADO

Meatless chili is gaining in popularity for a good reason: It is highly nutritious and inexpensive. Better yet, this recipe cooks in one pot in under 30 minutes! *Makes 4 or 5 servings*

Prep: 15 minutes Cook: 25 minutes

1 cup chopped onion (1 large)
2 teaspoons dried oregano, crushed
2 teaspoons cooking oil or olive oil
2 14.5-ounce cans diced tomatoes, undrained
1 15-ounce can black beans or kidney beans, rinsed and drained
1 15-ounce can pinto beans, rinsed and drained
½ cup bottled salsa
1 ripe medium avocado, seeded, peeled, and chopped
¼ cup snipped fresh cilantro or parsley

1. In a large saucepan cook onion and oregano in hot oil over medium-high heat about 3 minutes or until onion is tender, stirring occasionally. Stir in undrained tomatoes, drained black beans, drained pinto beans, and salsa.

2. Bring to boiling; reduce heat. Simmer, uncovered, about 25 minutes or until chili reaches desired consistency. Top each serving with avocado and cilantro.

Per serving: 325 cal., 10 g total fat (1 g sat. fat), 0 mg chol., 985 mg sodium, 50 g carbo., 15 g fiber, 14 g pro.

Barley VEGETABLE SOUP

Be a dinnertime hero with this long-simmered soup and crusty whole grain bread for a tantalizing supper.

Makes 6 servings

Prep: **25 minutes** Cook: **Low 8 hours, High 4 hours**

2 cups sliced fresh mushrooms

1 15-ounce can red beans, rinsed and drained

1 14.5-ounce can stewed tomatoes, undrained

1 10-ounce package frozen whole kernel corn

1 cup chopped onion (1 large)

½ cup coarsely chopped carrot (1 medium)

½ cup coarsely chopped celery (1 stalk)

½ cup regular barley

2 teaspoons dried Italian seasoning, crushed

1½ teaspoons bottled minced garlic (3 cloves)

¼ teaspoon ground black pepper

5 cups vegetable broth or reduced-sodium chicken broth

1. In a 3½- to 5-quart slow cooker, combine mushrooms, drained beans, undrained tomatoes, frozen corn, onion, carrot, celery, barley, Italian seasoning, garlic, and pepper. Pour broth over mixture in cooker.

2. Cover and cook on low-heat setting for 8 to 10 hours or on high-heat setting for 4 to 5 hours.

Per serving: 228 cal., 2 g total fat (0 g sat. fat), 0 mg chol., 1,211 mg sodium, 47 g carbo., 8 g fiber, 9 g pro.

IN-A-PINCH TIPS!

VEGGIE SCRAPS: SAVE ALL THE ENDS OF ONIONS, CARROT PEELINGS, AND CELERY LEAVES IN A FREEZER BAG IN YOUR FREEZER; ADD THEM TO THE COOKING LIQUID WHEN YOU MAKE HOMEMADE BROTH.

Cheese
ENCHILADA CHOWDER

This richly satisfying soup will impress everyone in the family. Set out the chowder along with bowls and containers of toppings, and let everyone serve themselves. *Makes 6 servings*

Prep: **25 minutes**   Cook: **Low 6 hours, High 3 hours**

1   15-ounce can black beans, rinsed and drained
1   14.5-ounce can diced tomatoes, drained
1   10-ounce package frozen whole kernel corn
½   cup chopped onion (1 medium)
½   cup chopped yellow, green, or red sweet pepper (1 small)
1   small fresh jalapeño chile pepper, seeded (if desired) and finely chopped (see note, page 22)
1   10.75-ounce can condensed cream of chicken soup
1   10-ounce can enchilada sauce
2   cups milk
1   cup shredded Monterey Jack cheese (4 ounces)
1   cup shredded cheddar cheese (4 ounces)
    Dairy sour cream (optional)
    Purchased guacamole (optional)
    Coarsely broken tortilla chips (optional)

1. In a 3½- to 5-quart slow cooker, combine drained beans, drained tomatoes, frozen corn, onion, sweet pepper, and jalapeño pepper. In a large bowl combine soup and enchilada sauce. Gradually stir in milk. Pour soup mixture over mixture in cooker.

2. Cover and cook on low-heat setting for 6 to 8 hours or on high-heat setting for 3 to 4 hours. Gradually add Monterey Jack cheese and cheddar cheese, stirring until cheeses are melted.

3. If desired, top each serving with sour cream, guacamole, and tortilla chips.

Per serving: 374 cal., 18 g total fat (10 g sat. fat), 47 mg chol., 1,536 mg sodium, 37 g carbo., 6 g fiber, 21 g pro.

Cream
OF VEGETABLE SOUP

This isn't an ordinary vegetable soup. Garbanzo beans and potatoes make it hefty enough to stand in for a full meal when served with hearty bread and a salad. *Makes 6 to 8 servings*

Prep: **20 minutes** Cook: **Low 7 hours, High 3½ hours; plus 15 minutes on High**

1 16-ounce package frozen
    small whole onions
2 cups cubed potato
    (2 medium)
2 cups sliced carrot
    (4 medium)
1 15-ounce can garbanzo
    beans (chickpeas) or navy
    beans, rinsed and drained
1 10-ounce package frozen
    whole kernel corn
1 cup sliced celery (2 stalks)
½ teaspoon salt
½ teaspoon paprika
½ teaspoon ground black
    pepper
2 14-ounce cans vegetable
    broth or chicken broth
1½ cups half-and-half or
    light cream
¼ cup all-purpose flour
    Salt and ground black pepper

1. In a 4½- to 5½-quart slow cooker combine frozen onions, potato, carrot, drained beans, frozen corn, celery, the ½ teaspoon salt, the paprika, and the ½ teaspoon pepper. Pour broth over mixture in cooker.
2. Cover and cook on low-heat setting for 7 to 9 hours or on high-heat setting for 3½ to 4½ hours. If using low-heat setting, turn to high-heat setting.

3. In a medium bowl gradually stir half-and-half into flour; stir into mixture in cooker. Cover and cook for 15 minutes more. Season to taste with salt and pepper.

Per serving: 282 cal., 9 g total fat (4 g sat. fat), 22 mg chol., 1,079 mg sodium, 48 g carbo., 8 g fiber, 9 g pro.

Hearty
ONION-LENTIL SOUP

A combination French onion and bean soup, this mix tastes great ladled over melted cheese-topped toasts. *Makes 6 servings*

Prep: **20 minutes** Cook: **Low 6 hours, High 3 hours**

4 cups water

2 10.5-ounce cans condensed French onion soup

2 cups sliced celery (4 stalks) or carrot (4 medium)

1 cup lentils, rinsed and drained

6 ¾-inch slices crusty country French bread, toasted

1 cup shredded Swiss or Gruyère cheese (4 ounces)

1. In a 3½- or 4-quart slow cooker, combine the water, soup, celery, and lentils.

2. Cover and cook on low-heat setting for 6 to 8 hours or on high-heat setting for 3 to 4 hours.

3. Before serving, preheat broiler. Arrange toasted bread slices on a baking sheet; sprinkle with cheese. Broil 3 to 4 inches from the heat for 2 to 3 minutes or until cheese is light brown and bubbly.

4. Divide cheese-topped bread among 6 soup bowls; ladle soup over bread.

Per serving: 345 cal., 9 g total fat (4 g sat. fat), 19 mg chol., 1,130 mg sodium, 48 g carbo., 12 g fiber, 20 g pro.

Vegetarian
GUMBO

Okra and gumbo are a perfect culinary marriage. Okra makes this stew taste special and also helps to thicken it. See photo on page 281. *Makes 6 servings*

Prep: 10 minutes   Cook: Low 6 hours, High 3 hours

2 15-ounce cans black beans, rinsed and drained
1 28-ounce can diced tomatoes, undrained
1 16-ounce package frozen sweet pepper stir-fry vegetables
2 cups frozen cut okra
2 to 3 teaspoons Cajun seasoning
3 cups hot cooked white or brown rice (optional)
Chopped green onion (optional)

1. In a 3½- to 4½-quart slow cooker combine drained beans, undrained tomatoes, frozen stir-fry vegetables, frozen okra, and Cajun seasoning.

2. Cover and cook on low-heat setting for 6 to 8 hours or on high-heat setting for 3 to 4 hours. If desired, serve over hot cooked rice and sprinkle with green onion.

Per serving: 153 cal., 0 g total fat (0 g sat. fat), 0 mg chol., 639 mg sodium, 31 g carbo., 10 g fiber, 12 g pro.

Easy Chicken and Dumplings
Recipe on page 194

Pulled Chicken Sandwich

Recipe on page 196

Salmon Confetti Chowder

Recipe on page 252

Chicken and Pasta Salad

Recipe on page 343

Creamed Corn Casserole

Recipe on page 368

Peanut Butter Swirl Ice Cream Cake

Recipe on page 398

Fettuccine
AND VEGETABLES ALFREDO

Keep all the ingredients for this satisfying dish on hand in the pantry for a fix-it-fast weeknight meal.

Makes 4 servings

Start to Finish: **20 minutes**

1 16-ounce package frozen
   sugar snap pea stir-fry
   vegetables
1 cup frozen shelled sweet
   soybeans (edamame)
1 9-ounce package
   refrigerated fettuccine
1 16-ounce jar Alfredo pasta
   sauce
½ cup finely shredded
   Parmesan cheese
   (2 ounces)
¼ cup milk
2 tablespoons refrigerated
   basil pesto

1. In a 4-quart Dutch oven, bring a large amount of water to boiling. Add stir-fry vegetables and soybeans; cook for 3 minutes. Add fettuccine. Cook about 3 minutes more or until fettuccine is tender but still firm; drain. Return fettuccine mixture to Dutch oven.

2. Meanwhile, in a medium saucepan combine pasta sauce, ¼ cup of the cheese, the milk, and pesto. Cook and stir until heated through. Add cheese mixture to fettuccine mixture; toss gently to coat.

3. Divide fettuccine mixture among 4 dinner plates. Sprinkle with the remaining ¼ cup cheese.

Per serving: 691 cal., 37 g total fat (16 g sat. fat), 117 mg chol., 1107 mg sodium, 61 g carbo., 7 g fiber, 28 g pro.

Easy
CHEESY PASTA

Do what Italian cooks do: Save a small amount of pasta water to stir into the pasta mixture if it is too thick and dry. *Makes 4 servings*

Start to Finish: **20 minutes**

8 ounces dried penne, rotini, or gemelli pasta

2 cups frozen cauliflower, broccoli, and carrots

1 10-ounce container refrigerated light Alfredo pasta sauce

¼ cup milk

1 cup shredded cheddar cheese (4 ounces)

½ cup finely shredded Parmesan cheese (2 ounces)

¼ cup chopped walnuts, toasted

1. In a 4-quart Dutch oven, cook pasta according to package directions, adding frozen vegetables during the last 4 minutes of cooking; drain. Return pasta mixture to Dutch oven.

2. Meanwhile, in a medium saucepan combine pasta sauce and milk. Cook and stir over medium heat just until bubbly. Reduce heat to low. Gradually add cheddar cheese and Parmesan cheese, stirring until cheeses are melted.

3. Add cheese mixture to pasta mixture; toss gently to coat. Heat through. Sprinkle each serving with walnuts.

Per serving: 586 cal., 28 g total fat (15 g sat. fat), 70 mg chol., 1,054 mg sodium, 57 g carbo., 3 g fiber, 26 g pro.

Tofu MANICOTTI

Vegetarians in your crowd will be grateful when you serve a meatless version of this ever-favorite casserole. *Makes 4 servings*

Prep: **40 minutes** Bake: **32 minutes** Stand: **10 minutes** Oven: **350°F**

8 dried manicotti shells
  Nonstick cooking spray
1 cup chopped fresh
  mushrooms
½ cup chopped green onion (4)
1 teaspoon dried Italian
  seasoning, crushed
1 12.3- or 16-ounce package
  soft tofu (fresh bean curd),
  drained
1 egg, lightly beaten
¼ cup finely shredded
  Parmesan cheese (1 ounce)
1 14.5-ounce can diced
  tomatoes with basil, garlic,
  and oregano, undrained
1 11-ounce can condensed
  tomato bisque soup
⅛ teaspoon ground black
  pepper
¾ cup shredded Italian cheese
  blend (3 ounces)

1. Preheat oven to 350°F. Cook manicotti shells according to package directions; drain. Rinse with cold water; drain again.
2. Meanwhile, coat a medium skillet with cooking spray; heat skillet over medium heat. Add mushrooms and green onion; cook until tender, stirring occasionally. Stir in Italian seasoning; set aside.
3. In a medium bowl mash tofu. Stir in mushroom mixture, egg, and Parmesan cheese. Gently spoon about ¼ cup of the tofu mixture into each manicotti shell. Arrange stuffed shells in a single layer in an ungreased 3-quart rectangular baking dish.

4. In a medium bowl combine undrained tomatoes, soup, and pepper. Pour tomato mixture over stuffed shells.
5. Bake, uncovered, about 30 minutes or until heated through. Sprinkle with Italian cheese. Bake, uncovered, about 2 minutes more or until cheese is melted. Let stand for 10 minutes before serving.

Per serving: 411 cal., 13 g total fat (6 g sat. fat), 74 mg chol., 1,383 mg sodium, 53 g carbo., 4 g fiber, 21 g pro.

VEGETABLE LASAGNA

Roasting brings out the earthy flavors of the vegetables that pack this delicious nonmeat lasagna with lots of pizzazz. *Makes 9 servings*

Prep: **30 minutes** Bake: **50 minutes** Broil: **12 minutes** Stand: **10 minutes** Oven: **375°F**

12 dried lasagna noodles

4 cups bite-size pieces zucchini

2½ cups thinly sliced carrot (5 medium)

2 cups fresh mushrooms, halved

1½ cups coarsely chopped red or green sweet pepper (2 medium)

¼ cup olive oil

1 tablespoon dried Italian seasoning, crushed

½ teaspoon salt

½ teaspoon ground black pepper

1 egg, lightly beaten

1 12-ounce carton cream-style cottage cheese, undrained

½ cup grated Parmesan cheese

1 26-ounce jar marinara sauce

3 cups shredded mozzarella cheese (12 ounces)

1. Cook lasagna noodles according to package directions; drain. Rinse with cold water; drain again. Place noodles in a single layer on a piece of foil; set aside.

2. Meanwhile, preheat broiler. In a very large bowl combine zucchini, carrot, mushrooms, and sweet pepper. Drizzle vegetables with oil. Sprinkle with Italian seasoning, salt, and black pepper; toss gently to combine.

3. Transfer vegetables to a shallow roasting pan. Broil 5 to 6 inches from the heat for 12 to 14 minutes or until vegetables are tender and light brown, stirring once halfway through broiling. Set vegetables aside.

4. Reduce oven temperature to 375°F. Grease a 3-quart rectangular baking dish or 13×9×2-inch baking pan; set aside. In a medium bowl combine egg, undrained cottage cheese, and ¼ cup of the Parmesan cheese.

5. To assemble, spread one-third of the marinara sauce in the bottom of the prepared baking dish. Layer 4 of the cooked noodles in the dish. Top with half of the roasted vegetables, one-third of the marinara sauce, and one-third of the mozzarella cheese. Add 4 more noodles, all of the cottage cheese mixture, and one-third of the mozzarella cheese. Add the remaining 4 noodles, the remaining vegetables, the remaining marinara sauce, and the remaining mozzarella cheese. Sprinkle with the remaining ¼ cup Parmesan cheese.

6. Bake, covered, for 30 minutes. Bake, uncovered, about 20 minutes more or until heated through. Let stand for 10 minutes before serving.

Per serving: 420 cal., 21 g total fat (8 g sat. fat), 3 mg chol., 1,020 mg sodium, 37 g carbo., 3 g fiber, 22 g pro.

Greek
PASTA CASSEROLE

Cooks from countries bordering the Mediterranean know how to stretch meat—or leave it out entirely—and still serve fully satisfying, full-flavored meals. This lively Greek-inspired casserole is proof positive!

Makes 6 servings

Prep: **25 minutes** Bake: **20 minutes** Stand: **10 minutes** Oven: **375°F**

12 ounces dried rotini pasta

1 15-ounce can tomato sauce

1 10.75-ounce can condensed tomato soup

2 cups crumbled feta cheese (8 ounces)

1 15-ounce can cannellini (white kidney) beans or garbanzo beans (chickpeas), rinsed and drained

1 cup coarsely chopped, pitted Greek black olives

½ cup seasoned fine dry bread crumbs

2 tablespoons butter or margarine, melted

2 tablespoons grated Parmesan cheese

1. Preheat oven to 375°F. Lightly grease a 3-quart rectangular baking dish; set aside. Cook pasta according to package directions; drain. In a very large bowl, combine cooked pasta, tomato sauce, and soup. Stir in feta cheese, drained beans, and olives. Transfer pasta mixture to the prepared baking dish.

2. In a small bowl combine bread crumbs, melted butter, and Parmesan cheese; sprinkle over pasta mixture.

3. Bake, uncovered, for 20 to 25 minutes or until heated through and top is light brown. Let stand for 10 minutes before serving.

Per serving: 553 cal., 19 g total fat (10 g sat. fat), 52 mg chol., 1,890 mg sodium, 74 g carbo., 7 g fiber, 24 g pro.

Company Macaroni
AND CHEESE

You can use cavatelli, gnocchi, or campanelle pasta instead of the elbow macaroni called for in this hearty version of macaroni and cheese. *Makes 4 to 6 servings*

Prep: **25 minutes** Bake: **30 minutes** Stand: **10 minutes** Oven: **350°F**

12 ounces dried tricolor bow tie, penne, and/or rotini pasta
2 tablespoons butter or margarine
1 teaspoon bottled minced garlic (2 cloves)
2 tablespoons all-purpose flour
2 cups milk
2 cups shredded smoked or regular Gouda cheese (8 ounces)
1 cup shredded American cheese (4 ounces)
2 tablespoons snipped fresh oregano or 1 teaspoon dried oregano, crushed
½ cup soft whole wheat bread crumbs

1. Preheat oven to 350°F. Cook pasta according to package directions; drain.

2. Meanwhile, in a large saucepan melt butter over medium heat. Add garlic; cook and stir for 30 seconds. Stir in flour. Gradually stir in milk. Cook and stir until thickened and bubbly; reduce heat to low. Gradually add Gouda cheese and American cheese, stirring until cheeses are melted. Remove from heat. Stir in cooked pasta and oregano.

3. Transfer pasta mixture to an ungreased 2-quart casserole. Sprinkle with bread crumbs. Bake, uncovered, about 30 minutes or until heated through. Let stand for 10 minutes before serving.

Per serving: 794 cal., 36 g total fat (22 g sat. fat), 123 mg chol., 1,111 mg sodium, 77 g carbo., 3 g fiber, 38 g pro.

Butternut

SQUASH LASAGNA

This recipe is based on a classic Italian ravioli-filled squash dish that is time-consuming to prepare. Not so here. No-cook lasagna noodles are layered with a squash mixture for a meatless main dish with the same great taste. *Makes 8 to 10 servings*

Prep: **45 minutes** Bake: **50 minutes** Stand: **10 minutes** Oven: **425°F/375°F**

3 pounds butternut squash, seeded, peeled, and cut into ¼- to ½-inch slices

3 tablespoons olive oil

½ teaspoon salt

¼ cup butter or margarine

1 tablespoon bottled minced garlic (6 cloves)

¼ cup all-purpose flour

½ teaspoon salt

4 cups milk

1 tablespoon snipped fresh rosemary or 1 teaspoon dried rosemary, crushed

9 no-boil lasagna noodles

1⅓ cups finely shredded Parmesan cheese

1 cup whipping cream

1. Preheat oven to 425°F. Lightly grease a 15×10×1-inch baking pan. Place squash in the prepared baking pan. Add oil and ½ teaspoon salt; toss gently to coat. Spread squash in an even layer. Roast, uncovered, for 25 to 30 minutes or until squash is tender, stirring once. Reduce oven temperature to 375°F.

2. Meanwhile, for sauce, in a large saucepan melt butter over medium heat. Add garlic; cook and stir for 1 minute. Stir in flour and ½ teaspoon salt. Gradually stir in milk. Cook and stir until thickened and bubbly. Stir in squash and rosemary.

3. To assemble, lightly grease a 3-quart rectangular baking dish or 13×9×2-inch baking pan. Spread about 1 cup of the sauce in the bottom of the prepared baking dish. Top with 3 of the lasagna noodles, one-third of the remaining sauce, and ⅓ cup of the cheese. Repeat layering noodles, sauce, and cheese two more times. Pour cream evenly over layers in dish. Sprinkle with the remaining ⅓ cup cheese.

4. Bake lasagna, covered, for 40 minutes. Bake, uncovered, about 10 minutes more or until edges are bubbly and top is light brown. Let stand for 10 minutes before serving.

Make-Ahead Directions: **Prepare as directed through Step 3. Cover unbaked lasagna with foil; chill for 2 to 24 hours. To serve, preheat oven to 375°F. Bake, covered, for 45 minutes. Bake, uncovered, for 10 to 15 minutes more or until edges are bubbly and top is light brown. Let stand for 10 minutes before serving.**

Per serving: 525 cal., 29 g total fat (15 g sat. fat), 76 mg chol., 628 mg sodium, 53 g carbo., 4 g fiber, 16 g pro.

Vegetable
FRIED RICE

With this no-hassle recipe, you can enjoy a Chinese classic at home in just minutes. *Makes 4 servings*

Start to Finish: **20 minutes**

1 teaspoon toasted sesame oil
   or cooking oil
2 eggs, lightly beaten
⅓ cup rice vinegar
¼ cup soy sauce
⅛ teaspoon ground ginger
⅛ teaspoon crushed red pepper
1 tablespoon cooking oil
1 cup sliced fresh mushrooms
1 teaspoon bottled minced
   garlic (2 cloves)
2 8.8-ounce pouches cooked
   long grain rice
½ cup frozen peas
1 2-ounce jar diced pimiento,
   drained
¼ cup chopped peanuts
   (optional)

1. In a large skillet heat sesame oil over medium heat. Add half of the egg, lifting and tilting skillet to form a thin layer (egg may not completely cover bottom of skillet). Cook about 1 minute or until set. Invert skillet over a baking sheet to remove cooked egg; cut into strips and set aside. Repeat with the remaining egg.

2. In a small bowl stir together vinegar, soy sauce, ginger, and crushed red pepper; set aside.

3. In the same skillet heat the 1 tablespoon cooking oil over medium-high heat. Add mushrooms and garlic; cook about 3 minutes or until mushrooms are tender, stirring occasionally. Stir in vinegar mixture, rice, peas, and pimiento.

4. Cook and stir about 2 minutes or until heated through and liquid is nearly evaporated. Stir in egg strips. If desired, sprinkle each serving with peanuts.

Per serving: 314 cal., 10 g total fat (1 g sat. fat), 106 mg chol., 999 mg sodium, 45 g carbo., 3 g fiber, 10 g pro.

IN-A-PINCH TIPS!

EGG MATH: THE EGGS USED IN TESTING OUR RECIPES WERE LARGE EGGS.
FOR EGG SUBSTITUTIONS:
2 LARGE EGGS=2 EXTRA-LARGE, 2 MEDIUM, OR 3 SMALL EGGS
3 LARGE EGGS=3 EXTRA-LARGE, 3 MEDIUM, OR 4 SMALL EGGS
4 LARGE EGGS=4 EXTRA-LARGE, 5 MEDIUM, OR 5 SMALL EGGS
5 LARGE EGGS=4 EXTRA-LARGE, 6 MEDIUM, OR 7 SMALL EGGS
6 LARGE EGGS=5 EXTRA-LARGE, 7 MEDIUM, OR 8 SMALL EGGS

Savory
STUFFED PORTOBELLOS

Portobello mushrooms have a rich flavor and dense, meaty texture. The stems tend to be woody so trim and discard them. *Makes 6 servings*

Prep: **35 minutes** Bake: **15 minutes** Oven: **350°F**

Nonstick cooking spray
½ cup chopped onion
  (1 medium)
2 teaspoons bottled minced
  garlic (4 cloves)
1 6.75- to 8-ounce package
  rice pilaf with lentil mix
1 6-ounce jar marinated
  artichoke hearts, undrained
6 medium fresh portobello
  mushroom caps (about
  4 inches in diameter)
¼ cup finely shredded
  Parmesan cheese (1 ounce)
  (optional)

1. Preheat oven to 350°F. Coat a medium saucepan with cooking spray; heat saucepan over medium-high heat. Add onion and garlic; cook until tender, stirring occasionally. In the same saucepan with the onion and garlic, cook rice pilaf mix according to package directions.
2. Meanwhile, drain artichokes, reserving marinade. Coarsely chop artichokes; set aside. If desired, remove gills from undersides of mushrooms. Brush mushrooms with some of the reserved marinade; discard any remaining marinade.

3. Place mushroom caps, stemmed sides up, in an ungreased shallow baking pan. Bake, uncovered, for 15 to 20 minutes or until mushrooms are tender. Transfer to 6 dinner plates.
4. Add artichokes and, if desired, cheese to hot rice pilaf; stir to combine. Spoon pilaf into baked mushrooms.

Per serving: 288 cal., 14 g total fat (5 g sat. fat), 16 mg chol., 817 mg sodium, 31 g carbo., 4 g fiber, 20 g pro.

Fruited Couscous
AND BEANS

Golden raisins and mixed dried fruit bits lend subtle sweetness to this pinto bean and couscous combo.

Makes 6 servings

Prep: **20 minutes**   Cook: **Low 6 hours, High 3 hours**   Stand: **5 minutes**

2 15-ounce cans Great Northern beans or pinto beans, rinsed and drained

1 cup finely chopped onion (1 large)

1 cup golden raisins

1 cup mixed dried fruit bits

2 teaspoons grated fresh ginger

¾ teaspoon salt

¼ teaspoon crushed red pepper

1 14-ounce can vegetable broth or chicken broth

1¾ cups unsweetened pineapple juice

1 10-ounce package couscous

1 tablespoon olive oil

½ cup sliced almonds, toasted
Sliced green onion (optional)

1. In a 3½- or 4-quart slow cooker, combine drained beans, onion, raisins, fruit bits, ginger, salt, and crushed red pepper. Pour broth and pineapple juice over mixture in cooker.

2. Cover and cook on low-heat setting for 6 to 7 hours or on high-heat setting for 3 to 3½ hours.

3. Remove liner from cooker, if possible, or turn off cooker. Stir in couscous and oil. Let stand, covered, for 5 to 10 minutes or until couscous is tender. Fluff with a fork. Sprinkle each serving with almonds and, if desired, green onion.

Per serving: 623 cal., 9 g total fat (1 g sat. fat), 0 mg chol., 596 mg sodium, 120 g carbo., 14 g fiber, 22 g pro.

Brown
RICE PRIMAVERA

Flecks of colorful zucchini, sweet peppers, and tomatoes dress up brown rice in this cheesy one-dish slow cooker meal. *Makes 6 servings*

Prep: **25 minutes** Cook: **High 2½ hours**

1 medium eggplant (1 pound), peeled (if desired) and cubed

2 medium zucchini, halved lengthwise and cut into ½-inch pieces

1 medium onion, cut into thin wedges

1 14-ounce can vegetable broth

2 cups thin bite-size strips red and/or yellow sweet pepper (2 medium)

1 14.5-ounce can diced tomatoes with basil, garlic, and oregano, drained

1 cup uncooked instant brown rice

2 cups crumbled feta cheese (8 ounces)

1. In a 5- to 6-quart slow cooker, combine eggplant, zucchini, and onion. Pour broth over mixture in cooker. Cover and cook on high-heat setting for 2 to 2½ hours.

2. Stir in sweet pepper, drained tomatoes, and brown rice. Cover and cook for 30 minutes more. Sprinkle each serving with cheese.

Per serving: 212 cal., 9 g total fat (6 g sat. fat), 34 mg chol., 1,045 mg sodium, 26 g carbo., 5 g fiber, 9 g pro.

Meatless
SHEPHERD'S PIE

The mix of white kidney beans and soybeans packs in lots of protein for this potato-topped one-dish meal. You can substitute lima beans for the edamame. *Makes 8 servings*

Prep: **25 minutes**   Cook: Low 10 hours, High 5 hours; plus 30 minutes on High

2 19-ounce cans cannellini (white kidney) beans, rinsed and drained
1 14.5-ounce can diced tomatoes, drained
1 12-ounce package frozen shelled sweet soybeans (edamame)
1 12-ounce jar mushroom gravy
1½ cups sliced carrot (3 medium)
1 large onion, cut into wedges
1 teaspoon bottled minced garlic (2 cloves)
1 24-ounce package refrigerated mashed potatoes
1 cup shredded cheddar cheese (4 ounces)

1. In a 5- to 6-quart slow cooker, combine drained beans, drained tomatoes, frozen soybeans, gravy, carrot, onion, and garlic.

2. Cover and cook on low-heat setting for 10 to 12 hours or on high-heat setting for 5 to 6 hours.

3. If using low-heat setting, turn to high-heat setting. Spoon mashed potatoes in mounds on top of bean mixture. Sprinkle with cheese. Cover and cook about 30 minutes more or until potatoes are heated through.

Per serving: 320 cal., 9 g total fat (3 g sat. fat), 15 mg chol., 805 mg sodium, 47 g carbo., 13 g fiber, 20 g pro.

IN-A-PINCH TIPS!

EDAMAME SUBSTITUTE: USE FROZEN BABY LIMA BEANS INSTEAD; COOKING TIME IS THE SAME.

*Rice-Stuffed*

PEPPERS

Select sweet peppers that have flat bottoms or trim a small amount off the bottom so they won't tip over during cooking. *Makes 4 servings*

Prep: **25 minutes** Cook: **Low 5 hours, High 2½ hours**

4 medium red, green, and/or yellow sweet peppers
1½ cups frozen shelled sweet soybeans (edamame)
1 cup cooked converted rice
½ cup shredded carrot (1 medium)
¼ cup stir-fry sauce
½ cup water
1 tablespoon sesame seeds, toasted

1. Remove tops, seeds, and membranes from sweet peppers; set peppers aside. Chop enough of the tops to equal ⅓ cup. In a medium bowl combine the ⅓ cup chopped pepper, frozen soybeans, cooked rice, carrot, and stir-fry sauce. Spoon rice mixture into pepper shells.
2. Pour the water into a 4- to 5-quart slow cooker. Place sweet peppers, filled sides up, in the cooker.

3. Cover and cook on low-heat setting for 5 to 6 hours or on high-heat setting for 2½ to 3 hours.
4. Transfer sweet peppers to a serving platter. Sprinkle with sesame seeds.

Per serving: 184 cal., 3 g total fat (0 g sat. fat), 1 mg chol., 385 mg sodium, 30 g carbo., 8 g fiber, 10 g pro.

Meatless
BURRITOS

Everyone likes burritos, and this recipe makes enough to serve a crowd. For easy accompaniments pick up a fruit salad from the deli and a package or two of Mexican-style rice mix. *Makes 8 servings*

Prep: **20 minutes** Cook: Low 6 hours, High 3 hours

3 15-ounce cans red kidney beans and/or black beans, drained and rinsed
1 14.5-ounce can diced tomatoes, undrained
1½ cups bottled salsa or picante sauce
1 11-ounce can whole kernel corn with sweet peppers, drained
1 tablespoon seeded and finely chopped fresh jalapeño chile pepper (see note, page 22) (optional)
2 teaspoons chili powder
1 teaspoon bottled minced garlic (2 cloves)
16 8- to 10-inch flour tortillas, warmed
2 cups shredded lettuce
1 cup shredded taco cheese or cheddar cheese (4 ounces)
Sliced green onion and/or dairy sour cream (optional)

1. In a 3½- or 4-quart slow cooker, combine drained beans, undrained tomatoes, salsa, drained corn, jalapeño pepper (if desired), chili powder, and garlic.
2. Cover and cook on low-heat setting for 6 to 8 hours or on high-heat setting for 3 to 4 hours.

3. To assemble, spoon bean mixture onto tortillas just below the centers. Top with lettuce, cheese, and, if desired, green onion and/or sour cream. Fold bottom edge of each tortilla up and over filling. Fold in opposite sides; roll up tortilla.

Per serving: 417 cal., 5 g total fat (4 g sat. fat), 14 mg chol., 1,126 mg sodium, 69 g carbo., 12 g fiber, 17 g pro.

IN-A-PINCH TIPS!

FRESH JALAPEÑO OPTION: USE BOTTLED HOT PEPPER SAUCE OR GROUND RED PEPPER.

Skillet
EGGPLANT PARMIGIANA

This speedy stove-top version is as satisfying as the classic baked casserole. Best of all, this one-skillet recipe makes for extra easy cleanup. *Makes 4 servings*

Start to Finish: **30 minutes**

1 medium eggplant (1 pound)
1 egg, lightly beaten
1 tablespoon water
½ cup grated Parmesan cheese
¼ cup seasoned fine dry bread crumbs
2 tablespoons olive oil or cooking oil
1¼ cups bottled meatless spaghetti sauce
1 cup shredded mozzarella cheese (4 ounces)
¼ cup snipped fresh basil
2 tablespoons finely chopped walnuts

1. If desired, peel eggplant. Cut eggplant into ¾-inch slices. In a shallow dish combine egg and the water. In another shallow dish combine ¼ cup of the Parmesan cheese and the bread crumbs. Dip eggplant into egg mixture, then into crumb mixture, turning to coat.

2. In a 12-inch skillet heat oil over medium heat. Add eggplant; cook for 6 to 8 minutes or until golden brown, turning once. Add spaghetti sauce; sprinkle with mozzarella cheese and the remaining ¼ cup Parmesan cheese. Reduce heat to medium-low. Cover; cook for 5 minutes.

3. Before serving, sprinkle with basil and walnuts.

Per serving: 295 cal., 20 g total fat (7 g sat. fat), 48 mg chol., 850 mg sodium, 18 g carbo., 5 g fiber, 15 g pro.

LOOK!

MONEY-SAVING TIPS and HINTS

 **Shred to save! Purchasing shredded cheese may cost up to 20% more than if you shred your own.**

$ Use a less expensive brand of wine for cooking. There are some great buys at discount stores and superstores. $

Yes! Only need ½ cup of broth? Rather than open a can, add ½ teaspoon bouillon granules to ½ cup water.

Want to skip the deli and save? Make your own cole slaw. In a large bowl combine a bag of purchased coleslaw and desired amount of bottled coleslaw dressing. Toss to combine.

CHEAP! Purchase whole mushrooms and slice them for all recipes that call for sliced mushrooms.

$AVE SOME BREAD!

Larger grocery chains often offer store brand refrigerated biscuit varieties in the same size packages as those made by name brand manufacturers for significantly less money.

Substitute your colors. When out of season, red, yellow, and/or orange sweet peppers are 2 to 3 times the cost of green sweet peppers. Substitute green sweet peppers any time.

Sale! **Shop the day-old section of your local bakery for hoagie buns. They are perfect for any toasted sandwich—especially sandwiches that call for soaking up flavorful au jus. (French Dip Sandwich, page 311.)** *Sale!*

 **$AVE!** **Worth the trip! A greater variety of salsas, chiles, and other specialty items are available in Mexican markets and they are usually cheaper than those in the grocery store.**

CHAPTER 8

COOK ONCE, EAT TWICE

Economical slow cookers are the perfect appliance for cooking large quantities of food. Besides their time and energy efficiency, slow cookers transform inexpensive cuts of meat into juicy, full-of-flavor main dishes. This unsupervised long, slow cooking is what today's hectic lifestyles demand. With these recipes, plan to cook two meals at the same time.

Herb-Rubbed
POT ROAST

This is the easy but special slow-cooked pot roast recipe that is so desirable. Serve it with rice or try hot buttered pasta tossed with a little Parmesan cheese. *Makes 6 servings + reserves*

Prep: **20 minutes** Cook: **Low 11 hours, High 5½ hours**

1 teaspoon dried oregano, crushed
1 teaspoon dried basil, crushed
1 teaspoon fennel seeds, crushed
1 teaspoon ground black pepper
½ teaspoon salt
½ teaspoon dried thyme, crushed
2 1½- to 2-pound boneless beef chuck pot roasts
1 tablespoon olive oil
4 medium carrots, cut into 1-inch pieces
3 medium parsnips, peeled and cut into 1-inch pieces
1 large onion, sliced
⅓ cup beef broth
⅓ cup dry red wine or beef broth
3 tablespoons quick-cooking tapioca
2 tablespoons tomato paste
2 teaspoons bottled minced garlic (4 cloves)
3 cups hot cooked rice

1. For rub, in a small bowl combine oregano, basil, fennel seeds, pepper, salt, and thyme. Set aside. Trim fat from meat. Brush oil over all sides of meat. Sprinkle rub evenly over meat; rub in with your fingers.

2. In a 5- to 6-quart slow cooker, combine carrot, parsnip, onion, broth, wine, tapioca, tomato paste, and garlic. Add meat.

3. Cover and cook on low-heat setting for 11 to 12 hours or on high-heat setting for 5½ to 6 hours.

4. Remove meat from cooker. Chop enough of the meat to make 2½ cups; store as directed below. Transfer the remaining meat and all of the vegetables to a serving platter. Skim fat from cooking liquid. Serve meat, vegetables, and cooking liquid with hot cooked rice.

To store reserves: Place meat in an airtight container. Seal and chill for up to 3 days. (Or freeze for up to 3 months. Thaw in refrigerator overnight before using.) Use in Beef Enchilada Casserole, page 307.

Per serving: 430 cal., 8 g total fat (2 g sat. fat), 89 mg chol., 346 mg sodium, 48 g carbo., 6 g fiber, 37 g pro.

Beef ENCHILADA CASSEROLE

This is a family-friendly casserole for a Mexican-food-loving family. The bottled salsa is optional, but using your favorite brand of salsa is a great way to personalize this dish. *Makes 6 servings*

Prep: **30 minutes** Bake: **40 minutes** Oven: **350°F**

1 cup chopped onion (1 large)
1½ teaspoons bottled minced garlic (3 cloves)
1 tablespoon olive oil
2 10-ounce cans mild or hot enchilada sauce
 Reserved meat from Herb-Rubbed Pot Roast* (see recipe, 306)
½ teaspoon ground cumin
¼ teaspoon ground cinnamon
1½ cups shredded Monterey Jack cheese or cheddar cheese (6 ounces)
10 6-inch corn tortillas, cut into 1-inch strips
 Dairy sour cream (optional)
 Bottled salsa (optional)

1. Preheat oven to 350°F. Grease a 2-quart rectangular baking dish; set aside.

2. In a large saucepan cook onion and garlic in hot oil over medium heat until tender, stirring occasionally. Reserve ½ cup of the enchilada sauce; set aside. Stir the remaining enchilada sauce, the reserved meat, the cumin, and cinnamon into onion mixture. Bring to boiling; remove from heat.

3. Spoon half of the meat mixture into the prepared baking dish. Sprinkle with ½ cup of the cheese. Top with half of the tortilla strips. Spoon the remaining meat mixture over tortillas. Sprinkle with ½ cup of the cheese. Top with the remaining tortilla strips. Pour the reserved ½ cup enchilada sauce over tortillas.

4. Bake, covered, about 35 minutes or until heated through. Sprinkle with the remaining ½ cup cheese. Bake, uncovered, for 5 to 7 minutes more or until cheese is melted. If desired, serve with sour cream and salsa.

*Note: There should be 2½ cups reserved chopped meat.

Per serving: 382 cal., 16 g total fat (7 g sat. fat), 70 mg chol., 615 mg sodium, 33 g carbo., 2 g fiber, 26 g pro.

Moroccan-Spiced
BEEF

Does your pot roast need a makeover? Use Moroccan seasonings to spice this slow-cooker standby. Couscous makes a quick and natural accompaniment. *Makes 6 servings + reserves*

Prep: **25 minutes** Cook: **Low 10 hours, High 5 hours**

1 3½- to 4-pound boneless beef chuck pot roast
1 tablespoon curry powder
2 teaspoons ground cumin
1½ teaspoons salt
¼ teaspoon ground black pepper
⅛ teaspoon cayenne pepper
2 medium onions, cut into thin wedges
2 14.5-ounce cans diced tomatoes, undrained
½ cup beef broth
3 cups hot cooked couscous

1. Trim fat from meat. For rub, in a small bowl stir together curry powder, cumin, salt, black pepper, and cayenne pepper. Sprinkle rub evenly over all sides of meat; rub in with your fingers.

2. Place onion in a 5- to 6-quart slow cooker. Add meat. Pour undrained tomatoes and broth over meat and onion.

3. Cover and cook on low-heat setting for 10 to 11 hours or on high-heat setting for 5 to 5½ hours.

4. Remove meat from cooker. Skim fat from tomato mixture. Reserve half of the meat and half of the tomato mixture; store as directed below. Serve the remaining meat and the remaining tomato mixture over hot cooked couscous.

To store reserves: **Shred meat by pulling two forks through it in opposite directions. Place meat and tomato mixture in an airtight container. Seal and chill for up to 3 days. (Or freeze for up to 3 months. Thaw in refrigerator overnight before using.) Use in Beef and Vegetables over Rice, page 309.**

Per serving: 278 cal., 5 g total fat (2 g sat. fat), 78 mg chol., 534 mg sodium, 23 g carbo., 2 g fiber, 32 g pro.

Beef
AND VEGETABLES OVER RICE

Add a few well-chosen, flavor-packed ingredients to reserved Moroccan-Spiced Beef, and a satisfying stew is the result. *Makes 6 servings*

Start to Finish: **20 minutes**

Reserved Moroccan-Spiced
Beef* (see recipe, 308)
1½ cups thinly sliced carrot
(3 medium)
1 tablespoon olive oil
½ cup golden raisins
⅓ cup mango chutney
2 tablespoons snipped fresh
cilantro or parsley
3 cups hot cooked rice
2 tablespoons pine nuts,
toasted

1. Remove any fat from surface of the reserved meat mixture. In a large skillet cook carrot in hot oil over medium heat about 4 minutes or until tender, stirring occasionally. Stir in meat mixture, raisins, and chutney; heat through. Stir in cilantro.
2. Serve meat mixture over hot cooked rice. Sprinkle with pine nuts.

*Note: There should be about 1¼ pounds reserved shredded meat mixed with about 2½ cups reserved tomato mixture.

Per serving: 406 cal., 9 g total fat (2 g sat. fat), 78 mg chol., 591 mg sodium, 48 g carbo., 3 g fiber, 33 g pro.

IN-A-PINCH TIPS !

FOR EASY CHUTNEY, CORE, PEEL, AND CHOP ANY TREE FRUIT SUCH AS APPLES, APRICOTS, OR PEARS. COOK WITH SUGAR AND A LITTLE WATER UNTIL FRUIT SOFTENS. REMOVE FRUIT AND ADD A SMALL AMOUNT OF VINEGAR AND CURRY POWDER TO SAUCEPAN; CONTINUE BOILING UNTIL LIQUID BECOMES SYRUPY.

Mushroom-Onion
POT ROAST

This is a pot roast just the way you love it, with fork-tender meat that falls apart easily and a richly flavored sauce laced with mushrooms. *Makes 4 servings + reserves*

Prep: **30 minutes**   Cook: **Low 10 hours, High 5 hours**

1 3-pound boneless beef chuck pot roast
½ teaspoon salt
¼ teaspoon ground black pepper
2 tablespoons cooking oil
3 cups sliced fresh mushrooms (8 ounces)
2 large onions, halved and sliced ¼ inch thick
1 10.5-ounce can condensed beef broth
½ cup dry red wine
2 teaspoons bottled minced garlic (4 cloves)
1 teaspoon dried thyme, crushed
2 tablespoons cornstarch
2 tablespoons cold water
2 cups hot mashed potatoes

1. Trim fat from meat. If necessary, cut meat to fit into a 5- to 6-quart slow cooker. Sprinkle meat with salt and pepper. In a very large skillet, cook meat in hot oil over medium-high heat until brown on all sides. Drain off fat.

2. In the cooker combine mushrooms and onion. Add meat. In a medium bowl stir together broth, wine, garlic, and thyme. Pour over mixture in cooker.

3. Cover and cook on low-heat setting for 10 to 12 hours or on high-heat setting for 5 to 6 hours.

4. Remove meat from cooker. Reserve one-third of the meat (about 9 ounces). Transfer the remaining meat to a serving platter; cover and keep warm. Using a slotted spoon, remove 1 cup of the vegetables. Remove 1½ cups of the cooking liquid. Store the reserved meat, vegetables, and cooking liquid as directed below.

5. For sauce, in a medium saucepan combine cornstarch and the cold water; stir in the remaining cooking liquid. Cook and stir over medium heat until thickened and bubbly. Cook and stir for 2 minutes more. Serve meat and sauce over hot mashed potatoes.

To store reserves: Shred meat by pulling two forks through it in opposite directions (about 1½ cups). Place meat, vegetables, and cooking liquid in separate airtight containers. Seal and chill for up to 3 days. Use in French Dip Sandwiches with Red Wine au Jus, page 311.

Per serving: 523 cal., 18 g total fat (5 g sat. fat), 135 mg chol., 958 mg sodium, 30 g carbo., 3 g fiber, 55 g pro.

SANDWICHES WITH RED WINE AU JUS

When it comes to French dip sandwiches, the moister the better! This version finds extra richness from reserved mushrooms and onions and slices of provolone cheese. *Makes 4 sandwiches*

Start to Finish: **20 minutes**

4 French-style rolls or hoagie buns, split
   Reserved Mushroom-Onion Pot Roast* (see recipe, page 310)
8 slices provolone cheese (6 ounces)

1. Preheat broiler. Hollow out bottoms of rolls. Divide the reserved meat, the reserved vegetables, and the cheese among bottoms of rolls.

2. Broil 3 to 4 inches from the heat for 3 to 4 minutes or until sandwiches are heated through and cheese is melted. Replace tops of rolls.

3. Meanwhile, in a small microwave-safe bowl microwave the reserved cooking liquid on 100 percent power (high) about 1 minute or until heated though. Serve sandwiches with the hot cooking liquid for dipping.

*Note: There should be about 1½ cups reserved shredded meat, 1 cup reserved vegetables, and 1½ cups reserved cooking liquid.

Per sandwich: 718 cal., 24 g total fat (10 g sat. fat), 96 mg chol., 1,500 mg sodium, 73 g carbo., 5 g fiber, 49 g pro.

Beef Stew

IN RICH RED WINE SAUCE

Stew perfection is tender beef, vegetables, and just the right amount of herbs served with mashed potatoes to soak up the wine-enhanced broth. *Makes 4 servings + reserves*

Prep: **25 minutes** Cook: **Low 8 hours, High 4 hours**

3 pounds beef stew meat, cut into ¾-inch pieces

2 tablespoons cooking oil

2 cups sliced carrot (4 medium)

2 cups sliced celery (4 stalks)

2 medium onions, cut into wedges

I cup dry red wine or beef broth

I cup beef broth

3 tablespoons quick-cooking tapioca

2 teaspoons bottled minced garlic (4 cloves)

I teaspoon salt

I teaspoon dried basil, crushed

I teaspoon dried thyme, crushed

I teaspoon dried rosemary, crushed

I teaspoon ground black pepper

4 cups hot cooked mashed potatoes

I. In a very large skillet, cook meat, half at a time, in hot oil over medium-high heat until brown. Drain off fat. Transfer meat to a 5- to 6-quart slow cooker. Stir in carrot, celery, onion, wine, broth, tapioca, garlic, salt, basil, thyme, rosemary, and pepper.

2. Cover and cook on low-heat setting for 8 to 10 hours or on high-heat setting for 4 to 5 hours.

3. Reserve 4 cups of the stew; store as directed below. Serve the remaining stew over hot cooked mashed potatoes.

To store reserves: **Place stew in an airtight container. Seal and chill for up to 3 days. (Or freeze for up to 3 months. Thaw in refrigerator overnight before using.) Use in Sherried Beef Stroganoff, page 313.**

Per serving: 549 cal., 13 g total fat (4 g sat. fat), 125 mg chol., 1,309 mg sodium, 50 g carbo., 5 g fiber, 49 g pro.

Sherried

BEEF STROGANOFF

Classic stroganoff ingredients combine with the Beef Stew in Rich Red Wine Sauce for an elegant and savory main dish. *Makes 4 servings*

Start to Finish: **25 minutes**

1 8-ounce carton dairy
   sour cream
1 tablespoon all-purpose flour
2 cups sliced fresh mushrooms
1½ cups frozen small whole
   onions
1 tablespoon cooking oil
   Reserved Beef Stew in Rich
   Red Wine Sauce* (see
   recipe, page 312)
¼ cup dry sherry or beef broth
2 cups hot cooked egg noodles

1. In a small bowl stir together sour cream and flour; set aside. In a large skillet cook mushrooms and onions in hot oil over medium heat for 5 to 7 minutes or until onions are tender. Stir in the reserved stew and the sherry; heat through.

2. Stir in sour cream mixture. Cook and stir until thickened and bubbly. Cook and stir for 1 minute more. Serve over hot cooked noodles.

*Note: There should be 4 cups reserved stew.

Per serving: 563 cal., 25 g total fat (10 g sat. fat), 132 mg chol., 507 mg sodium, 38 g carbo., 3 g fiber, 38 g pro.

Braised Corned
BEEF DINNER

This is slow cooking at its best! Everything—main dish and sides—cooks in one pot for a spectacular meal. Be sure to use light beer instead of regular beer that can result in a bitter taste. *Makes 4 servings + reserves*

Prep: **20 minutes** Cook: **Low 10 hours, High 5 hours**

1 3-pound corned beef brisket with juices and spice packet
4 medium red potatoes, quartered
4 carrots, cut into 1½-inch pieces
2 medium onions, cut into thin wedges
2 teaspoons dried thyme, crushed
1 bay leaf
1 12-ounce bottle light beer

1. Trim fat from meat, reserving juices and spices from packet. If necessary, cut meat to fit into a 5- to 6-quart slow cooker. Set aside.

2. In the cooker combine potato, carrot, onion, thyme, and bay leaf. Add meat. Pour the meat juices and the spices from packet over meat. Pour beer over mixture in cooker.

3. Cover and cook on low-heat setting for 10 to 11 hours or on high-heat setting for 5 to 5½ hours. Remove bay leaf.

4. Transfer meat to a cutting board. Thinly slice meat across the grain. Reserve half of the sliced meat (about 1 pound); store as directed below.

5. Transfer the remaining meat to a serving platter. Using a slotted spoon, transfer vegetables to the platter. Drizzle meat and vegetables with some of the cooking liquid; pass the remaining liquid.

To store reserves: Place meat in an airtight container. Seal and chill for up to 2 days. Use in Rueben Panini, page 315.

Per serving: 478 cal., 21 g total fat (6 g sat. fat), 86 mg chol., 1,195 mg sodium, 37 g carbo., 5 g fiber, 29 g pro.

Reuben

PANINI

Reuben sandwiches are a classic and succulent way to use leftover corned beef. The beverage of choice is also a no-brainer: A beer is perfect! Round out the meal with a good deli potato salad. *Makes 4 sandwiches*

Prep: 10 minutes   Grill: 5 minutes

¼ cup bottled Thousand Island
  salad dressing
8 slices rye bread
  Reserved meat from Braised
  Corned Beef Dinner* (see
  recipe, page 314)
1 cup canned sauerkraut,
  rinsed and drained
4 slices Swiss cheese (3 to
  4 ounces)

1. Spread salad dressing on 4 of the bread slices. Top with the reserved meat, the sauerkraut, cheese, and the remaining 4 bread slices.

2. Lightly grease the rack of a covered indoor electric grill. Preheat grill to medium heat. Place sandwiches on grill rack; close the lid. Grill for 5 to 10 minutes or until bread is toasted and cheese is melted. (Or lightly grease a large heavy skillet; heat skillet over medium heat. Place sandwiches, half at a time if necessary, in hot skillet; top with a heavy cast-iron skillet. Cook for 5 to 10 minutes or until bread is toasted and cheese is melted, turning once.)

*Note: There should be about 1 pound reserved sliced meat.

Per sandwich: 594 cal., 34 g total fat (10 g sat. fat), 110 mg chol., 3,176 mg sodium, 35 g carbo., 8 g fiber, 36 g pro.

Barbecue
PULLED PORK

Inexpensive pork shoulder roast is a prime candidate for the slow cooker because all-day simmering makes it richer and more tender. Its bold flavors stand up to the robust homemade barbecue sauce.

Makes 8 servings + reserves

Prep: 15 minutes Cook: Low 12 hours, High 6 hours

- 1 4-pound boneless pork shoulder roast
- 1 sweet onion, cut into thin wedges
- 1 12-ounce bottle chili sauce
- 1 cup cola
- ½ cup ketchup
- 2 tablespoons yellow mustard
- 1 tablespoon chili powder
- 1 tablespoon cider vinegar
- 2 teaspoons ground cumin
- 1½ teaspoons bottled minced garlic (3 cloves)
- 1 teaspoon paprika
- ½ teaspoon salt
- ½ teaspoon ground black pepper
- ¼ teaspoon crushed red pepper
- 8 hamburger buns, split and toasted
- Deli coleslaw (optional)

1. Trim fat from meat. In a 5- to 6-quart slow cooker place meat and onion. In a medium bowl combine chili sauce, cola, ketchup, mustard, chili powder, vinegar, cumin, garlic, paprika, salt, black pepper, and crushed red pepper. Pour over meat and onion in cooker.

2. Cover and cook on low-heat setting for 12 to 13 hours or on high-heat setting for 6 to 6½ hours.

3. Transfer meat to a cutting board. Using a slotted spoon, transfer onion to a medium bowl, reserving cooking liquid. Thinly slice or shred meat. Add meat to onion; stir gently to combine. Reserve half of the meat mixture (about 3½ cups); store as directed below.

4. Toss the remaining meat mixture with enough of the reserved cooking liquid to moisten. (If necessary, return meat mixture to cooker. Cover and cook on high-heat setting about 15 minutes or until heated through.) Serve meat mixture in buns with, if desired, coleslaw.

To store reserves: Place meat mixture in an airtight container. Seal and chill for up to 3 days. (Or freeze for up to 3 months. Thaw in refrigerator overnight before using.) Use in Pulled Pork Turnovers, page 317.

Per serving: 332 cal., 10 g total fat (3 g sat. fat), 76 mg chol., 760 mg sodium, 31 g carbo., 3 g fiber, 27 g pro.

 *Pulled*

PORK TURNOVERS

Transform Barbecue Pulled Pork into tasty little turnovers with a soft, tender pastry. They taste great with a steaming bowl of cheese soup for a casual Saturday lunch or Sunday night supper. *Makes 8 servings*

Prep: **20 minutes**   Bake: **15 minutes**   Oven: **350°F**

Reserved Barbecue Pulled
   Pork* (see recipe, 316)
1 16.3-ounce package (8)
   refrigerated large Southern-
   style biscuits
1 egg, lightly beaten
1 tablespoon water
   Bottled barbecue sauce,
   warmed (optional)

1. Preheat oven to 350°F. Lightly grease a baking sheet; set aside. In a medium saucepan bring the reserved meat mixture to simmering. Remove from heat.

2. Meanwhile, on a lightly floured surface, roll each biscuit into a 6-inch circle. In a small bowl combine egg and the water. Spoon a scant ½ cup of the meat mixture onto each biscuit circle, placing mixture on half of each circle. Brush edges of dough with egg mixture. Fold dough over meat mixture to opposite edge. Press edges with a fork to seal. Place turnovers on the prepared baking sheet.

3. Bake, uncovered, for 15 to 17 minutes or until golden brown. If desired, serve with warm barbecue sauce.

*Note: There should be about 3½ cups reserved meat mixture.

Per serving: 411 cal., 18 g total fat (5 g sat. fat), 102 mg chol., 1,153 mg sodium, 34 g carbo., 2 g fiber, 28 g pro.

Adobo
PORK TOSTADAS

The smoky flavor of the canned chipotle chiles and the spice of the adobo sauce (made from ground chiles, herbs, and vinegar) create a spicy, smoky flavor in these attractively layered tostadas. The slow cooker simmers the meat until it is tender and juicy. *Makes 4 servings + reserves*

Prep: **30 minutes**   Cook: **Low 10 hours, High 5 hours**

1   3- to 3½-pound boneless pork shoulder roast
1   15-ounce can tomato sauce
½   cup chicken broth
2   tablespoons finely chopped canned chipotle chile pepper in adobo sauce (see note, page 22)
1   tablespoon bottled minced garlic (6 cloves)
½   teaspoon salt
½   teaspoon ground cumin
½   teaspoon ground coriander
¼   teaspoon ground black pepper
1   cup canned refried beans
8   tostada shells
1   cup shredded lettuce
1   cup chopped tomato (2 medium)
1   medium avocado, seeded, peeled, and sliced
1   cup shredded Monterey Jack cheese (4 ounces)
½   cup dairy sour cream

1. Trim fat from meat. Cut meat into chunks. Place meat in a 4- to 5-quart slow cooker. For sauce, in a medium bowl stir together tomato sauce, broth, chipotle pepper, garlic, salt, cumin, coriander, and black pepper. Pour sauce over meat in cooker.

2. Cover and cook on low-heat setting for 10 to 12 hours or on high-heat setting for 5 to 6 hours.

3. Remove meat from cooker. Shred meat by pulling two forks through it in opposite directions. Reserve half of the meat (about 3 cups) and 2 cups of the sauce; store as directed below. In a medium bowl combine the remaining meat and ½ cup of the sauce. Discard any remaining sauce.

4. Spread refried beans over tostada shells. Top with meat mixture. Divide lettuce, tomato, and avocado among tostadas. Top with cheese and sour cream.

To store reserves: Place meat and sauce in separate airtight containers. Seal and chill for up to 3 days. (Or freeze for up to 3 months. Thaw in refrigerator overnight before using.) Use in Chipotle Pork Tamale Casserole, page 319.

Per serving: 720 cal., 38 g total fat (14 g sat. fat), 151 mg chol., 1,378 mg sodium, 44 g carbo., 9 g fiber, 49 g pro.

Chipotle Pork
TAMALE CASSEROLE

Polenta used to be tricky to make. Then along came the convenient tube of refrigerated polenta, a terrific ingredient in casseroles inspired by Mexican tamales. *Makes 4 servings*

Prep: 15 minutes   Bake: 35 minutes   Oven: 375°F

1 16-ounce tube refrigerated
  cooked polenta, sliced
  ½ inch thick
  Reserved meat and sauce
  from Adobo Pork Tostadas*
  (see recipe, page 318)
1 cup shredded cheddar
  cheese (4 ounces)
½ cup chopped tomato
  (1 medium)
¼ cup sliced green onion (2)

1. Preheat oven to 375°F. In an ungreased 2-quart square baking dish, arrange polenta slices, overlapping as necessary. Top with the reserved meat. Remove any fat from surface of the reserved sauce. Spoon ½ cup of the reserved sauce over meat.
2. Bake, covered, for 30 minutes. Sprinkle with cheese. Bake, uncovered, about 5 minutes more or until cheese is melted.
3. Meanwhile, heat the remaining 1½ cups reserved sauce. Sprinkle tomato and green onion over casserole. Serve with warm sauce.

*Note: There should be about 3 cups reserved shredded meat and 2 cups reserved sauce.

Per serving: 488 cal., 21 g total fat (10 g sat. fat), 143 mg chol., 1,215 mg sodium, 27 g carbo., 4 g fiber, 44 g pro.

Classic
MEAT LOAF

Here it is—the meat loaf topped with ketchup and brown sugar, loved by generations. Serve it with mashed potatoes, gravy, and canned green beans for a tasty trip down memory lane. You need a large oval slow cooker for this recipe. *Makes 6 servings + reserves*

Prep: **30 minutes** Cook: Low 7 hours, High 3½ hours

3 eggs, lightly beaten
¾ cup milk
2 cups soft bread crumbs
1 cup finely chopped onion
   (1 large)
2 teaspoons salt
½ teaspoon ground black
   pepper
1½ pounds lean ground beef
1½ pounds ground pork
¼ cup ketchup
2 tablespoons packed
   brown sugar
1 teaspoon dry mustard

1. In a large bowl combine eggs and milk. Stir in bread crumbs, onion, salt, and pepper. Add ground beef and ground pork; mix well. Shape meat mixture into two 5-inch round loaves.

2. Tear off two 18-inch square pieces of heavy foil; cut each into thirds. Fold each piece of foil in half lengthwise to make strips. Crisscross 3 of the strips and place 1 meat loaf in the center of the foil crisscross. Bringing up the foil strips, lift the ends of the strips to transfer the meat loaf to a 6- to 7-quart oval slow cooker. Leave foil strips under loaf. Repeat with the remaining foil strips and the remaining meat loaf.

3. Cover and cook on low-heat setting for 7 to 8 hours or on high-heat setting for 3½ to 4 hours.

4. Using the foil strips, carefully lift 1 meat loaf out of cooker; discard foil strips. Store meat loaf as directed below. Transfer the second meat loaf to a serving platter; discard foil strips.

5. In a small bowl stir together ketchup, brown sugar, and dry mustard. Spread over meat loaf on platter.

To store reserves: **Place meat loaf in an airtight container. Seal and chill for up to 3 days. (Or freeze for up to 3 months. Thaw in refrigerator overnight before using.) Use in Meat Loaf Parmesan, page 321.**

Per serving: 239 cal., 11 g total fat (4 g sat. fat), 116 mg chol., 617 mg sodium, 13 g carbo., 0 g fiber, 20 g pro.

Meat Loaf
PARMESAN

If you enjoy chicken Parmesan and eggplant Parmesan, why not give the treatment to meat loaf? The side-dish accompaniment could go either way: Italian with pasta or American with mashed potatoes.

Makes 6 servings

Prep: 15 minutes   Bake: 35 minutes   Oven: 350°F

Reserved Classic Meat Loaf*
    (see recipe, page 320)
2 eggs, lightly beaten
¼ cup milk
½ cup seasoned fine dry
    bread crumbs
¼ cup grated Parmesan cheese
1 26- or 28-ounce jar tomato
    pasta sauce
1 cup shredded mozzarella
    cheese (4 ounces)

1. Preheat oven to 350°F. Cut the reserved meat loaf into 6 slices; set aside.

2. In a shallow dish combine eggs and milk. In another shallow dish stir together bread crumbs and Parmesan cheese. Dip meat loaf slices into egg mixture, then into crumb mixture, turning to coat. Place slices in a single layer in an ungreased 3-quart rectangular baking dish.

3. Bake, uncovered, for 20 minutes. Pour pasta sauce evenly over meat loaf; sprinkle with mozzarella cheese. Bake, uncovered, about 15 minutes more or until sauce is heated through and cheese is melted.

*Note: There should be 1 reserved meat loaf.

Per serving: 469 cal., 22 g total fat (9 g sat. fat), 205 mg chol., 33 g carbo., 4 g fiber, 31 g pro.

Chipotle
MEATBALLS

Here's a cure for the common pasta-and-meatball combo. Liven the dish up with a sauce spiked with zippy beer and chipotle chili powder. Orzo, a rice-shape pasta, makes a good choice for the pasta option.

Makes 4 servings + reserves

Prep: **35 minutes**   Bake: **25 minutes**   Cook: **Low 4 hours, High 2 hours**   Oven: **350°F**

 2 eggs, lightly beaten
1⅓ cups ketchup
 ¾ cup quick-cooking rolled oats
1¼ to 1½ teaspoons chipotle chili powder
 ½ teaspoon salt
 ½ teaspoon garlic powder
 1 pound lean ground beef
 1 pound ground pork
 1 12-ounce can beer
 ¼ cup packed brown sugar
 1 tablespoon quick-cooking tapioca, crushed
 8 ounces desired dried pasta

1. Preheat oven to 350°F. In a large bowl combine eggs, ⅓ cup of the ketchup, the oats, 1 teaspoon of the chili powder, the salt, and garlic powder. Add ground beef and ground pork; mix well. Shape meat mixture into 32 meatballs. Place meatballs in an ungreased 15×10×1-inch baking pan. Bake, uncovered, for 25 minutes. Drain off fat.

2. In a 3½- or 4-quart slow cooker combine the remaining 1 cup ketchup, the remaining ¼ to ½ teaspoon chili powder, the beer, brown sugar, and tapioca. Add meatballs.

3. Cover and cook on low-heat setting for 4 to 5 hours or on high-heat setting for 2 to 2½ hours. Using a slotted spoon, remove meatballs from cooker. Reserve half of the meatballs (16 meatballs) and ½ cup of the sauce; store as directed below.

4. Cook pasta according to package directions; drain. Serve the remaining meatballs and the remaining sauce over hot cooked pasta.

To store reserves: Place meatballs and sauce in separate airtight containers. Seal and chill for up to 3 days. (Or freeze for up to 3 months. Thaw in refrigerator overnight before using.) Use in Meatball Hoagies, page 323.

Per serving: 544 cal., 12 g total fat (5 g sat. fat), 115 mg chol., 827 mg sodium, 76 g carbo., 3 g fiber, 28 g pro.

Meatball
HOAGIES

The meatballs pack a combination of sweet and heat. If you savored them in the Chipotle Meatballs recipe, you will love them in a sandwich topped with melty Monterey Jack cheese. *Makes 4 servings*

Prep: 15 minutes Broil: 5 minutes

Reserved Chipotle Meatballs*
  (see recipe, page 322)
4 hoagie buns, split
1 cup shredded Monterey Jack
  cheese (4 ounces)

1. Preheat broiler. In a small saucepan bring the reserved sauce to simmering over medium heat. Reduce heat to low; cover and keep warm.
2. Meanwhile, place the reserved meatballs in a single layer on a microwave-safe plate. Microwave, uncovered, on 100 percent power (high) for 2 to 3 minutes or until heated through.
3. Place buns, cut sides up, on an ungreased baking sheet. Broil 4 to 6 inches from the heat about 3 minutes or until toasted. Remove tops of buns from baking sheet.

4. Cut meatballs in half; arrange on bottoms of buns. Drizzle with warm sauce; sprinkle with cheese. Broil about 2 minutes more or until cheese is melted. Replace tops of buns.

*Note: There should be 16 reserved meatballs and ½ cup reserved sauce.

Per serving: 761 cal., 28 g total fat (12 g sat. fat), 140 mg chol., 1,321 mg sodium, 89 g carbo., 5 g fiber, 38 g pro.

Honey
CURRY CHICKEN

Curry powders are available in degrees of heat levels. For mild curry flavor, use conventional curry powder. To take it up several notches, try madras or red curry powder. *Makes 6 servings + reserves*

Prep: **20 minutes**   Cook: **Low 5 hours, High 2½ hours**

8 bone-in chicken breast halves (about 4½ pounds total)

1 large onion, halved and sliced

½ teaspoon salt

¼ teaspoon ground black pepper

¼ cup honey

¼ cup Dijon-style mustard

2 tablespoons butter or margarine, melted

1 tablespoon curry powder

2 large red sweet peppers, seeded and cut into bite-size strips

3 cups hot cooked white or brown rice

1. Remove skin from chicken; set chicken aside. Place onion in a 5- to 6-quart slow cooker. Add chicken. Sprinkle chicken with salt and black pepper. In a small bowl stir together honey, mustard, melted butter, and curry powder; pour over chicken in cooker. Add sweet pepper.

2. Cover and cook on low-heat setting for 5 to 6 hours or on high-heat setting for 2½ to 3 hours.

3. Using a slotted spoon, remove chicken and vegetables from cooker, reserving cooking liquid. Strain liquid through a fine-mesh sieve. Reserve 2 chicken breast halves, 1 cup vegetables, and ½ cup cooking liquid; store as directed below.

4. Serve the remaining chicken and vegetables with hot cooked rice. Spoon enough of the remaining cooking liquid over chicken and vegetables to moisten.

To store reserves: Place chicken, vegetables, and cooking liquid in separate airtight containers. Seal and chill for up to 3 days. Use in Asian Chicken Salad, page 325.

Per serving: 367 cal., 5 g total fat (2 g sat. fat), 104 mg chol., 435 mg sodium, 36 g carbo., 1 g fiber, 43 g pro.

CHICKEN SALAD

Made from leftover chicken, this colorful salad delivers eye appeal as well as great savings.

Makes 4 servings

Start to Finish: **20 minutes**

Reserved Honey Curry Chicken* (see recipe, page 324)

½ cup mayonnaise or salad dressing

3 cups shredded iceberg lettuce

½ cup chopped carrot (I medium)

½ cup chopped, peeled jicama or carrot

½ cup fresh snow pea pods, thinly sliced lengthwise

½ cup chow mein noodles

I. In a small bowl whisk together the reserved cooking liquid and the mayonnaise until smooth; set aside. Remove meat from the reserved chicken, discarding bones. Chop chicken and the reserved vegetables.

2. In a large bowl combine the reserved chicken, the reserved vegetables, the lettuce, carrot, jicama, and pea pods. Stir mayonnaise mixture, then add to chicken mixture; gently toss to coat.

3. Sprinkle each serving with chow mein noodles.

*Note: There should be 2 reserved chicken breast halves, I cup reserved vegetables, and ½ cup reserved cooking liquid.

Per serving: 406 cal., 27 g total fat (6 g sat. fat), 62 mg chol., 439 mg sodium, 19 g carbo., 3 g fiber, 22 g pro.

Kickin'

CHICKEN CHILI

Chicken instead of beef, white beans instead of red, and a windfall of colorful vegetables—not to mention green salsa for extra kick—this is a whole new bowl of chili! *Makes 4 servings + reserves*

Prep: **25 minutes** Cook: **Low 4 hours, High 2 hours**

2 pounds skinless, boneless chicken breast halves or thighs, cut into I-inch pieces

2 teaspoons ground cumin

¼ teaspoon salt

I tablespoon olive oil or cooking oil

I 16-ounce package frozen sweet pepper stir-fry vegetables

I 16-ounce jar green salsa

I 15-ounce can cannellini (white kidney) beans, rinsed and drained

I 14.5-ounce can diced tomatoes with onion and garlic, undrained

Dairy sour cream (optional)

Shredded cheddar cheese (optional)

I. In a large bowl combine chicken, cumin, and salt; toss gently to coat. In a large skillet cook chicken, half at a time, in hot oil over medium-high heat until light brown. Drain off fat. Transfer chicken to a 4- to 5-quart slow cooker. Stir in frozen vegetables, salsa, drained beans, and undrained tomatoes.

2. Cover and cook on low-heat setting for 4 to 5 hours or on high-heat setting for 2 to 2½ hours. Reserve 3 cups of the chili; store as directed below.

3. Serve the remaining chili while warm. If desired, top each serving with sour cream and cheese.

To store reserves: Place chili in an airtight container. Seal and chill for up to 3 days. Use in Kickin' Chicken Taco Salad, page 327.

Per serving: 305 cal., 5 g total fat (I g sat. fat), 88 mg chol., 914 mg sodium, 24 g carbo., 6 g fiber, 4I g pro.

Kickin' Chicken
TACO SALAD

Give the usual taco salad extra kick by starting with Kickin' Chicken Chili. In a hurry? Use a bag of lettuce and don't bother halving the tomatoes. *Makes 4 servings*

Start to Finish: **30 minutes**

Reserved Kickin' Chicken
   Chili* (see recipe, page 326)
6 cups torn romaine lettuce
1 large avocado, seeded,
   peeled, and chopped
1 cup grape tomatoes or cherry
   tomatoes, halved
   (if desired)
1 cup chopped, peeled jicama
1½ cups coarsely crushed lime-
   flavor or plain tortilla chips
½ cup dairy sour cream
¼ cup snipped fresh cilantro
   or parsley

1. In a medium saucepan cook the reserved chili over medium-low heat until heated through, stirring occasionally. In a very large bowl, combine lettuce, avocado, tomato, and jicama. Add heated chili; toss gently to combine.

2. Divide mixture among 4 large salad bowls. Sprinkle with chips. In a small bowl stir together sour cream and cilantro; spoon onto salads.

*Note: There should be 3 cups reserved chili.

Per serving: 385 cal., 19 g total fat (5 g sat. fat), 54 mg chol., 565 mg sodium, 34 g carbo., 9 g fiber, 25 g pro.

Rosemary Turkey
ROAST WITH VEGETABLES

If you love turkey, why make it a holiday-only treat? Boneless turkey roasts are readily available and perfectly sized for anytime enjoyment. *Makes 6 servings + reserves*

Prep: **30 minutes** Cook: **Low 9 hours, High 4½ hours**

Nonstick cooking spray
1 pound small new potatoes, quartered
1 pound carrots, cut into 3-inch pieces
1 large onion, cut into ½-inch wedges
¼ cup water
1 teaspoon salt
1 teaspoon dried rosemary, crushed
¼ teaspoon garlic powder
¼ teaspoon dried thyme, crushed
¼ teaspoon ground black pepper
1 3-pound boneless turkey roast, thawed (do not remove cloth netting)*
Chicken broth
¼ cup all-purpose flour
Salt and ground black pepper

1. Lightly coat the inside of a 5- to 6-quart slow cooker with cooking spray. In the prepared cooker combine potato, carrot, onion, the water, the 1 teaspoon salt, the rosemary, garlic powder, thyme, and the ¼ teaspoon pepper. Add turkey.

2. Cover and cook on low-heat setting for 9 to 10 hours or on high-heat setting 4½ to 5 hours.

3. Transfer turkey to a cutting board. Cover loosely with foil; let stand for 15 minutes before removing netting and carving. Using a slotted spoon, remove vegetables from cooker; cover and keep warm.

4. Meanwhile, for gravy, strain cooking liquid into a 2-cup glass measuring cup. Add enough broth to the strained liquid to equal 2 cups. In a medium saucepan whisk together the 2 cups broth mixture and the flour. Cook and stir over medium heat until thickened and bubbly. Cook and stir for 1 minute more. Season to taste with additional salt and pepper.

5. Reserve one-third of the turkey (about 12 ounces) and 2 cups of the vegetables; store as directed below. Slice the remaining turkey. Serve the remaining turkey and the remaining vegetables with gravy.

To store reserves: **Place turkey and vegetables in separate airtight containers. Seal and chill for up to 3 days. Use in Perfect Fit Turkey Potpie, page 329.**

*Test Kitchen Tip: **Reserve giblets and/or gravy packet from turkey for another use.**

Per serving: 270 cal., 4 g total fat (1 g sat. fat), 81 mg chol., 1,611 mg sodium, 29 g carbo., 3 g fiber, 29 g pro.

Perfect Fit

TURKEY POT PIE

Could a homemade pot pie be any easier? Here, one pan does it all—you combine the ingredients in an oven-going skillet, top with a refrigerated piecrust, and bake—for a supper with loads of family-friendly appeal. *Makes 6 servings*

Prep: **25 minutes** Bake: **40 minutes** Stand: **10 minutes** Oven: **375°F**

½ of a 15-ounce package (1 crust) rolled refrigerated unbaked piecrust
  Reserved Rosemary Turkey Roast with Vegetables* (see recipe, 328)
2 10.75-ounce cans condensed cream of chicken soup
1 cup frozen peas
1 4-ounce jar diced pimiento, undrained
⅛ teaspoon ground black pepper

1. Preheat oven to 375°F. Let piecrust stand according to package directions.

2. Meanwhile, chop the reserved turkey. In a large oven-going skillet combine the reserved turkey, the reserved vegetables, the soup, peas, undrained pimiento, and pepper. Cook and stir over medium heat until mixture is bubbly. Remove from heat.

3. Unroll piecrust; cut slits in pastry to allow steam to escape. Carefully place pastry on top of turkey mixture. Press edges of pastry firmly against sides of skillet.

4. Bake, uncovered, for 40 to 45 minutes or until pastry is golden brown. Let stand for 10 minutes before serving.

*Note: There should be about 12 ounces reserved turkey and 2 cups reserved vegetables.

Per serving: 406 cal., 17 g total fat (6 g sat. fat), 55 mg chol., 1,572 mg sodium, 43 g carbo., 4 g fiber, 19 g pro.

Creamy Turkey
BOW TIES AND CHEESE

This is an opulent dish as it includes whipping cream. A vinaigrette-tossed salad starring chopped vegetables provides contrast to the creamy entrée. *Makes 6 servings + reserves*

Prep: **20 minutes**   Cook: **Low 3 hours**

4 cups chopped cooked turkey
2 cups chopped onion (2 large)
2 cups whipping cream
8 ounces American cheese, cubed
8 ounces process Swiss cheese slices, torn
1 teaspoon dried sage, crushed
½ teaspoon ground black pepper
16 ounces dried bow tie pasta

1. In a 4- to 5-quart slow cooker, combine turkey, onion, cream, American cheese, Swiss cheese, sage, and pepper.
2. Cover and cook on low-heat setting (do not use high-heat setting) for 3 to 4 hours.
3. Cook pasta according to package directions; drain. Stir cheese mixture in cooker. Stir in cooked pasta.
4. Reserve 2½ cups of the pasta mixture; store as directed below. Serve the remaining pasta mixture while warm.

To store reserves: Place pasta mixture in an airtight container. Seal and chill for up to 3 days. Use in Turkey and Asparagus Strata, page 331.

Per serving: 755 cal., 43 g total fat (25 g sat. fat), 186 mg chol., 886 mg sodium, 49 g carbo., 2 g fiber, 43 g pro.

Turkey AND ASPARAGUS STRATA

This clever rendition of the classic brunch dish is made extra hearty with pasta. A melon-and-apple salad could round out the menu. *Makes 6 servings*

Prep: 15 minutes   Bake: 1 hour   Stand: 10 minutes   Chill: 2 to 24 hours   Oven: 325°F

½ cups seasoned croutons
  Reserved Creamy Turkey
  Bow Ties and Cheese* (see
  recipe, page 330)
1 10-ounce package frozen cut
  asparagus, thawed and well
  drained
4 eggs, lightly beaten
1¼ cups milk
1 tablespoon dry mustard
½ teaspoon onion powder
⅛ teaspoon ground nutmeg

1. Grease a 2-quart square baking dish. Spread croutons in the prepared baking dish. In a medium bowl combine the reserved pasta mixture and asparagus. Spoon pasta mixture evenly over croutons.

2. In the same bowl combine eggs, milk, dry mustard, onion powder, and nutmeg. Pour evenly over pasta mixture in baking dish. Cover and chill for 2 to 24 hours.

3. Preheat oven to 325°F. Bake, covered, for 30 minutes. Bake, uncovered, for 30 to 45 minutes more or until the temperature of the strata reaches 170°F. Let stand for 10 minutes before serving.

*Note: There should be 2½ cups reserved pasta mixture.

Per serving: 389 cal., 21 g total fat (11 g sat. fat), 208 mg chol., 490 mg sodium, 28 g carbo., 2 g fiber, 23 g pro.

Marinara
SAUCE

This red sauce, full of veggies, calls for a refreshing accompaniment. How about a crisp green salad tossed with a vinaigrette dressing and topped with Gorgonzola cheese? *Makes 6 servings + reserves*

Prep: **30 minutes** Cook: **Low 10 hours, High 5 hours**

2 28-ounce cans Italian-style or regular whole peeled tomatoes in puree, cut up

3 cups shredded carrot (6 medium) or packaged coarsely shredded fresh carrot

2 cups thinly sliced celery (4 stalks)

2 cups chopped red and/or green sweet pepper

1½ cups finely chopped onion (3 medium)

2 6-ounce cans tomato paste

½ cup water

½ cup dry red wine

5 teaspoons dried Italian seasoning, crushed

4 teaspoons bottled minced garlic (8 cloves)

1 tablespoon sugar

2 teaspoons salt

¼ to ½ teaspoon ground black pepper

12 ounces dried penne pasta

⅓ cup grated Parmesan cheese

1. In a 6- to 7-quart slow cooker, stir together undrained tomatoes, carrot, celery, sweet pepper, onion, tomato paste, the water, wine, Italian seasoning, garlic, sugar, salt, and black pepper.

2. Cover and cook on low-heat setting for 10 to 12 hours or on high-heat setting for 5 to 6 hours.

3. Reserve 6 cups (about half) of the sauce; store as directed below.

4. Cook pasta according to package directions; drain. Serve the remaining sauce over hot cooked pasta. Sprinkle with cheese.

To store reserves: Place sauce in an airtight container. Seal and chill for up to 3 days. Use in Marinara-Sauced Shells, page 333.

Per serving: 327 cal., 3 g total fat (1 g sat. fat), 4 mg chol., 844 mg sodium, 62 g carbo., 5 g fiber, 13 g pro.

Marinara-Sauced
SHELLS

A good way to extend the ricotta is with the addition of silken-style tofu. The marinara sauce is a good foil so tofu abstainers will never know its presence in this recipe. *Makes 6 servings*

Prep: **30 minutes** Bake: **65 minutes** Stand: **10 minutes** Oven: **350°F**

18 dried jumbo macaroni shells*
1 12.3-ounce package firm, silken-style tofu (fresh bean curd)
1 15-ounce carton ricotta cheese
1 egg, lightly beaten
1/3 cup finely shredded Parmesan cheese
1 teaspoon dried basil, crushed
1/8 teaspoon ground black pepper
Reserved Marinara Sauce** (see recipe, page 332)
1 cup shredded mozzarella cheese (4 ounces)

1. Preheat oven to 350°F. Grease a 3-quart rectangular baking dish; set aside. Cook macaroni shells according to package directions; drain. Rinse with cold water; drain again.
2. Meanwhile, pat tofu dry with paper towels. In a medium bowl combine tofu and ricotta cheese; mash with a potato masher or fork. Stir in egg, Parmesan cheese, basil, and pepper.
3. Spoon about 3 tablespoons of the tofu mixture into each cooked macaroni shell. Arrange filled shells in the prepared baking dish. Top evenly with the reserved sauce.
4. Bake, covered, for 30 minutes. Bake, uncovered, for 30 to 35 minutes or until heated through. Sprinkle with mozzarella cheese. Bake, uncovered, about 5 minutes more or until cheese is melted. Let stand for 10 minutes before serving.

*Test Kitchen Tip: Cook 2 or 3 extra shells in case any tear while cooking.

**Note: There should be 6 cups reserved sauce.

Per serving: 444 cal., 18 g total fat (10 g sat. fat), 89 mg chol., 1,060 mg sodium, 44 g carbo., 4 g fiber, 26 g pro.

Cowboy Rice
AND BEANS

Beans pack a powerful one-two punch of fiber and protein. With three kinds of beans and brown rice, this dish makes a healthy meatless dinner. Thanks to spicy seasonings, it's an exciting one too.

Makes 4 servings + reserves

Prep: 15 minutes Cook: Low 5 hours, High 2½ hours; plus 30 minutes on High

2 15-ounce cans chili beans in chili gravy, undrained
1 15-ounce can butter beans, rinsed and drained
1 15-ounce can black beans, rinsed and drained
1 cup chopped onion (1 large)
¾ cup chopped green sweet pepper (1 medium)
¾ cup chopped red sweet pepper (1 medium)
1 fresh jalapeño chile pepper, seeded and finely chopped (see note, page 22)
1 18-ounce bottle barbecue sauce
1 cup vegetable broth
1 cup uncooked instant brown rice

1. In a 5- to 6-quart slow cooker, combine undrained chili beans in gravy, drained butter beans, drained black beans, onion, sweet peppers, and jalapeño pepper. Pour barbecue sauce and broth over mixture in cooker.
2. Cover and cook on low-heat setting for 5 to 6 hours or on high-heat setting for 2½ to 3 hours.
3. If using low-heat setting turn to high-heat setting. Stir in rice. Cover and cook about 30 minutes or until rice is tender.
4. Reserve 3 cups of the bean mixture; store as directed below. Serve the remaining bean mixture while warm.

To store reserves: Place bean mixture in an airtight container. Seal and chill for up to 3 days. Use in Baked Cowboy Chimichangas, page 335.

Per serving: 365 cal., 3 g total fat (0 g sat. fat), 0 mg chol., 1,676 mg sodium, 68 g carbo., 17 g fiber, 19 g pro.

COWBOY CHIMICHANGAS

Baking chimichangas is easier than frying them. Add a spoonful of sour cream and your favorite purchased salsa to this Mexican standby, and you may never again want the traditional fried version.

Makes 4 servings

Prep: 15 minutes   Bake: 15 minutes   Oven: 350°F

Reserved Cowboy Rice
and Beans* (see recipe,
page 334)
8 8-inch flour tortillas
1 8-ounce package shredded
Mexican cheese blend
(2 cups)
Dairy sour cream (optional)
Bottled salsa (optional)

1. Preheat oven to 350°F. Spoon a generous ⅓ cup of the reserved bean mixture down the center of each tortilla. Top each with ¼ cup of the cheese. Fold in opposite sides of each tortilla; roll up tortilla. If necessary, secure with wooden toothpicks.

2. Place filled tortillas, seam sides down, on an ungreased baking sheet. Bake, uncovered, for 15 to 20 minutes or until tortillas are crisp and brown.

3. If desired, serve with sour cream and salsa.

*Note: There should be 3 cups reserved bean mixture.

Per serving: 580 cal., 24 g total fat (11 g sat. fat), 50 mg chol., 1,558 mg sodium, 66 g carbo., 9 g fiber, 26 g pro.

Cheesy Cauliflower,
BROCCOLI, AND CORN SOUP

Add a few vegetables to the slow cooker and let this soup simmer to creamy perfection. Recipes like this make the slow cooker a favorite appliance. *Makes 6 servings + reserves*

Prep: **20 minutes** Cook: **Low 6 hours, High 3 hours; plus 30 minutes on High**

2 10-ounce packages frozen cauliflower, thawed and well drained

2 10-ounce packages frozen cut broccoli, thawed and well drained

1 10-ounce package frozen whole kernel corn, thawed and well drained

2 teaspoons dried dill

3 14-ounce cans vegetable broth

16 ounces American cheese, cubed

1. In a 5- to 6-quart slow cooker, combine cauliflower, broccoli, corn, and dill. Stir in broth.

2. Cover and cook on low-heat setting for 6 to 7 hours or on high-heat setting for 3 to 3½ hours.

3. If using low-heat setting, turn to high-heat setting. Stir in cheese. Cover and cook about 30 minutes more or until cheese is melted.

4. Using a slotted spoon, remove 4 cups of the vegetables. Remove 1 cup of the cooking liquid. Store the reserved vegetables and cooking liquid as directed below. Serve the remaining soup while warm.

To store reserves: **Place vegetables and cooking liquid in an airtight container. Seal and chill for up to 3 days. Use in Cheese and Vegetable Rice Casserole, page 337.**

Per serving: 295 cal., 20 g total fat (12 g sat. fat), 58 mg chol., 1,609 mg sodium, 15 g carbo., 4 g fiber, 17 g pro.

Cheese and
VEGETABLE RICE CASSEROLE

A casserole studded with rice, beans, and vegetables is one of the most satisfying ways to go meatless. Here diced green chile peppers and roasted red sweet peppers boost the flavor impact. *Makes 6 servings*

Prep: **20 minutes** Bake: **35 minutes** Stand: **10 minutes** Oven: **350°F**

Reserved vegetable mixture from Cheesy Cauliflower, Broccoli, and Corn Soup* (see recipe, page 336)
4 cups cooked rice
1 15-ounce can black beans, rinsed and drained
1 12-ounce jar roasted red sweet peppers, drained and coarsely chopped
2 4-ounce cans diced green chile peppers, drained
1 cup shredded cheddar cheese (4 ounces)
½ cup seasoned fine dry bread crumbs
2 tablespoons butter or margarine, melted

1. Preheat oven to 350°F. Lightly grease a 3-quart rectangular baking dish; set aside.
2. In a large bowl stir together the reserved vegetable mixture, the cooked rice, drained beans, roasted pepper, and drained chile peppers. Spread mixture in the prepared baking dish. Sprinkle with cheese.
3. In a small bowl combine bread crumbs and melted butter; toss gently to coat. Sprinkle over mixture in baking dish.

4. Bake, uncovered, for 35 to 40 minutes or until heated through and top is golden brown. Let stand for 10 minutes before serving.

*Note: There should be 4 cups reserved vegetables mixed with 1 cup reserved cooking liquid.

Per serving: 446 cal., 17 g total fat (10 g sat. fat), 47 mg chol., 1,080 mg sodium, 57 g carbo., 7 g fiber, 21 g pro.

LOOK!

MONEY-SAVING TIPS and HINTS

Instead of bagged greens and cabbage, purchase whole heads and tear or cut them for salads or coleslaw.

Produce at local farmers' markets is often <u>less</u> expensive and is of good quality.

AMAZING!

Fresh fruits and vegetables are at the lowest price when in season.

TIP! **TIP!** Produce in large bags or in bulk is at least half the price of individually bagged produce. Be sure to carefully inspect for bruised or spoiled items. **Tip!** **Tip!**

Purchase and slice mushrooms, sweet peppers, carrots, and/or desired vegetables instead of buying them precut.

$AVE! Buy fresh herbs in bulk at your local farmers' market or grow your own herbs. Herb pots are available in local garden centers and farmers' markets and the quality is often superior.

CHEAP! **Use leftover cooked peas and/or carrots with some mayo and chopped celery for a fresh, quick salad.**

 **Save vegetable peels and trimmings in a freezer bag in the freezer for making broth.**

Make your own salad dressing. It is fresh and fast. For vinaigrette, use three parts oil to one part vinegar. Turning your vinaigrette into a creamy dressing is an easy way to use up small dabs of mayo, sour cream, cheese ends, or yogurt.

CHAPTER 9

FRESH AND FRUGAL SALADS

The introduction of bagged salad greens and mixes transformed salads into convenience foods. But let's face it, they can be costly. To control grocery spending, start with individual heads of lettuce instead. And as every frugal cook knows, salads are a great way to use up bits of leftovers. Even better, they still look and taste garden-fresh.

Taco
SALAD

If you prefer, omit the crisp salad shells and serve this satisfying salad in individual serving bowls with a side of taco chips for crunch. *Makes 6 servings*

Start to Finish: **30 minutes**

8 ounces lean ground beef or uncooked ground turkey
1½ teaspoons bottled minced garlic (3 cloves)
1 15-ounce can dark red kidney beans, rinsed and drained
1 8-ounce jar taco sauce
¾ cup frozen whole kernel corn, thawed (optional)
6 cups shredded leaf lettuce or iceberg lettuce
1 cup chopped green sweet pepper
1 cup chopped tomato (2 medium)
½ cup thinly sliced green onion (4)
6 baked crisp salad shells*
1 medium avocado, seeded, peeled, and chopped
¾ cup shredded sharp cheddar cheese (3 ounces)
Dairy sour cream (optional)

1. In a medium saucepan cook ground beef and garlic over medium-high heat until meat is brown. Drain off fat. Stir in drained beans, taco sauce, and, if desired, corn. Bring to boiling; reduce heat. Simmer, covered, for 10 minutes.

2. Meanwhile, in a very large bowl, combine lettuce, sweet pepper, tomato, and green onion.

3. To serve, divide lettuce mixture among salad shells. Top with meat mixture, avocado, and cheese. If desired, serve with sour cream.

Per serving: 412 cal., 18 g total fat (6 g sat. fat), 35 mg chol., 632 mg sodium, 45 g carbo., 8 g fiber, 21 g pro.

*Test Kitchen Tip: If you can't find purchased salad shells, prepare your own shells using flour tortillas. Preheat oven to 350°F. Lightly brush one side of six 9- to 10-inch flour tortillas with a little water or lightly coat with nonstick cooking spray. Coat 6 small ovenproof bowls or 16-ounce individual casseroles with nonstick cooking spray. Press tortillas, coated sides up, into the prepared bowls. Place a ball of foil in each tortilla shell. Bake, uncovered, for 15 to 20 minutes or until light brown. Remove foil; let tortilla shells cool. Remove shells from bowls. To store, place in an airtight container for up to 5 days.

Chef's
SALAD

Originally this salad received its name because the chef chose whatever leftover ingredients he wanted to use for the salad. Now ham, cheese, and egg are almost expected. But as the chef, you can use whatever is at hand. *Makes 4 servings*

Start to Finish: **30 minutes**

4 cups torn iceberg lettuce or leaf lettuce

4 cups torn romaine lettuce or fresh spinach

1 cup bite-size strips cooked ham, chicken, beef, or pork

1 cup bite-size strips Swiss, cheddar, or American cheese

2 hard-cooked eggs, sliced

2 medium tomatoes, cut into wedges, or 8 cherry tomatoes, halved

1/2 cup bite-size strips green or red sweet pepper

1 cup purchased croutons (optional)

1/2 cup bottled French or desired salad dressing

1. In a large bowl combine iceberg lettuce and romaine lettuce; toss gently to combine. Divide greens among 4 large salad plates.

2. Arrange meat, cheese, hard-cooked eggs, tomato, and sweet pepper on top of greens. If desired, sprinkle with croutons.

3. Drizzle desired amount of dressing over salads. Pass any remaining dressing.

Per serving: 368 cal., 27 g total fat (9 g sat. fat), 148 mg chol., 730 mg sodium, 15 g carbo., 3 g fiber, 18 g pro.

Maple-Pork
WILTED SALAD

Springtime spinach pairs well with pork and a maple syrup-sweetened dressing. *Makes 4 servings*

Start to Finish: **30 minutes**

8 cups packaged fresh baby spinach or torn fresh spinach

1½ cups peeled, seeded, and chopped cucumber (1 medium)

⅓ cup slivered red onion

12 ounces pork tenderloin

¼ teaspoon salt

¼ teaspoon ground black pepper

2 tablespoons olive oil

2 tablespoons finely chopped shallot or onion

¼ cup cider vinegar

¼ cup maple syrup

⅓ cup shredded cheddar cheese

¼ cup toasted sliced almonds or butter toffee-glazed sliced almonds

1. In a large bowl combine spinach, cucumber, and red onion; set aside.

2. Trim fat from meat. Cut meat into ¼-inch slices. Sprinkle with ¼ teaspoon salt and ¼ teaspoon pepper. In a large skillet heat 1 tablespoon of the oil over medium-high heat. Add meat; cook for 2 to 3 minutes or until meat is slightly pink in center, turning once. Add meat to spinach mixture in bowl; set aside.

3. In the same skillet cook shallot in the remaining 1 tablespoon oil over medium heat about 2 minutes or until tender. Add vinegar and maple syrup. Simmer, uncovered, for 1½ to 2 minutes or until slightly thickened. Pour over spinach mixture; toss gently to coat.

4. Sprinkle each serving with cheese and almonds.

Per serving: 305 cal., 15 g total fat (4 g sat. fat), 65 mg chol., 292 mg sodium, 20 g carbo., 2 g fiber, 24 g pro.

Chicken
AND PASTA SALAD

To save time and energy, roast two chickens at the same time; use one for dinner tonight; refrigerate the other for this fruity salad in a day or two. See photo on page 282. *Makes 6 servings*

Prep: 30 minutes Chill: 4 to 24 hours

1½ cups dried radiatore, mostaccioli, and/or medium shell pasta

3 cups chopped cooked chicken

3 cups seedless grapes, halved

1½ cups halved or quartered small strawberries

1 8-ounce can sliced water chestnuts, drained

⅔ cup bottled cucumber ranch salad dressing

⅛ teaspoon cayenne pepper

1 to 2 tablespoons milk (optional)

Leaf lettuce

Sliced almonds, toasted (optional)

1. Cook pasta according to package directions; drain. Rinse with cold water; drain again.

2. In a large bowl combine cooked pasta, chicken, grapes, strawberries, and drained water chestnuts.

3. For dressing, in a small bowl stir together bottled dressing and cayenne pepper. Pour dressing over pasta mixture; toss gently to coat. Cover and chill for 4 to 24 hours.

4. If necessary, stir enough of the milk into the pasta mixture to moisten. Line 6 large salad plates with lettuce. Mound pasta mixture on top of lettuce. If desired, sprinkle with almonds.

Per serving: 447 cal., 19 g total fat (3 g sat. fat), 62 mg chol., 265 mg sodium, 44 g carbo., 3 g fiber, 25 g pro.

Turkey AND ARTICHOKE TOSS

Bottled artichokes have a robust flavor that marries well with spinach and turkey in this zesty main-dish salad. _Makes 4 servings_

Start to Finish: **25 minutes**

1 12- or 14-ounce jar quartered marinated artichoke hearts, undrained

¼ cup bottled roasted garlic vinaigrette salad dressing or creamy Parmesan-basil salad dressing

1 tablespoon honey

1 5-ounce package fresh baby spinach

2¼ cups cubed roasted turkey

1 cup cherry tomatoes, halved

½ cup shredded carrot (1 medium)

¼ cup sliced almonds, toasted

1. Drain artichokes, reserving ¼ cup of the marinade. For dressing, in a small bowl stir together the reserved ¼ cup marinade, the bottled dressing, and honey. Set aside.

2. In a large salad bowl combine artichokes, spinach, turkey, tomato, carrot, and almonds. Pour dressing over spinach mixture; toss gently to coat.

Per serving: 342 cal., 20 g total fat (2 g sat. fat), 54 mg chol., 459 mg sodium, 19 g carbo., 3 g fiber, 25 g pro.

Salad
NIÇOISE
Cook and chill the beans and potatoes for this French-inspired salad a day before serving. *Makes 4 servings*

Prep: **35 minutes** Chill: **2 to 24 hours**

8 ounces fresh green beans, trimmed

12 ounces tiny new potatoes, sliced

Butterhead (Boston or bibb) lettuce leaves

8 ounces cooked tuna or salmon, broken into chunks (about 1½ cups), or one 9.25-ounce can chunk white tuna (water pack), drained and broken into chunks

2 medium tomatoes, cut into wedges

2 hard-cooked eggs, sliced

½ cup pitted ripe olives (optional)

¼ cup thinly sliced green onion (2)

4 anchovy fillets, rinsed, drained, and patted dry (optional)

Fresh tarragon sprigs (optional)

1 recipe Niçoise Dressing or ½ cup bottled balsamic vinaigrette salad dressing

1. In a covered large saucepan, cook green beans and potato in a small amount of boiling, lightly salted water for 10 to 15 minutes or just until tender; drain. Transfer vegetables to a medium bowl. Cover and chill for 2 to 24 hours.
2. To serve, line 4 large salad plates with lettuce. Arrange chilled vegetables, tuna, tomato, hard-cooked eggs, and, if desired, olives on plates. Sprinkle with green onion. If desired, top salads with anchovies and garnish with tarragon. Drizzle salads with Niçoise Dressing.

Niçoise Dressing: In a screw-top jar combine ¼ cup olive oil or salad oil; ¼ cup white wine vinegar or white vinegar; 1 teaspoon honey; 1 teaspoon snipped fresh tarragon or ¼ teaspoon dried tarragon, crushed; 1 teaspoon Dijon-style mustard; ¼ teaspoon salt; and dash ground black pepper. Cover and shake well. Makes about ½ cup.

Per serving: 348 cal., 17 g total fat (3 g sat. fat), 139 mg chol., 228 mg sodium, 24 g carbo., 4 g fiber, 24 g pro.

Tuna, Cheese, AND PASTA SALAD

Three-color pasta, cheese, albacore tuna, and roasted red peppers blend for a fun pasta salad with a hint of summer freshness from the basil and romaine. Sprinkle the salad with cashews for crunch.

Makes 4 servings

Prep: **30 minutes** Chill: **2 to 8 hours**

2 cups dried tri-color fusilli, rotini, or tiny shell pasta
¾ cup cubed Swiss, cheddar, or American cheese (3 ounces)
⅔ cup frozen peas
½ cup sliced celery (1 stalk)
2 tablespoons thinly sliced fresh basil
½ cup bottled creamy roasted garlic or peppercorn ranch salad dressing
1 7-ounce pouch chunk white albacore tuna (water pack), undrained
1 7-ounce jar roasted red sweet peppers, drained and coarsely chopped
Romaine lettuce leaves
⅓ cup dry-roasted cashews, coarsely chopped

1. Cook pasta according to package directions; drain. Rinse with cold water; drain again. Transfer pasta to a large bowl. Stir in cheese, frozen peas, celery, and basil.

2. Pour salad dressing over pasta mixture; toss gently to coat. Add undrained tuna and roasted pepper; toss gently to coat. Cover and chill for 2 to 8 hours.

3. If necessary, stir a few tablespoons additional salad dressing or milk into pasta mixture to moisten. Line 4 large salad plates or shallow bowls with lettuce. Mound pasta mixture on top of lettuce. Sprinkle with cashews.

Per serving: 596 cal., 30 g total fat (8 g sat. fat), 43 mg chol., 594 mg sodium, 54 g carbo., 4 g fiber, 28 g pro.

Panzanella
(BREAD SALAD)

A favorite with Italians, this salad is a time-honored way to use day-old bread. Juicy seasonal tomatoes contribute some of the moisture that softens the bread. *Makes 4 servings*

Prep: 20 minutes   Stand: 15 minutes

3 cups dried Italian bread
  cubes*

1½ cups coarsely chopped
  seeded tomato (3 medium)

½ of a medium red onion,
  cut into thin wedges and
  separated

¼ cup snipped fresh basil or
  Italian (flat-leaf) parsley

2 tablespoons red or white
  wine vinegar

2 tablespoons olive oil

1 teaspoon bottled minced
  garlic (2 cloves)

¼ teaspoon salt

¼ teaspoon ground black
  pepper

4 cups torn or chopped
  romaine lettuce

1. In a large bowl combine bread cubes, tomato, red onion, and basil. Set aside.
2. For dressing, in a screw-top jar combine vinegar, oil, garlic, salt, and pepper. Cover and shake well. Pour dressing over bread mixture; toss gently to coat.
3. Let stand for 15 minutes to allow the flavors to blend. Serve bread mixture over lettuce.

*Test Kitchen Tip: To dry bread, spread fresh bread cubes in an ungreased shallow baking pan. Let stand at room temperature overnight, stirring once or twice. Or preheat oven to 300°F. Bake, uncovered, for 8 to 10 minutes or until dry but not toasted, stirring once or twice.

Per serving: 213 cal., 9 g total fat (1 g sat. fat), 0 mg chol., 417 mg sodium, 29 g carbo., 4 g fiber, 6 g pro.

IN-A-PINCH TIPS!

TO SAVE TIME, SUBSTITUTE ¼ TO ⅓ CUP BOTTLED ITALIAN SALAD DRESSING FOR THE HOMEMADE DRESSING.

Spring Greens
WITH SUGARED NUTS

A simple technique, sugar-coating nuts, turns an ordinary salad into something spectacular.

Makes 6 servings

Start to Finish: **30 minutes**

Nonstick cooking spray
½ cup coarsely chopped
   walnuts or pecans
2 tablespoons sugar
⅛ teaspoon salt
1 teaspoon butter
5 cups torn romaine lettuce
⅓ cup thin wedges red onion or
   sliced green onion
¼ cup dried cherries or
   cranberries
⅓ cup bottled reduced-calorie
   raspberry vinaigrette salad
   dressing or raspberry-
   walnut vinaigrette salad
   dressing
½ cup shaved or shredded
   Asiago cheese or crumbled
   blue cheese (2 ounces)

1. Preheat oven to 325°F. Line a baking sheet with foil. Lightly coat foil with cooking spray; set baking sheet aside. Spread nuts evenly in an ungreased shallow baking pan. Bake, uncovered, about 10 minutes or until toasted, stirring once.

2. Meanwhile, for sugared nuts, place sugar and salt in a 6-inch heavy skillet. Heat over medium-high heat, shaking skillet several times to heat sugar evenly (do not stir). Heat until some of the sugar is melted (it should look syrupy). Start to stir only the melted sugar to keep it from overbrowning and stirring in the remaining sugar as it melts. Reduce heat to low. Continue to cook and stir until all of the sugar is melted and golden brown. Stir in butter.

3. Add warm nuts to skillet, stirring to coat. Pour nut mixture onto the prepared baking sheet. Using two forks, separate nut mixture into clusters while still warm. Cool.

4. In a large bowl combine lettuce, onion, and dried cherries. Drizzle dressing over lettuce mixture; toss gently to coat. Divide lettuce mixture among 6 salad plates. Top with sugared nuts and cheese.

Test Kitchen Tip: **If you prefer use ½ cup purchased glazed walnuts or almonds instead of making your own sugared nuts.**

Per serving: 182 cal., 13 g total fat (3 g sat. fat), 12 mg chol., 283 mg sodium, 14 g carbo., 2 g fiber, 5 g pro.

Spicy
BLT SALAD

This is a great salad for anyone who loves the flavor of the classic sandwich but wants to hold the bread.

Makes 4 to 6 servings

Start to Finish: **25 minutes**

8 cups torn mixed salad greens

1 11-ounce can whole kernel corn with sweet peppers, drained

1 large tomato, coarsely chopped

²⁄₃ cup snipped fresh cilantro or parsley

8 slices bacon, crisp-cooked, drained, and crumbled

½ cup bottled ranch salad dressing

1 canned chipotle chile pepper in adobo sauce, finely chopped (see note, page 22)

1. In a large salad bowl, combine salad greens, drained corn, tomato, cilantro, and bacon.

2. For dressing, in a small bowl combine bottled dressing and chipotle pepper. Pour over greens mixture; toss gently to coat.

Per serving: 288 cal., 22 g total fat (4 g sat. fat), 27 mg chol., 868 mg sodium, 15 g carbo., 4 g fiber, 9 g pro.

Apple-Pecan
SALAD

The least expensive apples work just fine for this salad that contrasts warm apples with cold mixed greens. *Makes 6 servings*

Start to Finish: **30 minutes** Oven: **425°F**

Nonstick cooking spray

3 tablespoons packed brown sugar

3 tablespoons finely chopped pecans

3 small sweet apples, halved lengthwise and cored

1 tablespoon butter or margarine, melted

⅓ cup salad oil

¼ cup apple cider or apple juice

¼ cup cider vinegar

1 tablespoon honey

¼ teaspoon salt

¼ teaspoon ground black pepper

6 cups torn mixed salad greens

¼ cup coarsely chopped pecans, toasted (optional)

1. Preheat oven to 425°F. Line a baking sheet with foil. Lightly coat foil with cooking spray; set baking sheet aside. In a small bowl combine brown sugar and the 3 tablespoons pecans. Place apple halves, cut sides up, on the prepared baking sheet. Brush apples with melted butter; sprinkle with brown sugar mixture. Bake, uncovered, about 15 minutes or just until apples are tender.

2. Meanwhile, for dressing, in a screw-top jar combine oil, cider, vinegar, honey, salt, and pepper. Cover and shake well.

3. Arrange salad greens on a serving platter. Add apple halves; spoon any melted brown sugar mixture from baking sheet onto salad. Shake dressing; drizzle desired amount over salad. If desired, sprinkle with the ¼ cup pecans. Pass any remaining dressing.

Per serving: 380 cal., 30 g total fat (4 g sat. fat), 8 mg chol., 328 mg sodium, 28 g carbo., 4 g fiber, 4 g pro.

Corn Bread
SALAD

Corn bread adds delightful corn flavor to this make-ahead salad that is great any time of year.

Makes 10 to 12 servings

Prep: **20 minutes** Bake: **20 minutes** Chill: **2 to 24 hours** Oven: **400°F**

1 8.5-ounce package corn muffin mix
1 cup mayonnaise or salad dressing
1 8-ounce carton dairy sour cream
1 0.4-ounce envelope ranch dry salad dressing mix
2 15-ounce cans pinto beans, rinsed and drained
1 15.25-ounce can whole kernel corn, drained
1 cup chopped tomato (2 medium)
¾ cup chopped green sweet pepper (1 medium)
½ cup sliced green onion (4)
8 slices bacon, crisp-cooked, drained, and crumbled
2 cups shredded cheddar cheese (8 ounces)

1. Preheat oven to 400°F. Grease an 8-inch oven-proof cast-iron skillet; set aside. Prepare muffin mix according to package directions. Spread batter in the prepared skillet. Bake, uncovered, for 20 to 25 minutes or until a toothpick inserted near the center comes out clean. Cool on a wire rack. Coarsely crumble corn bread; set aside.

2. For dressing, in a medium bowl combine mayonnaise, sour cream, and salad dressing mix; set aside. In a large bowl combine drained beans, drained corn, tomato, sweet pepper, green onion, and bacon.

3. In a 3-quart glass bowl, layer half of the corn bread, half of the bean mixture, and half of the cheese. Spread half of the dressing over layers in bowl. Repeat layers. Cover and chill for 2 to 24 hours.

4. To serve, toss gently to coat corn bread and vegetables with dressing.

Per serving: 564 cal., 37 g total fat (13 g sat. fat), 68 mg chol., 1,126 mg sodium, 38 g carbo., 6 g fiber, 16 g pro.

IN-A-PINCH TIPS!

CHEESE EQUIVALENTS: FOR 2 CUPS OF PRE-PACKAGED SHREDDED CHEESE, SHRED AN 8-OUNCE BLOCK OF CHEESE.

24-Hour Layered
VEGETABLE SALAD

This eye-catching salad cleverly uses small bits of vegetables and cheese without screaming leftovers. The added bonus: Make it from 2 to 24 hours ahead of serving time. *Makes 4 servings*

Prep: 15 minutes   Chill: 2 to 24 hours

2 cups torn mixed salad greens
1 cup broccoli florets
¾ cup sliced carrot
3 slices bacon, crisp-cooked, drained, and crumbled
¾ cup shredded cheddar cheese (3 ounces)
½ cup bottled creamy Italian salad dressing
¼ cup thinly sliced green onion (2)

1. Place salad greens in a 1½-quart glass bowl. Layer ingredients on top of greens in the following order: broccoli, carrot, bacon, and ½ cup of the cheese. Spread dressing over salad. Sprinkle with the remaining ¼ cup cheese and the green onion. Cover and chill for 2 to 24 hours.

2. To serve, toss gently to coat greens and vegetables with dressing.

Per serving: 226 cal., 19 g total fat (7 g sat. fat), 26 mg chol., 467 mg sodium, 7 g carbo., 2 g fiber, 8 g pro.

Pepper
AND FOUR-BEAN SALAD

If you like three-bean salad, you will enjoy this colorful four-bean adaptation. A tangy tarragon vinaigrette gives it pizzazz. See photo on page 283. *Makes 14 servings*

Prep: **25 minutes** Chill: **4 to 24 hours**

4 cups fresh green and/or wax beans, trimmed and cut into 1½-inch pieces, or one 16-ounce package frozen cut green beans

3 cups thin strips green, red, and/or yellow sweet pepper (3 medium)

1 15-ounce can red kidney beans, rinsed and drained

1 15-ounce can garbanzo beans (chickpeas), rinsed and drained

1 small red or white onion, thinly sliced and separated into rings

½ cup vinegar

¼ cup olive oil

1 tablespoon sugar

2 teaspoons snipped fresh tarragon or thyme or ½ teaspoon dried tarragon or thyme, crushed

½ teaspoon ground black pepper

Lettuce leaves (optional)

1. In a covered large saucepan, cook fresh green and/or wax beans in a small amount of boiling water for 8 to 10 minutes or just until tender. (If using frozen green beans, cook according to package directions.) Drain beans. Immerse in a bowl of ice water to cool quickly; drain well.

2. In a large bowl combine green and/or wax beans, sweet pepper, drained kidney beans, drained garbanzo beans, and onion.

3. For dressing, in a medium bowl whisk together vinegar, oil, sugar, tarragon, and black pepper. Pour dressing over bean mixture; toss gently to coat. Cover and chill for 4 to 24 hours, stirring occasionally.

4. If desired, line a serving bowl with lettuce. Using a slotted spoon, spoon bean mixture into bowl.

Per serving: 117 cal., 4 g total fat (0 g sat. fat), 0 mg chol., 146 mg sodium, 17 g carbo., 5 g fiber, 5 g pro.

Broccoli, Cauliflower, AND RAISIN SALAD

This colorful and healthful salad totes well to picnics and potlucks. Keep the salad and dressing separate and transport them in a cooler with an ice pack. Then toss the salad and dressing together just before serving. Be sure to serve within 2 hours. *Makes 10 servings*

Prep: **30 minutes** Chill: **2 to 3 hours**

6 cups broccoli florets
3 cups cauliflower florets
½ cup golden raisins
⅓ cup broken walnuts, toasted
¼ cup olive oil or salad oil
¼ cup cider vinegar
1 teaspoon salt
1 teaspoon honey or sugar
½ teaspoon dried basil, crushed
½ teaspoon ground black
   pepper
¼ teaspoon crushed red pepper
   (optional)

1. In a large saucepan bring 2 inches of water to boiling. Add broccoli. Return to boiling; reduce heat. Cook, covered, about 2 minutes or until broccoli is crisp-tender; drain. Rinse with cold water; drain again.

2. In the same saucepan cook cauliflower in water as directed in Step I; drain. Rinse with cold water; drain again.

3. In a 2- to 2½-quart bowl, layer half of each of the following: broccoli, cauliflower, raisins, and walnuts. Repeat layers. Cover and chill for 2 to 3 hours.

4. For dressing, in a screw-top jar combine oil, vinegar, salt, honey, basil, black pepper, and, if desired, crushed red pepper. Cover and shake well.

5. Before serving, pour dressing over vegetable mixture; toss gently to coat.

Per serving: 128 cal., 8 g total fat (1 g sat. fat), 0 mg chol., 261 mg sodium, 13 g carbo., 3 g fiber, 3 g pro.

Sesame
NOODLE SLAW

The ramen noodles are crunchy when you first make this cabbage salad. If you prefer softer noodles, chill the salad to give the noodles time to absorb some of the soy-vinegar dressing. *Makes 8 servings*

Prep: **25 minutes** Chill: **30 minutes to 4 hours** Oven: **300°F**

½ cup slivered almonds

2 tablespoons sesame seeds

1 3-ounce package chicken-flavor ramen noodles

⅓ cup salad oil

3 tablespoons vinegar

2 tablespoons reduced-sodium soy sauce

1 tablespoon sugar

¼ teaspoon ground black pepper

6 cups shredded cabbage

⅓ to ½ cup thinly sliced green onion (3 to 4)

I. Preheat oven to 300°F. Spread almonds and sesame seeds in an ungreased shallow baking pan. Bake, uncovered, about IO minutes or until toasted, stirring once. Cool.

2. Meanwhile, break noodles into small pieces; set aside. For dressing, in a screw-top jar combine seasoning packet from noodles, oil, vinegar, soy sauce, sugar, and pepper. Cover and shake well.

3. In a large bowl combine almonds, sesame seeds, noodles, cabbage, and green onion. Pour dressing over cabbage mixture; toss gently to coat. Cover and chill for 30 minutes to 4 hours.

Per serving: 2II cal., I6 g total fat (3 g sat. fat), 0 mg chol., 360 mg sodium, I4 g carbo., 3 g fiber, 4 g pro.

Sesame Chicken and Noodle Slaw: Prepare as directed, except toss 1½ cups chopped cooked chicken or pork with the cabbage mixture. Makes 4 servings.

Per serving: 523 cal., 37 g total fat (7 g sat. fat), 47 mg chol., 450 mg sodium, 28 g carbo., 6 g fiber, 24 g pro.

Spring
WALDORF SALAD

Though some people may only admit it secretly, they love this salad not because it is economical to make but because it tastes so good. *Makes 6 servings*

Start to Finish: **25 minutes**

2 medium Granny Smith apples, cored and cut into wedges
1 tablespoon lemon juice
1 head butterhead (Boston or bibb) lettuce, separated into leaves
2 heads green and/or red Belgian endive, separated into leaves
¾ cup seedless green grapes, halved
¼ cup blanched whole almonds, toasted
1 recipe Lemon Dressing

1. In a medium bowl combine apple and lemon juice; toss gently to coat.
2. Arrange lettuce and endive on 6 salad plates. Top with apple, grapes, and almonds. Spoon Lemon Dressing over salads.

Lemon Dressing: In a small bowl stir together one 6-ounce carton lemon low-fat yogurt, 1 tablespoon snipped fresh dill or ¼ teaspoon dried dill, 1 tablespoon cider vinegar, ¼ teaspoon salt, and ¼ teaspoon ground black pepper. Makes about ⅔ cup.

Per serving: 112 cal., 4 g total fat (0 g sat. fat), 1 mg chol., 120 mg sodium, 19 g carbo., 2 g fiber, 4 g pro.

Spring Waldorf Chicken Salad: Prepare as directed, except add 2 cups chopped cooked chicken or ham with the fruit and almonds.

Per serving: 200 cal., 7 g total fat (1 g sat. fat), 43 mg chol., 160 mg sodium, 18 g carbo., 2 g fiber, 17 g pro.

Marinated
CUCUMBERS

For added color and flavor, stir in I cup halved cherry tomatoes and I medium green, red, or yellow sweet pepper, cut into strips. *Makes 6 servings*

Prep: 15 minutes Chill: 4 to 24 hours

2 tablespoons vinegar
2 tablespoons salad oil
½ teaspoon sugar
½ teaspoon salt
¼ teaspoon celery seeds
1 large cucumber, peeled (if desired), halved lengthwise, and thinly sliced
1 small onion, thinly sliced

1. In a medium bowl combine vinegar, oil, sugar, salt, and celery seeds. Add cucumber and onion; toss gently to coat. Cover and chill for 4 to 24 hours, stirring occasionally.

Per serving: 54 cal., 5 g total fat (1 g sat. fat), 0 mg chol., 195 mg sodium, 3 g carbo., 1 g fiber, 0 g pro.

Basil
AND TOMATO PASTA SALAD

During tomato and basil season, this is the salad to serve with grilled chicken or burgers.

Makes 12 to 16 servings

Prep: **30 minutes** Chill: **4 to 24 hours**

8 ounces dried rotini, cavatelli, or penne pasta

6 ounces fresh green beans, trimmed and cut into 1-inch pieces, or 1 cup frozen cut green beans

3 medium tomatoes, cut into thin wedges

¾ cup finely shredded Parmesan cheese (3 ounces)

½ cup sliced, pitted kalamata olives or ripe olives

½ cup finely shredded fresh basil

1 cup desired bottled vinaigrette salad dressing
Shaved Parmesan cheese (optional)

1. Cook pasta according to package directions, adding green beans during the last 5 minutes of cooking; drain. Rinse with cold water; drain again.

2. In a very large bowl, combine pasta mixture, tomato, the ¾ cup cheese, the olives, and basil. Pour dressing over pasta mixture; toss gently to coat. Cover and chill for 4 to 24 hours.

3. Before serving, gently toss again. If desired, top with shaved cheese.

Per serving: 170 cal., 8 g total fat (2 g sat. fat), 4 mg chol., 384 mg sodium, 19 g carbo., 2 g fiber, 5 g pro.

Southwestern Corn,
BEAN, AND RICE SALAD

Toss this side salad together using leftover rice and canned veggies from your pantry. *Makes 6 servings*

Start to Finish: **30 minutes**

1 15-ounce can black beans or pinto beans, rinsed and drained

1½ cups cooked rice, chilled

1 cup seeded and chopped tomato (2 medium)

1 cup frozen whole kernel corn, thawed

1 4-ounce can diced green chile peppers, drained

¼ cup chopped red onion or green onion

2 tablespoons snipped fresh cilantro or parsley

1 recipe Garlic Dressing or ⅓ cup bottled Italian salad dressing

1 recipe Tortilla Strips or crushed tortilla chips

1. In a large bowl stir together drained beans, rice, tomato, corn, drained chile peppers, onion, and cilantro.
2. Pour Garlic Dressing over rice mixture; toss gently to coat.
3. To serve, top salad with Tortilla Strips.

Garlic Dressing: In a screw-top jar combine 3 tablespoons white wine vinegar, 2 tablespoons olive oil or salad oil, 1 tablespoon water, ¼ teaspoon salt, ¼ teaspoon garlic powder, and ¼ teaspoon ground black pepper. Cover and shake well. Makes about ⅓ cup.

Tortilla Strips: Preheat oven to 350°F. Roll up 2 plain, spinach, and/or tomato flour tortillas and slice crosswise into ¼- to ½-inch strips. Lightly coat strips with nonstick cooking spray; spread on an ungreased baking sheet. Bake, uncovered, for 10 to 15 minutes or until golden brown. Cool.

Make-Ahead Directions: Prepare as directed through Step 2. Cover and chill for up to 24 hours. Serve as directed.

Per serving: 205 cal., 6 g total fat (1 g sat. fat), 0 mg chol., 369 mg sodium, 34 g carbo., 5 g fiber, 8 g pro.

LOOK!

MONEY-SAVING TIPS and HINTS

Purchase store-brand canned vegetables and fruits, or purchase them at discount dollar stores which often have specials on these items.

If you use potatoes regularly, 10-pound bags of potatoes are a better buy than either 5-pound bags or purchasing potatoes individually.

Instead of buying the expensive steam bags of frozen veggies, buy your own plastic steam bags for cooking veggies.

CHEAP!

Fun-shape pasta on sale adds interest to skillet pasta dinners and pasta salads.

$AVE! $AVE!

Use leftover veggies to your advantage. Chop, season, and stir them into hot cooked rice for a tasty pilaf.

$AVE! $AVE!

Sale! Save leftover rolls and/or bread to cut into cubes, drizzle with butter, and toast for homemade croutons. Or use a food processor or blender to make fresh bread crumbs for casserole toppings.

Purchase bulk rice and pasta, especially when on sale.

Loose-pack frozen vegetables and fruits are far more economical than those packaged in smaller boxes.

Overly ripe bananas are perfect for banana bread and/or banana muffins.

CHAPTER 10

ON-THE-CHEAP SIDES

A smart way to stretch your food dollar: reduce the amount of protein food, such as meat, poultry, and fish, that you serve and fill in with one of these 21 good side dishes. No one will be the wiser. In addition to saving money, you're rounding out dinner with good nutrition from vegetables and breads.

Green Bean–
RED PEPPER CASSEROLE

Roasted red sweet peppers refresh this traditional casserole, updated with an onion-crumb topping.

Makes 8 servings

Prep: **20 minutes** Bake: **35 minutes** Oven: **350°F**

½ cup finely chopped onion
   (1 medium)
2 tablespoons butter or
   margarine
⅓ cup fine dry bread crumbs
1 10.75-ounce can condensed
   cream of mushroom soup
⅓ cup bottled roasted red
   sweet peppers, drained
   and chopped
¼ cup slivered almonds,
   toasted
½ teaspoon salt
⅛ teaspoon ground black
   pepper
2 16-ounce packages frozen
   French-cut green beans,
   thawed and drained

1. Preheat oven to 350°F. In a small saucepan cook onion in hot butter over medium heat until tender. Remove from heat. Add bread crumbs; toss gently to coat. Set aside.

2. In a large bowl combine soup, roasted pepper, almonds, salt, and black pepper. Stir in green beans. Transfer to an ungreased 2-quart casserole. Sprinkle with crumb mixture.

3. Bake, uncovered, for 35 to 40 minutes or until beans are tender.

Per serving: 140 cal., 8 g total fat (3 g sat. fat), 9 mg chol., 556 mg sodium, 17 g carbo., 4 g fiber, 4 g pro.

Orange-Sauced Broccoli
AND PEPPERS

Choose a red or yellow pepper depending on price and how it complements the rest of your meal. Broccoli is widely available year-round and is a good value. *Makes 6 servings*

Start to Finish: **35 minutes**

3½ cups broccoli florets
 1 cup bite-size strips red or yellow sweet pepper (1 medium)
 1 tablespoon butter or margarine
 2 tablespoons finely chopped onion
 ½ teaspoon bottled minced garlic (1 clove)
 1½ teaspoons cornstarch
 ⅔ cup orange juice

1. In a covered medium saucepan cook broccoli and sweet pepper in a small amount of boiling water about 8 minutes or until broccoli is crisp-tender; drain. Cover and keep warm.

2. For sauce, in a small saucepan melt butter over medium heat. Add onion and garlic; cook about 5 minutes or until onion is tender. Stir in cornstarch. Slowly stir in orange juice. Cook and stir until thickened and bubbly. Cook and stir for 2 minutes more.

3. To serve, pour sauce over broccoli mixture; toss gently to coat.

Per serving: 57 cal., 2 g total fat (1 g sat. fat), 5 mg chol., 32 mg sodium, 9 g carbo., 2 g fiber, 2 g pro.

Broccoli
AND RICE BAKE

Rice, broccoli, and a savory soup-based sauce bake together for a true fix-and-forget favorite.

Makes 6 servings

Prep: **15 minutes** Bake: **65 minutes** Stand: **5 minutes** Oven: **350°F**

1 10.75-ounce can condensed cream of broccoli soup or cream of chicken soup
1¼ cups milk
1 8-ounce carton dairy sour cream
1 teaspoon dried basil, crushed
¼ teaspoon salt
⅛ teaspoon ground black pepper
1 16-ounce package frozen cut broccoli
1½ cups uncooked instant white rice
½ cup shredded Swiss cheese (2 ounces)

1. Preheat oven to 350°F. In a large bowl whisk together soup, milk, sour cream, basil, salt, and pepper. Stir in frozen broccoli and rice. Transfer mixture to an ungreased 2-quart rectangular baking dish.

2. Bake, covered, about 65 minutes or until heated through. Sprinkle with cheese. Let stand, covered, for 5 minutes before serving.

Per serving: 295 cal., 13 g total fat (8 g sat. fat), 31 mg chol., 511 mg sodium, 33 g carbo., 2 g fiber, 10 g pro.

Caramelized
BRUSSELS SPROUTS

These autumn, green nuggets are a good value through fall and winter. You will win over sprout haters with the caramelized sugar and vinegar sauce. *Makes 4 servings*

Start to Finish: **45 minutes**

1 pound small Brussels sprouts
2 tablespoons sugar
1 tablespoon butter or
   margarine
2 tablespoons red wine vinegar
¼ cup water
¼ teaspoon salt

1. Trim stems and remove any wilted outer leaves from Brussels sprouts. Set aside.
2. In a large skillet heat sugar over medium-high heat until it starts to melt, shaking pan occasionally to heat sugar evenly. Once sugar starts to melt, reduce heat and cook until sugar starts to turn brown. Add butter; stir until melted. Add vinegar. Cook and stir for 1 minute.

3. Carefully add the water and salt. Bring to boiling; stir in Brussels sprouts. Return to boiling; reduce heat. Simmer, covered, for 6 minutes. Simmer, uncovered, about 15 minutes more or until most of the liquid has been absorbed and the sprouts are glazed, gently stirring occasionally.

Per serving: 94 cal., 3 g total fat (2 g sat. fat), 8 mg chol., 191 mg sodium, 15 g carbo., 4 g fiber, 3 g pro.

Ginger-Honey
GLAZED CARROTS

Fast and flavorful, these glazed carrots are the ideal accompaniment for more time-consuming main dishes. Just cook, glaze, and serve! *Makes 4 servings*

Start to Finish: **20 minutes**

2 cups water
½ teaspoon salt
1 pound packaged peeled baby carrots
1 tablespoon butter or margarine
1 tablespoon honey
¾ teaspoon ground ginger

1. In a 10-inch heavy skillet, combine the water and salt. Bring to boiling. Add carrots. Return to boiling; reduce heat. Simmer, covered, for 10 to 12 minutes or until carrots are tender. Drain, removing carrots from skillet.

2. In the same skillet combine butter, honey, and ginger. Cook and stir over medium heat until butter is melted. Stir in carrots. Cook and stir for 2 to 3 minutes or until carrots are heated through and glazed.

Per serving: 91 cal., 3 g total fat (2 g sat. fat), 8 mg chol., 169 mg sodium, 15 g carbo., 3 g fiber, 1 g pro.

Curried
CARROTS

Keep a supply of frozen vegetables, such as carrots, on hand for speedy side dishes.

Makes 6 servings

Start to Finish: 15 minutes

1 16-ounce package frozen
   crinkle-cut carrots
¼ cup chopped onion
2 tablespoons butter or
   margarine
1 teaspoon sugar
1 teaspoon curry powder
½ teaspoon salt
⅛ teaspoon cayenne pepper
   Dash ground allspice
   or nutmeg

1. In a covered medium saucepan cook carrots and onion in a small amount of boiling salted water for 5 to 7 minutes or until crisp-tender. Drain, removing vegetables from pan.

2. In the same saucepan melt butter over medium heat. Stir in sugar, curry powder, salt, cayenne pepper, and allspice. Stir in vegetables; heat through.

Per serving: 73 cal., 4 g total fat (2 g sat. fat), 11 mg chol., 275 mg sodium, 9 g carbo., 2 g fiber, 1 g pro.

Creamed
CORN CASSEROLE

You have two choices for cooking this casserole—either in an oven or in a slow cooker. Use the method that fits your lifestyle. See photo on page 284. *Makes 12 servings*

Prep: **20 minutes** Bake: **50 minutes** Oven: **375°F**

Nonstick cooking spray

2 16-ounce packages frozen whole kernel corn

2 cups chopped red and/or green sweet pepper

1 cup chopped onion (1 large)

1 tablespoon butter or margarine

¼ teaspoon ground black pepper

1 10.75-ounce can condensed cream of celery soup

1 8-ounce tub cream cheese spread with chive and onion or cream cheese spread with garden vegetables

¼ cup milk

1. Preheat oven to 375°F. Coat a 2-quart casserole with cooking spray; set aside. Place corn in a colander and thaw by running under cool water; drain. Set aside.

2. In a large saucepan cook sweet pepper and onion in hot butter until tender. Stir in corn and black pepper. In a medium bowl whisk together soup, cream cheese spread, and milk. Stir soup mixture into corn mixture. Transfer to the prepared casserole.

3. Bake, covered, for 50 to 55 minutes or until heated through, stirring once.

Slow Cooker Directions: **Do not thaw corn and omit butter. In a 3½- or 4-quart slow cooker combine frozen corn, sweet pepper, onion, and black pepper. In a medium bowl whisk together soup, cream cheese spread, and milk. Pour over corn mixture in cooker. Cover and cook on low-heat setting for 8 to 10 hours or on high-heat setting for 4 to 5 hours. Stir before serving.**

Per serving: 176 cal., 9 g total fat (5 g sat. fat), 22 mg chol., 280 mg sodium, 22 g carbo., 3 g fiber, 4 g pro.

Honestly Good
MASHED POTATOES

After french fries, mashed is the second most favorite way to serve potatoes. Make a double batch and freeze half for another meal. *Makes 6 to 8 servings*

Prep: **20 minutes**   Cook: **15 minutes**   Stand: **5 minutes**

2½ pounds potatoes (about
    5 medium), cut into
    ½-inch slices
¾ cup milk
½ cup whipping cream
6 tablespoons unsalted butter,
    cut up
  Salt
  Unsalted butter

1. In a covered large saucepan cook potatoes in enough boiling salted water to cover for 15 to 20 minutes or until tender. Set colander in sink. Pour potatoes into colander to drain. Let potatoes stand in colander for 5 minutes to dry and cool slightly. Transfer potatoes to a large bowl. Meanwhile, in a small saucepan combine the ¾ cup milk and the cream. Cook, uncovered, just until hot.

2. Beat potatoes with the whip attachment of a electric stand mixer just until potatoes break. Add 3 tablespoons of the cut-up butter; beat on low speed just until combined. Add the remaining 3 tablespoons cut-up butter; beat just until combined.

3. Gradually beat in hot milk mixture, beating on low speed and adding only as much as the potatoes can absorb. Beat on medium speed until potatoes are light and fluffy (do not overmix).

4. Season to taste with salt. If necessary, stir in a little more of the hot milk mixture to moisten. Top with additional butter before serving.

Test Kitchen Tip: If you are not serving the potatoes right away, cover and set aside. If you need to reheat them, transfer the mashed potatoes to a medium nonstick saucepan. Cook, uncovered, over medium-low heat until warm, gently stirring occasionally. You will probably need to moisten the potatoes with a little additional warm milk before serving.

You also may freeze mashed potatoes in a freezer container for up to 1 month. Thaw in the refrigerator overnight, then reheat as directed above.

Per serving: 295 cal., 20 g total fat (12 g sat. fat), 60 mg chol., 417 mg sodium, 27 g carbo., 2 g fiber, 4 g pro.

Parmesan
POTATO WEDGES
The cheesy coating accented with Italian seasoning and garlic embellishes baked potato wedges.

Makes 6 servings

Prep: **20 minutes** Bake: **30 minutes** Oven: **425°F**

6 medium baking potatoes
  (6 to 8 ounces each)
⅓ cup butter or margarine,
  melted
¼ cup grated Parmesan cheese
½ teaspoon dried Italian
  seasoning, crushed
½ teaspoon bottled minced
  garlic (I clove)
¼ teaspoon salt
⅛ teaspoon ground black
  pepper

I. Preheat oven to 425°F. Line a 15×10×1-inch baking pan with foil; set aside. Cut each potato lengthwise into 8 wedges.

2. In a large bowl combine melted butter, cheese, Italian seasoning, garlic, salt, and pepper. Add potato wedges; stir gently to coat. Transfer wedges to the prepared baking pan.

3. Bake, uncovered, about 30 minutes or until tender.

Per serving: 194 cal., 12 g total fat (6 g sat. fat), 31 mg chol., 232 mg sodium, 19 g carbo., 2 g fiber, 4 g pro.

Roasted Baby
POTATOES WITH CARAMELIZED ONIONS

While the potatoes are oven roasting, cook the onions on the stovetop. Then combine the two just before serving. *Makes 10 to 12 servings*

Start to Finish: **45 minutes**   Oven: **425°F**

Nonstick cooking spray
1½ pounds small new red
    potatoes
1½ pounds small new white
    potatoes
¼ cup olive oil
1 tablespoon snipped fresh
    rosemary
2 teaspoons salt
½ teaspoon ground black
    pepper
4 cups thinly sliced onion
1 tablespoon sugar

1. Preheat oven to 425°F. Coat a 15×10×1-inch baking pan with cooking spray; set aside. Halve or quarter any large potatoes.

2. In a large bowl combine potatoes, 2 tablespoons of the oil, the rosemary, 1½ teaspoons of the salt, and ¼ teaspoon of the pepper; toss gently to coat. Arrange in a single layer in the prepared baking pan. Roast, uncovered, about 30 minutes or until tender and brown, stirring occasionally.

3. Meanwhile, for caramelized onions, in a very large nonstick skillet heat the remaining 2 tablespoons oil over medium-high heat. Add onion and sugar. Cook about 20 minutes or until golden brown, stirring occasionally. Remove from heat. Stir in the remaining ½ teaspoon salt and the remaining ¼ teaspoon pepper.

4. In a very large bowl combine potatoes and caramelized onions. Transfer to a serving bowl.

Make-Ahead Directions: **Prepare as directed. Cover and chill for up to 24 hours.**

To reheat in the oven, preheat oven to 350°F. Transfer potato mixture to an ungreased 13×9×2-inch baking pan. Bake, covered, about 20 minutes or until heated through, stirring once.

To reheat in the microwave oven, transfer half of the potato mixture to a 2-quart microwave-safe casserole. Microwave, covered, on 100 percent power (high) for 6 minutes, stirring twice. Repeat with the remaining potato mixture.

Per serving: 192 cal., 6 g total fat (1 g sat. fat), 0 mg chol., 480 mg sodium, 33 g carbo., 4 g fiber, 4 g pro.

Cheese-Potato
SOUP

Enjoy a hassle-free bowl of soup tonight. Place ingredients in a slow cooker and head off to work. Add the cheese when you return home. *Makes 8 servings*

Prep: 20 minutes   Cook: Low 8 hours, High 4 hours; plus 15 minutes on High

6 cups peeled and cubed
   potato (6 medium)
1 cup chopped onion (1 large)
1 cup chopped carrot
   (2 medium)
1 teaspoon bottled minced
   garlic (2 cloves)
¼ teaspoon ground black
   pepper
3 14-ounce cans vegetable
   broth or chicken broth
1 cup shredded Monterey
   Jack cheese with jalapeño
   peppers (4 ounces)
   Milk (optional)

1. In a 4- to 5-quart slow cooker combine potato, onion, carrot, garlic, and pepper. Pour broth over mixture in cooker.

2. Cover and cook on low-heat setting for 8 to 9 hours or on high-heat setting for 4 to 4½ hours. Ladle soup into a large bowl; cool slightly.

3. Transfer about one-third of the soup at a time to a blender. Cover and blend until smooth. Return to cooker.

4. If using low-heat setting, turn to high-heat setting. Stir in cheese. Cover and cook for 15 minutes more. Stir until cheese is nearly melted. If desired, stir in a little milk to reach desired consistency.

Per serving: 167 cal., 5 g total fat (3 g sat. fat), 15 mg chol., 696 mg sodium, 26 g carbo., 3 g fiber, 6 g pro.

Mashed Sweet
POTATOES AND PARSNIPS

Sweet potatoes and parsnips cook together in a slow cooker until tender for tasty results. The harvest-orange color contrasts well with chicken or turkey. *Makes 6 to 8 servings*

Prep: **20 minutes** Cook: **Low 7 hours, High 3½ hours**

Nonstick cooking spray
4 cups peeled and cubed sweet potato
3 medium parsnips, peeled and cubed
½ cup chicken broth
2 tablespoons butter or margarine, melted
½ teaspoon onion salt
½ teaspoon ground sage
⅛ teaspoon ground black pepper

1. Lightly coat the inside of a 3½- or 4-quart slow cooker with cooking spray. Add sweet potato, parsnip, broth, melted butter, onion salt, sage, and pepper.

2. Cover and cook on low-heat setting for 7 to 8 hours or on high-heat setting for 3½ to 4 hours.

3. Using a potato masher, mash sweet potato mixture until fluffy.

Per serving: 166 cal., 5 g total fat (3 g sat. fat), 11 mg chol., 273 mg sodium, 30 g carbo., 5 g fiber, 2 g pro.

Acorn Squash
WITH ORANGE-CRANBERRY SAUCE

A few basic ingredients bestow amazing flavor on this side dish. No matter whether you serve the festive cranberry-sauced squash with roasted pork, grilled poultry, or broiled fish, it is a top-notch way to round out a meal. *Makes 4 to 6 servings*

Prep: 15 minutes Cook: Low 6 hours, High 3 hours

- 2 medium acorn squash (about 2 pounds)
- 1 16-ounce can jellied cranberry sauce
- ¼ cup orange marmalade
- ¼ cup raisins
- ¼ teaspoon ground cinnamon
  Salt and ground black pepper

1. Cut each squash in half lengthwise; remove seeds. Cut squash into 1-inch wedges. Arrange squash in a 3½- or 4-quart slow cooker.

2. In a small saucepan combine cranberry sauce, marmalade, raisins, and cinnamon. Cook and stir over medium heat until smooth. Pour over squash in cooker.

3. Cover and cook on low-heat setting for 6 to 7 hours or on high-heat setting for 3 to 3½ hours. Season to taste with salt and pepper.

Per serving: 328 cal., 0 g total fat (0 g sat. fat), 0 mg chol., 220 mg sodium, 83 g carbo., 5 g fiber, 2 g pro.

Saucepan
BAKED BEANS

Flavorful baked beans are an all-time-favorite side dish with an added bonus—they're economical.

Makes 6 servings

Prep: 10 minutes Cook: 10 minutes

1 15-ounce can pork and beans in tomato sauce, undrained
1 15-ounce can navy beans or Great Northern beans, rinsed and drained
¼ cup ketchup
2 tablespoons maple syrup or packed brown sugar
2 teaspoons dry mustard
2 slices bacon, crisp-cooked, drained, and crumbled

1. In a medium saucepan combine undrained pork and beans, drained navy beans, ketchup, maple syrup, and dry mustard.

2. Bring mixture to boiling; reduce heat. Simmer, uncovered, about 10 minutes or until mixture reaches desired consistency, stirring frequently. Stir in bacon.

Per serving: 191 cal., 2 g total fat (1 g sat. fat), 8 mg chol., 801 mg sodium, 35 g carbo., 6 g fiber, 10 g pro.

Corn
BREAD

You can have this freshly baked bread on your dinner table in less than 30 minutes. See photo on page 285. *Makes 8 to 10 servings*

Prep: 10 minutes Bake: 15 minutes Oven: 400°F

1 cup all-purpose flour
¾ cup cornmeal
2 to 3 tablespoons sugar
2½ teaspoons baking powder
¾ teaspoon salt
1 tablespoon butter or margarine
2 eggs, lightly beaten
1 cup milk
¼ cup cooking oil or melted butter
Honey (optional)

1. Preheat oven to 400°F. In a medium bowl stir together flour, cornmeal, sugar, baking powder, and salt. Set aside.

2. Add the 1 tablespoon butter to a 10-inch cast-iron skillet, a 9×1½-inch round baking pan, or an 8×8×2-inch baking pan. Place in oven and heat about 3 minutes or until butter is melted. Remove skillet or pan from oven; swirl butter in skillet or pan to coat bottom and sides of pan.

3. Meanwhile, in a small bowl combine eggs, milk, and oil. Add egg mixture all at once to flour mixture; stir just until moistened. Pour batter into the hot skillet or pan.

4. Bake, uncovered, for 15 to 20 minutes or until a toothpick inserted near the center comes out clean. Cut into wedges or squares. Serve warm. If desired, drizzle with honey.

Per serving: 219 cal., 10 g total fat (3 g sat. fat), 60 mg chol., 390 mg sodium, 26 g carbo., 1 g fiber, 5 g pro.

Double Corn Bread: Prepare as directed, except fold ½ cup frozen whole kernel corn, thawed, into the batter.

Per serving: 227 cal., 11 g fat (3 g sat. fat), 60 mg chol., 391 mg sodium, 28 g carbo., 2 g fiber, 5 g pro.

Green Chile Corn Bread: Prepare as directed, except fold 1 cup shredded cheddar cheese or Monterey Jack cheese (4 ounces) and one 4-ounce can diced green chile peppers, drained, into the batter.

Per serving: 279 cal., 15 g fat (6 g sat. fat), 74 mg chol., 517 mg sodium, 26 g carbo., 1 g fiber, 9 g pro.

Corn Muffins: Prepare as directed, except omit the 1 tablespoon butter. Spoon batter into 12 greased 2½-inch muffin cups, filling each cup about two-thirds full. Bake about 15 minutes or until light brown and a toothpick inserted near the centers comes out clean. Makes 12 muffins.

Per muffin: 137 cal., 6 g fat (1 g sat. fat), 37 mg chol., 250 mg sodium, 17 g carbo., 1 g fiber, 3 g pro.

Seeded
DINNER ROLLS

Personalize frozen dinner rolls by selecting the seed topping that fits your meal. *Makes 6 rolls*

Prep: 10 minutes Bake: 7 minutes Oven: 375°F

2 tablespoons butter or
   margarine, melted
1 to 2 tablespoons seeds
   (such as sesame seeds,
   poppy seeds, dill seeds,
   or caraway seeds)
6 frozen baked soft white
   dinner rolls

1. Preheat oven to 375°F. Place melted butter in a small shallow dish. Place seeds in another small shallow dish or on waxed paper. Dip tops of rolls into melted butter, then dip into seeds. Place rolls, seed sides up, on an ungreased baking sheet.

2. Bake, uncovered, for 7 to 9 minutes or until hot. Serve warm.

Per roll: 154 cal., 7 g total fat (2 g sat. fat), 11 mg chol., 299 mg sodium, 18 g carbo., 1 g fiber, 4 g pro.

Garlic
DINNER ROLLS

Transform refrigerated breadsticks into pretty fleur-de-lis or other shapes, then brush with garlic butter and top with tangy Romano cheese. *Makes 12 rolls*

Prep: 15 minutes   Bake: 13 minutes   Oven: 375°F

1 11-ounce package
    (12) refrigerated breadsticks
2 tablespoons purchased garlic
    butter spread, melted
½ cup grated Romano or
    Parmesan cheese
1 teaspoon dried parsley flakes
⅛ teaspoon cayenne pepper

1. Preheat oven to 375°F. Line a large baking sheet with foil; set aside. On a lightly floured surface, separate dough into 12 breadsticks. Cut each dough piece lengthwise into 3 strips, leaving ¾ inch uncut at one end.
2. To shape each fleur-de-lis roll, coil strips from cut end down toward uncut base, coiling outside strips away from the center and coiling the center strip in either direction. If necessary, pinch slightly to hold shape. Transfer to the prepared baking sheet.

3. Brush rolls with melted garlic butter spread. In a small bowl combine cheese, parsley flakes, and cayenne pepper; sprinkle generously over rolls.
4. Bake, uncovered, for 13 to 15 minutes or until golden brown. Serve warm.

Per roll: 112 cal., 5 g total fat (2 g sat. fat), 8 mg chol., 263 mg sodium, 12 g carbo., 0 g fiber, 3 g pro.

Cheese
BREAD

Buy day-old bread on sale for this easy meal accompaniment. It's great served with a bowl of soup.

Makes 4 servings

Start to Finish: 15 minutes

½ of a 1-pound loaf French bread, halved horizontally
2 tablespoons butter or margarine, softened
¾ cup shredded provolone cheese or mozzarella cheese (3 ounces)

1. Preheat broiler. Spread cut sides of the bread with butter. Place bread, cut sides up, on an ungreased baking sheet.

2. Broil 3 to 4 inches from the heat for 1 to 2 minutes or until brown. Sprinkle with cheese. Broil for 1 to 2 minutes more or until cheese is melted. Cut into slices. Serve warm.

Per serving: 281 cal., 13 g total fat (8 g sat. fat), 30 mg chol., 572 mg sodium, 30 g carbo., 2 g fiber, 10 g pro.

Easy
APPLE DUMPLINGS

Letting the dumplings cool for 30 minutes allows the syrup to thicken slightly. Use a crisp cooking apple such as a Granny Smith or Golden Delicious so the apples keep their shape. *Makes 8 servings*

Prep: 15 minutes Bake: 25 minutes Cool: 30 minutes Oven: 375°F

½ cup apple juice or apple cider
⅓ cup packed brown sugar
2 tablespoons butter
2 tablespoons granulated sugar
1 teaspoon ground cinnamon
1 large cooking apple, peeled (if desired), cored, and cut into 8 wedges
1 8-ounce package (8) refrigerated crescent rolls
1 teaspoon white coarse decorating sugar or granulated sugar
Vanilla or cinnamon ice cream (optional)

1. Preheat oven to 375°F. Lightly grease a 2-quart square baking dish; set aside. In a small saucepan combine apple juice, brown sugar, and butter. Cook over medium-low heat until butter is melted, stirring to dissolve brown sugar.

2. Meanwhile, in a medium bowl stir together granulated sugar and cinnamon. Add apple wedges; toss gently to coat. Unroll crescent rolls; separate at perforations. Place a coated apple wedge along the wide edge of each roll. Roll up dough around apple wedges. Place in the prepared baking dish. Slowly drizzle apple juice mixture over filled rolls. Sprinkle with coarse sugar.

3. Bake, uncovered, for 25 to 30 minutes or until rolls are golden brown and apples are tender. Cool about 30 minutes before serving. Serve warm. If desired, serve with ice cream.

Per serving: 201 cal., 9 g total fat (4 g sat. fat), 8 mg chol., 245 mg sodium, 28 g carbo., 1 g fiber, 2 g pro.

Rhubarb-Oatmeal
CRISP

This version of the old-fashioned dessert features one of spring's favorite fruits. The tart taste of rhubarb contrasts with a sweet oatmeal-crumb topping. *Makes 12 servings*

Prep: **30 minutes** Bake: **45 minutes** Oven: **325°F**

8 cups fresh or frozen unsweetened sliced rhubarb
2¾ cups packed brown sugar
1¼ cups all-purpose flour
¼ cup butter, cut into small pieces
2 cups quick-cooking rolled oats
1 cup butter
Whipped cream or vanilla ice cream (optional)

1. If rhubarb is frozen, thaw but do not drain. Preheat oven to 325°F. Grease a 13×9×2-inch baking pan; set aside. In a large bowl combine rhubarb, 1 cup of the brown sugar, ¼ cup of the flour, and the ¼ cup butter. Spread mixture evenly in the prepared baking pan.

2. For topping, in a medium bowl combine the remaining 1¾ cups brown sugar, the remaining 1 cup flour, and the oats. Using a pastry blender, cut in the 1 cup butter until mixture resembles coarse crumbs. Sprinkle topping over rhubarb mixture.

3. Bake, uncovered, for 45 to 50 minutes or until rhubarb is tender and topping is golden brown. Serve warm. If desired, top with whipped cream.

Per serving: 476 cal., 20 g total fat (12 g sat. fat), 51 mg chol., 154 mg sodium, 72 g carbo., 3 g fiber, 4 g pro.

Old-Fashioned
RICE PUDDING

No stirring or watching is needed when rice pudding is made in a slow cooker. This version is studded with raisins, dried cranberries, and/or dried cherries for a homey, comforting dessert. *Makes 12 to 14 servings*

Prep: 10 minutes Cook: Low 2 hours

Nonstick cooking spray
4 cups cooked rice
1 12-ounce can evaporated milk
1 cup milk
⅓ cup sugar
¼ cup water
1 cup raisins, dried cranberries, and/or dried cherries
3 tablespoons butter or margarine, softened
1 tablespoon vanilla
1 teaspoon ground cinnamon

1. Lightly coat the inside of a 3½- to 4-quart slow cooker with cooking spray; set aside.
2. In a large bowl combine cooked rice, evaporated milk, milk, sugar, and the water. Stir in raisins, dried cranberries, and/or dried cherries; butter; vanilla; and cinnamon. Transfer mixture to the prepared cooker.

3. Cover and cook on low-heat setting (do not use high-heat setting) for 2 to 3 hours. Before serving, gently stir mixture.

Per serving: 204 cal., 6 g total fat (3 g sat. fat), 18 mg chol., 73 mg sodium, 34 g carbo., 1 g fiber, 4 g pro.

IN-A-PINCH TIPS!

MILK OPTIONS: KEEP A BOX OF INSTANT DRY MILK POWDER ON HAND. USE IT IF YOU RUN OUT OF REGULAR MILK AND FOR BAKING. OR, TO REDUCE THE COST OF REGULAR MILK, RECONSTITUTE ENOUGH DRY MILK POWDER TO MAKE A QUART AND STIR IT INTO A QUART OF REGULAR MILK.

Black Forest
BREAD PUDDING

Remember this dessert when entertaining a crowd; it can be prepared ahead and baked just when the party begins. Chocolate and cherries are an unbeatable combination. *Makes 16 to 20 servings*

Prep: **25 minutes** Bake: **70 minutes** Cool: **45 minutes** Chill: **2 to 24 hours** Oven: **325°F**

12 ounces black rye bread, cut into ½-inch slices
⅓ cup butter, softened
1 12- or 16-ounce package frozen pitted dark sweet cherries
2 12-ounce packages semisweet chocolate pieces
½ teaspoon ground cinnamon
3¼ cups whipping cream
¾ cup sugar
8 eggs, lightly beaten
½ teaspoon almond extract
Whipped cream or vanilla ice cream (optional)
Sliced almonds, toasted (optional)

1. Lightly butter a 3-quart rectangular baking dish. Spread bread slices with the ⅓ cup butter. Place bread slices in the prepared baking dish, overlapping as necessary to fit. Sprinkle with frozen cherries, half of the chocolate, and the cinnamon. Set aside.

2. In a medium saucepan combine the remaining chocolate, 1 cup of the cream, and the sugar. Cook and stir just until chocolate is melted. Gradually stir in the remaining 2¼ cups cream. In a very large bowl, combine eggs and almond extract; stir in melted chocolate mixture. Gradually pour over bread in dish (dish will be very full). Cover and chill for 2 to 24 hours.

3. Preheat oven to 325°F. Uncover bread pudding and place dish on a foil-lined baking sheet. Bake for 70 to 80 minutes or until the temperature in the center reaches 160°F. Cool on a wire rack for at least 45 minutes. Serve warm. If desired, top with whipped cream and almonds.

Per serving: 546 cal., 38 g total fat (22 g sat. fat), 183 mg chol., 229 mg sodium, 51 g carbo., 4 g fiber, 8 g pro.

Applesauce CAKE

This moist cake, filled with raisins, nuts, and spices, could be called the multitude cake: for so little cost, it feeds many. It's a perennial favorite, especially when topped with Penuche Frosting, a brown sugar icing.

Makes 15 servings

Prep: **35 minutes**   Bake: **40 minutes**   Oven: **350°F**

2½ cups all-purpose flour
1½ teaspoons baking powder
1 teaspoon ground cinnamon
¾ teaspoon ground nutmeg
½ teaspoon salt
½ teaspoon ground cloves
¼ teaspoon baking soda
½ cup butter, softened
2 cups sugar
2 eggs
1½ cups applesauce
½ cup raisins
½ cup chopped walnuts
1 recipe Penuche Frosting

1. Preheat oven to 350°F. Grease a 13×9×2-inch baking pan; set aside. In a medium bowl stir together flour, baking powder, cinnamon, nutmeg, salt, cloves, and baking soda; set aside.

2. In a large mixing bowl beat butter with an electric mixer on medium to high speed for 30 seconds. Add sugar. Beat until combined, scraping sides of bowl occasionally. Add eggs, 1 at a time, beating well after each addition.

3. Alternately add flour mixture and applesauce to butter mixture, beating on low to medium speed after each addition just until combined. Stir in raisins and walnuts. Spread batter evenly in the prepared baking pan.

4. Bake, uncovered, for 40 to 45 minutes or until a toothpick inserted in the center comes out clean. Cool in pan on a wire rack. Quickly spread Penuche Frosting over cake.

Penuche Frosting: In a 2-quart saucepan melt ½ cup butter over medium heat; stir in 1 cup packed brown sugar. Cook and stir until bubbly. Remove from heat. Add ¼ cup milk and 1 teaspoon vanilla; beat vigorously with a wooden spoon until smooth. Add 3½ cups powdered sugar. Beat with the spoon about 5 minutes or until frosting reaches spreading consistency. Use immediately. (If frosting becomes too thick to spread, beat in hot water, a few drops at a time, until spreadable.) Makes 2 cups.

Make-Ahead Directions: **Prepare and bake as directed, except do not frost cake. Cover cooled cake tightly with heavy foil and freeze for up to 1 month. Thaw and frost cake before serving.**

Per serving: 517 cal., 16 g total fat (8 g sat. fat), 61 mg chol., 229 mg sodium, 93 g carbo., 1 g fiber, 2 g pro.

IN-A-PINCH TIPS !

DRIED FRUIT EQUALS: SUBSTITUTE EQUAL AMOUNTS OF DRIED CRANBERRIES OR OTHER DRIED FRUIT SUCH AS BLUEBERRIES, CHERRIES, OR SNIPPED DATES FOR RAISINS.

Caramel Apple
PUDDING CAKE

Surprise! The pudding forms on the bottom of the dish, and the cake floats to the top during baking. Serve the cake warm. *Makes 12 servings*

Prep: **25 minutes**   Bake: **35 minutes**   Oven: **350°F**

2 cups thinly sliced, peeled tart cooking apple (2 medium)

3 tablespoons lemon juice

½ teaspoon ground cinnamon

⅛ teaspoon ground nutmeg

¼ cup raisins or dried cherries

1 cup all-purpose flour

¾ cup packed brown sugar

1 teaspoon baking powder

¼ teaspoon baking soda

½ cup milk

2 tablespoons butter, melted

1 teaspoon vanilla

½ cup chopped pecans or walnuts

¾ cup caramel ice cream topping

½ cup water

1 tablespoon butter

Vanilla ice cream (optional)

1. Preheat oven to 350°F. Grease a 2-quart square baking dish. Arrange apple slices in bottom of dish; sprinkle with lemon juice, cinnamon, and nutmeg. Sprinkle with raisins.

2. In a large bowl combine flour, brown sugar, baking powder, and baking soda. Add milk, the 2 tablespoons melted butter, and the vanilla; mix well. Stir in pecans. Spread batter evenly over apple mixture.

3. In a small saucepan combine caramel topping, the water, and the 1 tablespoon butter. Bring to boiling. Pour mixture over batter in baking dish.

4. Bake, uncovered, about 35 minutes or until set in center. Serve warm. If desired, top with ice cream.

Per serving: 316 cal., 9 g total fat (3 g sat. fat), 11 mg chol., 176 mg sodium, 58 g carbo., 3 g fiber, 3 g pro.

IN-A-PINCH TIPS!

FOR VANILLA EXTRACT: SUBSTITUTE THE SAME AMOUNT OF RUM OR BRANDY FOR THE VANILLA.

Easy
SWIRL CHEESECAKE

You'd never believe that a cheesecake this pretty would be so easy to make. See photo on page 286.

Makes 10 servings

Prep: **25 minutes** Chill: **I to 24 hours**

I II.I-ounce package
　　cheesecake mix
2 tablespoons dry roasted
　　sunflower kernels
½ teaspoon finely shredded
　　orange peel
¼ cup semisweet chocolate
　　pieces
1½ teaspoons shortening
　　Sliced strawberries

I. Prepare cheesecake crust according to package directions, except stir in sunflower kernels. Press mixture onto the bottom of an ungreased 8-inch springform pan; set aside.

2. Prepare cheesecake filling according to package directions, except increase milk to 1¾ cups and stir in orange peel. Spoon filling into crust-lined pan, spreading evenly.

3. In a small microwave-safe bowl combine chocolate and shortening. Microwave, uncovered, on 100 percent power (high) for I minute. Stir until melted and smooth. Pour melted chocolate into a small resealable plastic bag; snip a small hole in one corner. Pipe chocolate over filling in a spiral pattern. Starting at the center of the cheesecake, pull a toothpick through the chocolate to create a swirl. Continue to create swirls around the entire cheesecake. Cover and chill for I to 24 hours.

4. Using a small sharp knife, loosen edge of cheesecake from side of pan. Remove side of pan. Before serving, arrange strawberries around top edge of cheesecake.

Per serving: 366 cal., 18 g total fat (9 g sat. fat), 34 mg chol., 452 mg sodium, 46 g carbo., 3 g fiber, 7 g pro.

IN-A-PINCH TIPS!

CHOCOLATE SISTERS: BITTERSWEET AND SEMISWEET CHOCOLATE CAN BE USED INTERCHANGEABLY IN RECIPES.

Gingerbread
CAKE

With its old-fashioned and comforting flavors, this cake is ideal when there is a chill in the air.

Makes 16 servings

Prep: **20 minutes** Bake: **40 minutes** Stand: **30 minutes** Cool: **30 minutes** Oven: **350°F**

½ cup butter
2 eggs
2⅓ cups all-purpose flour
1½ teaspoons baking powder
1 teaspoon ground ginger
½ teaspoon baking soda
½ teaspoon ground cinnamon
¼ teaspoon salt
¼ teaspoon ground cloves
½ cup granulated sugar
1 cup mild-flavor molasses
1¼ cups cold water
Powdered sugar

1. Allow butter and eggs to stand at room temperature for 30 minutes. Meanwhile, preheat oven to 350°F. Grease a 13×9×2-inch baking pan; set aside. In a medium bowl stir together flour, baking powder, ginger, baking soda, cinnamon, salt, and cloves; set aside.

2. In a large mixing bowl beat butter with an electric mixer on medium to high speed for 30 seconds. Add granulated sugar. Beat until combined, scraping sides of bowl occasionally. Add eggs, 1 at a time, beating well after each addition. Add molasses; beat until combined. Alternately add flour mixture and the cold water to butter mixture, beating on low speed after each addition just until combined. Spread batter evenly in the prepared baking pan.

3. Bake, uncovered, for 40 to 50 minutes or until a toothpick inserted near the center comes out clean. Cool in pan on a wire rack for 30 minutes. Sprinkle with powdered sugar. Serve warm.

Per serving: 213 cal., 7 g total fat (4 g sat. fat), 42 mg chol., 156 mg sodium, 36 g carbo., 1 g fiber, 1 g pro.

Pumpkin
PEAR CAKE

This cake makes its own "frosting." When you invert the pan, a delicious caramel topping oozes over the fruit-studded cake. *Makes 16 servings*

Prep: **25 minutes**   Bake: **35 minutes**   Cool: **35 minutes**   Oven: **350°F**

1 cup packed brown sugar
⅓ cup butter, melted
1½ teaspoons cornstarch
2 15-ounce cans pear halves in light syrup, undrained
½ cup coarsely chopped pecans
1 package 2-layer-size spice cake mix
1 cup canned pumpkin

1. Preheat oven to 350°F. In a small bowl combine brown sugar, melted butter, and cornstarch. Drain pears, reserving 3 tablespoons of the syrup. Stir the reserved 3 tablespoons syrup into brown sugar mixture. Pour mixture into an ungreased 13×9×2-inch baking pan. If desired, cut each pear half into a fan by making 3 or 4 lengthwise cuts ¼ inch from the stem end to the bottom. Arrange whole or fanned pear halves, cored sides down, on brown sugar mixture. Sprinkle with pecans.

2. Prepare cake mix according to package directions, except decrease the oil to 2 tablespoons and add the pumpkin. Slowly pour cake batter over pear halves, spreading evenly.

3. Bake, uncovered, for 35 to 40 minutes or until a toothpick inserted near the center comes out clean. Cool in pan on a wire rack for 5 minutes.

4. Run a thin metal spatula around edges of cake. Carefully invert cake into a 15×10×1-inch baking pan or onto a very large serving platter with slightly raised edges. Cool about 30 minutes before serving. Serve warm.

Per serving: 337 cal., 15 g total fat (4 g sat. fat), 51 mg chol., 254 mg sodium, 51 g carbo., 2 g fiber, 3 g pro.

Brownie

SURPRISE CUPCAKES

Tuck a mini candy in a brownie cupcake beneath layers of batter. Molten goodness awaits.

Makes 15 cupcakes

Prep: 15 minutes   Bake: 22 minutes   Oven: 350°F

1 19- to 21-ounce package
   fudge brownie mix
25 miniature chocolate-coated
   caramel-topped nougat bars
   with peanuts

1. Preheat oven to 350°F. Line fifteen 2½-inch muffin cups with paper bake cups; set aside.
2. Prepare brownie mix according to package directions. Spoon 1 tablespoon of the batter into each prepared muffin cup. Place a candy bar in each cup. Divide the remaining batter among cups. Chop the remaining candy bars; sprinkle on top.
3. Bake, uncovered, for 22 minutes. Cool in muffin cups on a wire rack. (Cupcakes may dip slightly in the centers.)

Per cupcake: 320 cal., 16 g total fat (4 g sat. fat), 30 mg chol., 163 mg sodium, 40 g carbo., 0 g fiber, 4 g pro.

Mint Surprise Cupcakes:
Prepare as directed, except place 2 miniature chocolate-covered cream-filled mint patties between batter layers in each cupcake (omit nougat bars with peanuts). Bake and cool as directed. Before serving, top cupcakes with canned vanilla frosting and, if desired, additional mint patties.

Per cupcake: 299 cal., 16 g total fat (5 g. sat. fat), 28 mg chol, 130 mg sodium, 37 g carbo., 0 g fiber, 3 pro.

Test Kitchen Tip: If all of the cupcakes do not fit in the oven at one time, refrigerate the unbaked extras until the first ones finish baking.

Cappuccino
BROWNIES

Double layers of frosting make these brownies doubly irresistible. Cappuccino icing is sandwiched between the brownie and the rich chocolate icing. *Makes 16 brownies*

Prep: **25 minutes** Bake: **30 minutes** Chill: **1 hour** Oven: **350°F**

⅔ cup all-purpose flour
¼ teaspoon baking soda
½ cup butter
3 ounces unsweetened chocolate, chopped
1 cup granulated sugar
2 eggs
1 teaspoon vanilla
1 recipe Cappuccino Frosting
1 recipe Chocolate Frosting

FOR UNSWEETENED CHOCOLATE: USE 3 TABLESPOONS UNSWEETENED COCOA AND 1 TABLESPOON VEGETABLE OIL FOR EACH 1-OUNCE SQUARE OF UNSWEETENED CHOCOLATE.

EXTRA CANDY: MAKE GOOD USE OF LEFTOVER HALLOWEEN OR HOLIDAY CHOCOLATE CANDY. STIR AN EQUAL AMOUNT OF THE CANDY, CUT UP, INTO BROWNIE BATTER INSTEAD OF CHOCOLATE CHIPS. BAKE AS USUAL.

1. Preheat oven to 350°F. Line an 8×8×2-inch baking pan with foil, extending foil over the edges of the pan; set aside. In a small bowl stir together flour and baking soda; set aside.
2. In a medium saucepan combine butter and chocolate. Cook and stir over low heat until melted. Remove from heat; cool slightly. Stir in granulated sugar. Add eggs, 1 at a time, beating with a wooden spoon after each addition. Stir in vanilla. Add flour mixture to chocolate mixture; stir just until combined. Spread batter evenly in the prepared baking pan.
3. Bake, uncovered, for 30 minutes. Spread Cappuccino Frosting over warm brownies. Cool in pan on a wire rack.
4. Spread Chocolate Frosting over cooled brownies. Chill about 1 hour or until frosting is set. Using the edges of the foil, lift the uncut block out of the pan. Cut into bars.

Cappuccino Frosting: In a small bowl stir together 1 tablespoon whipping cream and 1 teaspoon instant coffee crystals. Stir in 1 cup powdered sugar and 2 tablespoons softened butter. If necessary, stir in additional whipping cream to make a frosting of spreading consistency.

Chocolate Frosting: In a small saucepan combine 1 cup semisweet chocolate pieces and ⅓ cup whipping cream. Cook and stir over low heat until mixture is smooth and starts to thicken.

Per brownie: 264 cal., 16 g total fat (10 g sat. fat), 54 mg chol., 84 mg sodium, 32 g carbo., 2 g fiber, 2 g pro.

Black and White
BROWNIES

These oh-so-easy bars boast a drizzling of chocolate frosting and a sprinkling of white chocolate and pecans over a fudgy brownie layer. *Makes 36 brownies*

Prep: **25 minutes**   Bake: **31 minutes**   Oven: **350°F**

1 19- to 21-ounce package fudge brownie mix
1 10- to 12-ounce package white baking pieces
1 6-ounce package (1 cup) semisweet chocolate pieces
½ cup pecan pieces
¼ cup butter, melted
3 tablespoons hot water
2 cups powdered sugar
¼ cup unsweetened cocoa powder
1 teaspoon vanilla
¾ cup pecan pieces

1. Preheat oven to 350°F. Grease the bottom of a 13×9×2-inch baking pan; set aside. Prepare brownie mix according to package directions. Stir in half of the white baking pieces, all of the semisweet chocolate pieces, and the ½ cup pecans. Spread batter evenly in the prepared baking pan.

2. Bake, uncovered, about 30 minutes or until the center is set. Sprinkle with half of the remaining white baking pieces; bake for 1 minute more. Cool in pan on a wire rack.

3. For frosting, in a medium bowl combine melted butter and the hot water. Stir in powdered sugar, cocoa powder, and vanilla. Beat with a wooden spoon until smooth. Spoon over top of brownies. Sprinkle with the remaining white baking pieces and the ¾ cup pecans. Cool until frosting is set. Cut into bars.

Per brownie: 221 cal., 12 g total fat (4 g sat. fat), 18 mg chol., 67 mg sodium, 25 g carbo., 1 g fiber, 2 g pro.

IN-A-PINCH TIPS !

COCOA SAVVY: DUTCH PROCESS AND UNSWEETENED COCOA CAN BE USED INTERCHANGEABLY.

Lemon
BARS DELUXE

The sweet-tart taste of these lemon bars is a favorite on dessert tables everywhere. They also make a fresh-tasting, inexpensive hostess gift. *Makes 30 bars*

Prep: **20 minutes**   Bake: **45 minutes**   Oven: **350°F**

  2 cups all-purpose flour
 ½ cup powdered sugar
  I cup butter, softened
  4 eggs, lightly beaten
1½ cups granulated sugar
  I tablespoon finely shredded
      lemon peel
 ⅓ cup lemon juice
 ¼ cup all-purpose flour
      Powdered sugar

1. Preheat oven to 350°F. Line a 13×9×2-inch baking pan with foil, extending foil over the edges of the pan; set aside.

2. In a large bowl stir together the 2 cups flour and the ½ cup powdered sugar. Add butter. Beat with an electric mixer on low to medium speed just until mixture starts to cling together. Press evenly onto the bottom of the prepared baking pan. Bake about 25 minutes or until light brown.

3. In a medium bowl combine eggs, granulated sugar, lemon peel, and lemon juice. Stir in the ¼ cup flour. Pour evenly over baked crust.

4. Bake, uncovered, about 20 minutes more or until edges start to brown and center is set. Cool in pan on a wire rack. Using the edges of the foil, lift the uncut block out of the pan. Sift additional powdered sugar over top. Cut into bars. Store, covered, in the refrigerator.

Per bar: 147 cal., 7 g total fat (4 g sat. fat), 44 mg chol., 53 mg sodium, 20 g carbo., 0 g fiber, 2 g pro.

Candy Bar
COOKIE BARS

Is it a cookie or a candy? Not to worry. When it is your turn to provide the sweet for the next large gathering, this is the one to take. See photo on page 287. *Makes 48 bars*

Prep: **30 minutes**   Bake: **10 minutes**   Oven: **375°F**

1 cup packed brown sugar
⅔ cup butter
¼ cup dark- or light-color corn syrup
¼ cup peanut butter
1 teaspoon vanilla
3½ cups quick-cooking rolled oats
1 12-ounce package semisweet chocolate pieces
1 cup butterscotch-flavor pieces
⅔ cup peanut butter
½ cup chopped peanuts

1. Preheat oven to 375°F. Line a 13×9×2-inch baking pan with foil, extending foil over the edges of the pan; set aside.

2. In a medium saucepan combine brown sugar, butter, and corn syrup. Cook and stir over medium-low heat until combined. Remove from heat. Stir in the ¼ cup peanut butter and the vanilla until smooth.

3. For crust, place oats in a very large bowl. Pour brown sugar mixture over oats, stirring gently until combined. Press mixture evenly onto the bottom of the prepared baking pan. Bake, uncovered, for 10 to 12 minutes or until edges are light brown.

4. Meanwhile, in the same saucepan combine chocolate pieces and butterscotch pieces. Cook and stir over low heat until melted. Stir in the ⅔ cup peanut butter until mixture is smooth. Slowly pour mixture over the hot crust, spreading evenly. Sprinkle with peanuts.

5. Cool in pan on a wire rack until chocolate layer is firm. (If necessary, chill until chocolate layer is firm.) Using the edges of the foil, lift the uncut block out of the pan. Cut into bars.

Make-Ahead Directions: **Prepare as directed, except leave the cooled uncut block in the baking pan. Cover tightly with foil and chill for up to 3 days or freeze for up to 3 months.**

Per bar: 166 cal., 9 g total fat (4 g sat. fat), 7 mg chol., 64 mg sodium, 16 g carbo., 2 g fiber, 3 g pro.

IN-A-PINCH **TIPS!**

BROWN SUGAR SAVVY: SUBSTITUTE 1 CUP GRANULATED SUGAR AND 2 TABLESPOONS MOLASSES FOR 1 CUP PACKED BROWN SUGAR.

Whoopie
PIES

This black-and-white cookie is credited with originating in both New England and Pennsylvania Dutch country. But once tasted, the creamy-filled chocolate cookie has everybody everywhere claiming it as their own. *Makes 6 sandwich cookies*

Start to Finish: 15 minutes

¼ cup butter, softened

½ of an 8-ounce package reduced-fat cream cheese (Neufchâtel), softened

½ of a 7-ounce jar marshmallow creme

12 purchased soft chocolate cookies

1. For filling, in a medium mixing bowl combine butter and cream cheese. Beat with an electric mixer on medium to high speed until smooth and fluffy. Fold in marshmallow creme.

2. Spread filling evenly on the flat side of half of the cookies. Top with the remaining cookies, flat sides down, to make sandwiches. For a firmer filling, wrap and chill for 2 hours before serving.

Per sandwich cookie: 710 cal., 36 g total fat (16 g sat. fat), 55 mg chol., 423 mg sodium, 90 g carbo., 1 g fiber, 6 g pro.

CHOCOLATE-CARAMEL CLUSTERS

Kids call these cookies; adults call them candy. Regardless, they will be popular whatever they are called.

Makes about 28 clusters

Prep: **20 minutes** Chill: **30 minutes**

12 vanilla caramels
½ cup milk chocolate pieces
2 tablespoons water
2 cups honey graham cereal,
  slightly crushed
¾ cup peanuts

1. Line a large baking sheet with waxed paper; set aside. In a medium saucepan combine caramels, milk chocolate, and the water. Cook and stir over low heat until caramels are melted. Remove from heat. Stir in cereal and peanuts.

2. Quickly drop cereal mixture by teaspoons onto the prepared baking sheet. Chill about 30 minutes or until firm.

Per cluster: 71 cal., 4 g total fat (1 g sat. fat), 1 mg chol., 68 mg sodium, 9 g carbo., 0 g fiber, 1 g pro.

Peanut Butter
SWIRL ICE CREAM CAKE

With a combination of cookies, candy, and ice cream, is there any way you can go wrong serving this dessert? To reduce cost, use a generic brand of cream-filled sandwich cookies; they are crushed for crumbs and no one will know the difference. See photo on page 288. *Makes 16 servings*

Prep: **45 minutes** Freeze: **6 to 24 hours**

½ gallon vanilla ice cream
24 chocolate sandwich cookies with white filling
5 tablespoons butter or margarine, melted
30 chocolate-covered wafer cookies or your favorite chocolate-covered stick-shape candy bar
⅔ cup peanut butter (not reduced-fat)
¼ cup honey
2 tablespoons cooking oil
½ of an 8-ounce container frozen whipped dessert topping, thawed
½ cup bottled hot fudge sauce

1. Remove ice cream from freezer 30 minutes before using. Place sandwich cookies in a food processor. Cover and process into fine crumbs. Add melted butter; cover and process until combined.

2. Line the sides of a 9-inch springform pan with wafer cookies. Reserve ¾ cup of the chocolate crumb mixture. Press the remaining crumb mixture evenly onto the bottom of the pan.

3. In a small bowl stir together peanut butter, honey, and oil until combined.

4. Spoon half of the ice cream into the pan; spread evenly. Spoon half of the peanut butter mixture over ice cream and spread to edges. Sprinkle evenly with the remaining chocolate crumb mixture, pressing mixture down with the back of a spoon.

5. Top with the remaining ice cream; spread evenly. Top with the remaining peanut butter mixture, spreading to edges. Pipe whipped topping over cake. Place the cake on a baking sheet, cover loosely, and freeze for 6 to 24 hours.

6. To serve, in a small saucepan heat fudge sauce until warm. Remove side of pan from cake. Drizzle warm fudge sauce over cake. Slice cake into wedges.

Per serving: 539 cal., 33 g total fat (17 g sat. fat), 78 mg chol., 269 mg sodium, 54 g carbo., 1 g fiber, 7 g pro.

Cereal-Coated

ICE CREAM SUNDAES

You have lots of options with this dessert. Use whatever ice cream and fruit you have on hand. Cereal adds an unexpected crunch. *Makes 4 servings*

Start to Finish: 15 minutes

1 10-ounce package frozen red raspberries in syrup or strawberries in syrup
2 bananas
2 cups wheat cereal flakes, crushed
½ teaspoon ground cinnamon
1 pint desired-flavor ice cream

1. Thaw berries according to the quick-thaw directions on the package; set aside. Meanwhile, cut bananas into ½-inch slices. Divide banana slices among 4 dessert dishes; set aside.

2. Place cereal in a shallow dish; stir in cinnamon. Using an ice cream scoop, drop a scoop of ice cream into cereal mixture; roll ice cream in cereal mixture to coat. Place on top of banana slices in a dessert dish. Repeat with 3 more scoops of ice cream.

3. Sprinkle sundaes with any remaining cereal mixture. Spoon berries and their syrup over sundaes.

Per serving: 410 cal., 13 g total fat (8 g sat. fat), 68 mg chol., 174 mg sodium, 71 g carbo., 5 g fiber, 5 g pro.

Banana
SPLIT TRIFLES

This layered rendition of the classic trifle makes a deliciously fun way to end a meal. *Makes 4 servings*

Start to Finish: 15 minutes

2 to 3 cups tin roof sundae, chocolate chunk, or vanilla ice cream

4 soft-style oatmeal or chocolate chip cookies, crumbled

⅔ cup hot fudge ice cream topping and/or strawberry preserves

½ cup whipped cream

2 small bananas, halved lengthwise and cut into chunks

1. In a chilled medium bowl, stir ice cream just enough to soften, pressing it against the sides of the bowl with a wooden spoon.

2. To assemble, in 4 parfait glasses layer ingredients in the following order: half of the cookie crumbs, half of the ice cream, and half of the fudge topping and/or preserves.

3. Add the remaining cookie crumbs, the remaining ice cream, the whipped cream, banana chunks, and the remaining fudge topping and/or preserves.

Make-Ahead Directions: Prepare as directed. Cover and freeze for up to 1 hour.

Per serving: 524 cal., 23 g total fat (12 g sat. fat), 48 mg chol., 161 mg sodium, 73 g carbo., 3 g fiber, 6 g pro.

Kitty
CUPCAKE CONES

These cupcake cones are great for a kids' party. They're fun to make and easy to eat. If you like, let the guests frost and decorate their own cone. *Makes 24 cupcake cones plus about 12 regular cupcakes*

Prep: **45 minutes** Bake: **20 minutes per batch** Oven: **350°F**

24 ice cream cones with flat bottoms
1 package 2-layer-size desired-flavor cake mix
1 16-ounce can white frosting
12 to 15 drops desired food coloring
   Small jelly beans
   Candy corn
   Black shoestring licorice or pull-apart twist candy

1. Preheat oven to 350°F. Stand ice cream cones in twenty-four 2½-inch muffin cups. Prepare cake mix according to package directions. Fill each cone with 2 to 3 level tablespoons of batter.* (Bake any additional batter in muffin cups lined with paper bake cups according to package directions.)

2. Bake, uncovered, for 20 to 25 minutes or until a toothpick inserted in the centers comes out clean. Cool.

3. In a small bowl stir together frosting and enough food coloring to reach desired color. Frost tops of cupcakes.

4. To make kitty faces, use jelly beans for eyes and nose, candy corn for ears, and cut licorice strands for whiskers and mouth. Serve cupcake cones the same day they are prepared.

Per cupcake cone: 180 cal., 7 g total fat (2 g sat. fat), 18 mg chol., 140 mg sodium, 28 g carbo., 0 g fiber, 1 g pro.

*Test Kitchen Tip: Bake a few cones with each amount to see which amount works best. (Amount will vary among cake mix brands.)

Index

Note: Boldface page numbers indicate photographs.

Metric Information

The charts on this page provide a guide for converting measurements from the U.S. customary system, which is used throughout this book, to the metric system.

PRODUCT DIFFERENCES

Most of the ingredients called for in the recipes in this book are available in most countries. However, some are known by different names. Here are some common American ingredients and their possible counterparts:

- Sugar (white) is granulated, fine granulated, or castor sugar.
- Powdered sugar is icing sugar.
- All-purpose flour is enriched, bleached, or unbleached white household flour. When self-rising flour is used in place of all-purpose flour in a recipe that calls for leavening, omit the leavening agent (baking soda or baking powder) and salt.
- Light-colored corn syrup is golden syrup.
- Cornstarch is cornflour.
- Baking soda is bicarbonate of soda.
- Vanilla or vanilla extract is vanilla essence.
- Green, red, or yellow sweet peppers are capsicums or bell peppers.
- Golden raisins are sultanas.

VOLUME AND WEIGHT

The United States traditionally uses cup measures for liquid and solid ingredients. The chart, top right, shows the approximate imperial and metric equivalents. If you are accustomed to weighing solid ingredients, the following approximate equivalents will be helpful.

- 1 cup butter, castor sugar, or rice = 8 ounces = ½ pound = 250 grams
- 1 cup flour = 4 ounces = ¼ pound = 125 grams
- 1 cup icing sugar = 5 ounces = 150 grams

Canadian and U.S. volume for a cup measure is 8 fluid ounces (237 ml), but the standard metric equivalent is 250 ml.

1 British imperial cup is 10 fluid ounces.

In Australia, 1 tablespoon equals 20 ml, and there are 4 teaspoons in the Australian tablespoon.

Spoon measures are used for smaller amounts of ingredients. Although the size of the tablespoon varies slightly in different countries, for practical purposes and for recipes in this book, a straight substitution is all that's necessary. Measurements made using cups or spoons always should be level unless stated otherwise.

COMMON WEIGHT RANGE REPLACEMENTS

Imperial / U.S.	Metric
½ ounce	15 g
1 ounce	25 g or 30 g
4 ounces (¼ pound)	115 g or 125 g
8 ounces (½ pound)	225 g or 250 g
16 ounces (1 pound)	450 g or 500 g
1¼ pounds	625 g
1½ pounds	750 g
2 pounds or 2¼ pounds	1,000 g or 1 Kg

OVEN TEMPERATURE EQUIVALENTS

Fahrenheit Setting	Celsius Setting*	Gas Setting
300°F	150°C	Gas Mark 2 (very low)
325°F	160°C	Gas Mark 3 (low)
350°F	180°C	Gas Mark 4 (moderate)
375°F	190°C	Gas Mark 5 (moderate)
400°F	200°C	Gas Mark 6 (hot)
425°F	220°C	Gas Mark 7 (hot)
450°F	230°C	Gas Mark 8 (very hot)
475°F	240°C	Gas Mark 9 (very hot)
500°F	260°C	Gas Mark 10 (extremely hot)
Broil	Broil	Grill

*Electric and gas ovens may be calibrated using celsius. However, for an electric oven, increase celsius setting 10 to 20 degrees when cooking above 160°C. For convection or forced air ovens (gas or electric) lower the temperature setting 25°F/10°C when cooking at all heat levels.

BAKING PAN SIZES

Imperial / U.S.	Metric
9×1½-inch round cake pan	22- or 23×4-cm (1.5 L)
9×1½-inch pie plate	22- or 23×4-cm (1 L)
8×8×2-inch square cake pan	20×5-cm (2 L)
9×9×2-inch square cake pan	22- or 23×4.5-cm (2.5 L)
11×7×1½-inch baking pan	28×17×4-cm (2 L)
2-quart rectangular baking pan	30×19×4.5-cm (3 L)
13×9×2-inch baking pan	34×22×4.5-cm (3.5 L)
15×10×1-inch jelly roll pan	40×25×2-cm
9×5×3-inch loaf pan	23×13×8-cm (2 L)
2-quart casserole	2 L

U.S. / STANDARD METRIC EQUIVALENTS

⅛ teaspoon = 0.5 ml	⅓ cup = 3 fluid ounces = 75 ml
¼ teaspoon = 1 ml	½ cup = 4 fluid ounces = 125 ml
½ teaspoon = 2 ml	⅔ cup = 5 fluid ounces = 150 ml
1 teaspoon = 5 ml	¾ cup = 6 fluid ounces = 175 ml
1 tablespoon = 15 ml	1 cup = 8 fluid ounces = 250 ml
2 tablespoons = 25 ml	2 cups = 1 pint = 500 ml
¼ cup = 2 fluid ounces = 50 ml	1 quart = 1 litre